SOCIAL & BEHAVIORAL SCIENCES ▸ Political Science Political Theory

45-6431   JC423   2007-12303 CIP

Estlund, David M. **Democratic authority: a philosophical framework.**
Princeton, 2008. 309p bibl index afp ISBN 9780691124179, $29.95

Estlund (Brown Univ.) offers a thoughtful, philosophically dense discussion arguing for the legitimacy of democratic order. Estlund calls his theoretical justification of
democracy epistemic proceduralism. According to Estlund, this view differs from the
defenders of democracy who are proponents of social choice theory. To such proponents, democracy is only good as long as the procedures ensure choices most likely to
reflect majority sentiment and least likely to harm minorities. Estlund also examines
another account of democracy which he calls deliberative democracy, which emphasizes the processes for making choices. The discussion of theorists favoring deliberative democracy is quite strong, especially the section on Habermas. Estlund argues
that epistemic proceduralism is a superior justification for democracy because it shows
that democracies have the capacity to achieve good decisions that have legitimacy. His
comparison of the decisions of a democracy to those of a jury is particularly illuminating. The work includes careful discussion of many prominent democratic and liberal
theorists, such as Kenneth Arrow and John Rawls. **Summing Up:** Recommended.
Graduate and research collections.—*M. Coulter, Grove City College*

Democratic Authority

Democratic Authority

A PHILOSOPHICAL FRAMEWORK

David M. Estlund

PRINCETON UNIVERSITY PRESS

PRINCETON AND OXFORD

Library of Congress Cataloging-in-Publication Data

Estlund, David M.
Democratic authority : a philosophical framework / David M. Estlund.
p. cm.
Includes bibliographical references and index.
ISBN-13: 978-0-691-12417-9 (cloth : alk. paper)   1. Democracy.
2. Democracy—Philosophy.   3. Authority.   I. Title.
JC423E714   2007
321.8—dc22   2007012303

British Library Cataloging-in-Publication Data is available

This book has been composed in Palatino

Printed on acid-free paper. ∝

press.princeton.edu

Printed in the United States of America

1 2 3 4 5 6 7 8 9 10

To my mother, Ann Estlund,

and to the memory of my father, Bruce Estlund

Contents

CONTENTS

Preface

There are different kinds of philosophy books. While some are written over a relatively short time, say a year, this one grows out of papers written over twenty years. Many books, including this one, bear down on a question (or several), scrutinizing existing arguments in detail and proposing improvements. This book, in addition to that, tries to develop a relatively elaborate theoretical framework—what I call *epistemic proceduralism*. There are advantages and disadvantages of both of these features, but in any case, the reader deserves advance notice. The relation between this work and my previous papers is a close one, but not a simple one. Only a few chapters (noted below) are close to original papers, while in most cases the ideas from previous pieces are interspersed throughout. In general, where the treatment in the book differs from the papers, it supersedes them. On the other hand, material has often been left out here for the sake of brevity and readability (I have tried to provide references where appropriate), not in order to retract it. Perhaps most important, especially for those who work as specialists in normative democratic theory, this book is not by any means merely a restatement of my earlier views. The approach to democracy developed here goes well beyond what I have said before, for better or for worse.

As for the book's attempt to develop a new theoretical framework, not just a better argument for this or that point, one consequence is that there are places where I offer only tentative or preliminary argumentation. I think this is unavoidable if the shape of the general approach is to be laid out clearly. I hope there is enough argument to lend promise to the overall approach of epistemic proceduralism. If so, there is more work to be done. This disclaimer is separate from a further point, one with which the book begins, concerning the idea of a philosophical framework, one that steers relatively clear of engagement with empirical social science and stops short of prescribing many institutional specifics. I say more about that in chapter 1.

Having worked on these questions over a long time, it would be impossible to remember and thank all the people to whom thanks are owed. The acknowledgments would run back to teachers and fellow students in graduate school at Wisconsin; through students and colleagues at my first job at the University of California, Irvine; and those over the years at Brown, not to mention several visiting stints, and colloquia and conferences that were particularly helpful to me. I do owe many thanks to people in all those settings. I confine myself here to acknowledging several people who have been helpful in the later stages, as my views turned into a book. For facilitating the transition from views to a book, first thanks go to Nomy Arpaly, not only for the philosophical camaraderie of our weekly lunches, but for sharing some of her book-writing magic. Her books have virtues that mine lacks, but mine now has what she taught me was the primary one: existence. Nomy, Cindy Estlund, and Mariah Zeisberg gave me excellent comments on the first chapter, and thereby on the whole project. My graduate seminar at Brown in the fall of 2005 was where things began to take final form, thanks to the extremely high caliber of critical attention my draft received from the students. Among them was Jed Silverstein, whose additional excellent research assistance helped move the book from rough draft to less rough. Thanks also go to three students who helped with the final proof reading: Sean Aas, Derek Bowman, and Joshua Tropp.

John Tomasi and Corey Brettschneider, political theorists in political science here at Brown, are my partners in building a new swirl of activity and excitement in political philosophy here. I have benefited constantly from the discussions at our Political Philosophy Workshop, but also from their own comments on my work, and especially their encouragement. One event in particular, a workshop devoted to my manuscript, was John's generous idea. The commentators at that workshop—Russell Hardin, Philip Pettit, and Christian List—worked very hard on a difficult manuscript and helped me enormously. I had first gotten to know Philip during a Harsanyi Fellowship in 2001–2 that allowed me to spend a year at Australian National University. I am thankful for that support from ANU and the leave time from Brown, and for the frequent discussions there with Philip, Bob Goodin, Geoff Brennan, Gerry Mackie, John Dryzek, and Michael Smith, as well as the stellar students and vagabond scholars in the tea room at that amazing place. Thanks are also due to the National Endowment for the Humanities for two fellowships, one supporting a semester of research time in 1998–99, and the other supporting research during the summer of 2002. Thanks to Ian Malcolm for his enthusiasm and expert guidance at Princeton University Press.

For help of a deep but less specific kind, I must thank several people who were never my teachers or colleagues, but who took my ideas seriously when I was a young scholar just out of school (or even before).

Jerry Cohen, Josh Cohen, and the late John Rawls all paid me more supportive attention than I had any reason to expect. I owe much in my own thought to their distinguished work, but their early attention itself was formative.

For help of the deepest kind, I want to thank Meg Denton, Corey Estlund, Hannah Estlund, and Marshall Estlund for the years of working and playing together during the time when the book was produced, as were countless things of much greater value than this.

There is much new here, but there are also passages and ideas drawn from previously published papers. The bibliography lists most of my published articles that bear on democracy, but several chapters bear an especially close relation to the previously published versions, and I am grateful for permission to draw on them.

Chapter 5 is based closely on "Democracy," in *Oxford Handbook of Contemporary Philosophy*, ed. Frank Jackson and Michael Smith, (Oxford University Press, 2005), 208–30. Used by permission of Oxford University Press.

Chapter 7 is based on "Political Authority and the Tyranny of Nonconsent," *Philosophical Issues* 15 (2005): 351–67. Used by permission of Blackwell Publishing.

Chapter 11 is based on "Why Not Epistocracy?" in *Desire, Identity and Existence: Essays in Honor of T. M. Penner*, ed. Naomi Reshotko (Academic Printing and Publishing, 2003), 53–69. Used by permission of Academic Printing and Publishing.

Chapter 13 is based on "The Democracy/Contractualism Analogy," *Philosophy and Public Affairs* 31 (2003): 387–412. Used by permission of Blackwell Publishing.

Democratic Authority

Democratic Authority

> One of the two, as the wiser or better man, has a claim
> to superior weight: the difficulty is in ascertaining
> which of the two it is.
>   John Stuart Mill, *Considerations on Representative*
>   *Government*

DEMOCRACY CAN SEEM TO EMPOWER THE MASSES without regard for the
quality of the political decisions that will result. Concern for the quality
of decisions can seem to lead in an antidemocratic direction, toward
identifying and empowering those who know best. Partly for these reasons, philosophical treatments of democracy's value have often tried to
explain why politics should be democratic even though democracy has
no particular tendency to produce good decisions. I believe these accounts are weak, and I want to put democratic convictions on more secure footing. My goal is to show how a concern for the quality of political decisions, properly constrained by other principles, supports
democratic political arrangements. Rousseau pleads, "All my ideas are
consistent, but I cannot expound them all at once."[1] In this synoptic
essay I try to present, all at once, the broad shape and main points of a
more elaborate book-length argument. I hope it has some value as a
self-contained essay, but it is also intended as a prelude to the longer argument of the book, making certain points and terms available for easy
reference even before they are treated fully.

A FRAMEWORK

Before turning to democracy, I begin with the idea of a philosophical
framework. Political philosophy, as with some areas of ethics, is easily
distorted by the ever-present thought that it might be of practical importance. Practical applications of philosophical ideas require engagement with a lot of nonphilosophy, and the danger is not just that philosophers are not normally especially good at the relevant nonphilosophical

areas of inquiry. Even if they were, there are risks involved in trying to treat both kinds of questions in the same work. In the hurry to make a practical proposal it is easy to lose sight of the philosophical problems, and so to lose sight of whether and how they have been solved. Since even long-standing problems have, so often, not been solved (philosophy seems to be harder than science in this way), the idea that something is gained if political philosophers explain how to put their ideas into practice is hard to understand. If the more abstract arguments are of any value, then it would be good if someone takes up the further questions about what they might imply or recommend in practice, and I do not mean to denigrate that task. My main concern, however, is with the question whether certain points at a fairly abstract level are of value in the first place, whether they solve or at least contribute to the solution of important problems that lie at the more abstract level. As a result, few institutional specifics are offered here, and when they are they are mainly meant as illustrative examples, not as prescriptions.

There is a second aspect to the limitation I have in mind by providing only a philosophical framework: detailed factual information, while occasionally useful, is far from the center of our concerns. The focus of the argument is on very general questions of authority and legitimacy in a political community, terms that will be used in very specific ways. By *authority* I will mean the moral power of one agent (emphasizing especially the state) to morally require or forbid actions by others through commands. (To forbid x is to require not-x, and so I will usually simply speak of the moral power to require.) By *legitimacy* I will mean the moral permissibility of the state's issuing and enforcing its commands owing to the process by which they were produced. If the state's requiring you to pay taxes has no tendency to make you morally required to do so, then the state lacks authority in that case. And if the state puts you in jail for not paying, but it is morally wrong for it to do so, then it acts illegitimately. Even without authority or legitimacy, of course, the state might yet have enormous power. But we are not investigating brute power as such, since brute power is not a moral thing. Like a knife, it can be used rightly or wrongly. The moral questions about the use of knives are not much about the details of what knives are like, and the moral questions about the uses of power are not much about the exact nature of actual power.

Even without great emphasis on empirical studies about politics, or on the details of institutional design, the philosophical tasks alone lead to a rather elaborate theory. In this essay we look only at the main points and lines of argument.

Making Truth Safe for Democracy

The idea of democracy is not naturally plausible. The stakes of political decisions are high, and the ancient analogy is apt: in life-and-death medical decisions, what could be stupider than holding a vote? Most people do not know enough to make a wise medical decision, but a few people do, and it seems clear that the decisions should be made by those who know best.

While it makes good sense for us to defer to someone who we have reason to think is a medical expert, the doctor's right to make decisions and perform procedures on us comes mainly from our consent, not from the doctor's expertise. Politics is different, since most of us have never consented to the political authority of the government that rules over us. Authority would need some other basis, and expertise has long been a tempting one. It is important to see that authority does not simply follow from expertise. Even if we grant that there are better and worse political decisions (which I think we must), and that some people know better what should be done than others (we all think some are much worse than others), it simply does not follow from their expertise that they have authority over us, or that they ought to. This expert/boss fallacy is tempting, but someone's knowledge about what should be done leaves completely open what should be done about who is to rule. You might be correct, but what makes you boss? Perhaps this approach to political justification, which draws heavily on the views of John Rawls,[2] points in a democratic direction.

Consider religious points of view. One of the contending views might be correct, with all its implications about what should be done politically. Suppose your religious point of view is not the true one. If you think the knowers should rule—if expertise entails authority—then you must think that those with the true religious perspective, whoever they might be, should rule even over people like you who mistakenly doubt that they are the knowers. Their being experts (so to speak) certainly counts in favor of your *accepting* them as rulers, but as it happens, you do not realize they are experts. This doubt appears to block the inference from their expertise to their authority. The problem isn't exactly that you haven't consented, and we're not assuming that

3

consent would be required to legitimate rule. It's about what you believe: you do not believe that they are experts.

The problem that arises for this line of argument, however, is that there is not much that will be believed by everyone, and if legitimate authority depends on there being a justification accepted by everyone, it will be hard to find much legitimate authority. But this is not a plausible constraint anyway. Why should the objection of someone who is, say, crazy or vicious carry that much moral weight—enough to defeat a justification even if it is acceptable to everyone who is not crazy or vicious? Rather than say that a justification must be acceptable to everyone, we might try saying that it must be acceptable to everyone except the crazy, the vicious, and . . . well, there might be other things that it makes sense to put in here. We will finesse the details by simply saying that there will be some list of things that disqualify certain points of view for this purpose. That is, some points of view are such that objections that depend on those disqualified points of view are not capable of defeating a proposed political justification. People who believe that their own race has a right to rule other races, or who simply desire to subordinate other people to their power, will not accept certain principles about moral and political equality. But objections stemming from those unreasonable points of view are morally weightless.

By calling some views qualified and others disqualified, we tempt objectors to accuse us of being exclusive or elitist. This is a widespread confusion, in my view. Since all we've said so far is that not all points of view are qualified, a more inclusive view would have to say that all points of view are qualified. Justifications must simply be acceptable to everyone. This is an oddly amoral view, in which otherwise sensible lines of justification are unavailable if they are not acceptable to Nazis. If anyone believes this, we would need to hear a lot more in support of it.

The other argument against treating some grounds of objection as disqualified says that it is too inclusive—that it counts too many (not too few) lines of objection as qualified. In particular, some say that a point of view shouldn't defeat a proposed justification unless that point of view is true, whereas our approach allows that some views are qualified even though they are not true. This objection might seem to be the proper view for any lover of the truth. Some objections to proposed political justifications are correct and others are not, and lovers of truth should only care about the correct ones, so the story goes. But lovers of the truth want to know what the truth is about justification itself as well, and that requires that we determine whether only true points of view or also some others are qualified to defeat proposed justifications. If the truth is that justifications must be acceptable to all qualified points of view, including many that are not true, then lovers of the truth should accept this view of justification. We cannot settle it here, but this approach would explain the thought that even if the pope has a pipeline to God's will, it does not follow that atheists may permissibly be coerced on the basis of justifications drawn from Catholic doctrine. Some non-Catholic views should count as qualified for this purpose even if they are mistaken. This itself asserts a truth about justification, as lovable a truth as any other.

Fairness and Proceduralism

All this talk about truth will drive some readers crazy. Some will deny that there are any truths about what should be done politically, but few mean this in a way that would cause any difficulty for what I have said. The nature of truth is a fascinating philosophical matter, and truth in value judgments raises interesting questions of its own. But when I speak of moral truth here, I mean only the following very minimal thing: if gender discrimination is unjust, then it is *true* that gender discrimination is unjust. Not many readers will think nothing is just, unjust, right, wrong, and so forth, and so they accept that there are moral truths in the sense that concerns me.

Some will worry about whose view of the truth we are talking about. But we are not talking, initially, about anyone's view of the truth, but about the truth (whatever it might be). We are supposing that some things are unjust, some right, some things vicious, and so on, regardless of what anyone thinks about them. Then we say that some people have erroneous views about these matters, some other people less so. So far we are not endorsing any particular *view* of the truth. We have not said which things are true about these matters, or who might know the truths better.

This way of talking about truth makes it pretty hard to deny truth in political matters or to deny that some know it better than others. We cannot resist the move from expertise to authority by denying that there is expertise, then. I have proposed to avoid that move by denying that there is expertise that is generally acceptable in the right way even if it is genuine. But having acknowledged that there are truths about the high-stakes matters that are present in politics, we must ask whether its

5

discovery plays any role in the best account of how political authority and coercion would be justified. Is there an epistemic or truth-seeking dimension to the best account, or can we do without that?

I believe we cannot do without it, but there is a simple and influential approach that tries to. Why not understand democracy as a way of giving every (adult) person an equal chance to influence the outcome of the decision? The justification of the outcomes would be in terms of the familiar idea of the fairness of the procedure that produced the decision. That way we would not need to make any claims about the decision tending to be good or right or true. Democracy, after all, does seem like a fair way to make decisions, at least as an aspiration. People are given equal rights to express their political opinions, and equal rights to a vote. Should we say that the fairness of the procedure is the explanation of democracy's moral importance?

We have not said exactly what would make a procedure a fair one, but so far it looks like democracy is one fair procedure, and choosing between two proposals by flipping a coin is another one.[3] If that is right, and if fairness is the main basis of democracy's importance, then why not flip a coin instead? It is much cheaper and easier in so many ways. We would not need to expend resources on campaigns, televised debates, public political discussion, or all the time and work involved in holding a vote. For example, we could let the slate of candidates or issues be determined in whatever way they otherwise would, except at any stage that there would normally be a vote we substitute a random selection process, even at the final stage that would normally be an election or a referendum. It is a perfectly fair procedure, at least if this means giving each person an equal chance at changing the outcome. All have an equal chance, since no one has any. If the value of democracy is its fairness, this random procedure should be just as good.

Of course, this is impossible to accept. There is something about democracy other than its fairness that contributes to our sense that it can justify authority and legal coercion. A coin-flipping procedure would not justify these, at least not to the same extent. One natural hypothesis about why we actually want people's views taken account of by the process is that we expect people's views to be intelligent—maybe not to any high standard, but better than a coin flip. This introduces an epistemic dimension, and it is important to see what this would and would not commit us to.

EPISTEMIC PROCEDURALISM

The biggest objection to bringing in the epistemic dimension is that it might to tend to justify rule by the knowers—what we might call *epistocracy*. But I hope to have forestalled that worry by pointing out that even if there are knowers, it might well be that their status as knowers is not generally acceptable in the way that political justification would require. So now the question is how to bring in knowledge without privileging any class of knowers.

There is, however, the nagging thought that even if the knowers aren't generally acceptable, they do exist. And they might simply be a more accurate source of knowledge about what should be done than any democratic procedure could ever be. I don't want to deny this. The question is not how democracy might be the best epistemic device available, but how it might have some epistemic value in a way that could account for the degree of authority we think it should have. If you or someone whose opinions you trust is a knower, then the results of a modestly epistemic democratic procedure will not give you especially important epistemic reasons to believe the outcome is good or correct. But epistemic reasons are not what we need. The hope is to show how democracy yields moral reasons to obey the law and a moral permission to enforce it. We should not assume that there could only be such duties and permissions in cases where the procedure actually got the right answer. So we should not assume that authority and legitimacy lapse just whenever the procedure gets a wrong answer. That surely would not generate legitimacy and authority for the general run of democratically produced laws. Obviously, many of them are unjust or otherwise morally mistaken.

A good model for the structure I have in mind is a jury system. When it is properly done, a jury trial seems to produce a verdict with legal force, but also with some moral force. If the defendant is exonerated, then other people will have a moral duty not to carry out private punishments. If the defendant is convicted, then the duly appointed jailer will have a moral duty not to set him free. I assume that, at least within limits, these moral implications do not depend on the verdict being correct. If they did, then we should all ignore the verdict and use our own judgment about whether the defendant was guilty or not, and privately punish the truly guilty and open the cells of the innocent. Jailers who appoint themselves judge and jury, and vigilantes who appoint

7

themselves executioner, seem to be acting immorally when there has been a properly conducted (though always fallible) jury trial.

The jury trial would not have this moral force if it did not have its considerable epistemic virtues. The elaborate process of evidence, testimony, cross-examination, adversarial equality, and collective deliberation by a jury all contribute to the ability—certainly very imperfect—of trials to convict people only if they are guilty, and not to set too many criminals free. If it did not have this tendency, if it somehow randomly decided who is punished and who goes free, it is hard to see why vigilantes or jailers should pay it much heed. So its epistemic value is a crucial part of the story. Owing partly to its epistemic value, its decisions are (within limits) morally binding even when they are incorrect.

On this account, the bindingness and legitimacy of the decisions are not owed to the correctness of the decisions, but to the kind of procedure that produced them. Still, a central feature of the procedure in virtue of which it has this significance is its epistemic value. I call this theoretical structure *epistemic proceduralism*. This is just the structure I explore in the case of democratic procedures for making laws and policies generally. Democratically produced laws are legitimate and authoritative because they are produced by a procedure with a tendency to make correct decisions. It is not an infallible procedure, and there might even be more accurate procedures. But democracy is better than random and is epistemically the best among those that are generally acceptable in the way that political legitimacy requires. The authority and legitimacy of its laws often extends even to unjust laws, though there must be limits to this. The procedure does not give us great epistemic reasons for our opinions about justice. For that purpose we may each appeal to whatever sources and methods we think best, without the need for these to be generally acceptable.

Suppose the tax laws charge me more than is really just. But the laws were passed in a properly functioning democratic system with ample opportunity for discussion and debate. My objections were aired and answered, even though I think the answers were inadequate (and even suppose I'm right about this). The resulting laws charge me an unjust amount of tax. (Assume it does not take so much that I cannot still live a decent life. We will not try here to locate the limits, but there must be some.) According to epistemic proceduralism, the law is legitimate and binding on me even though it is unjust, and this is owed partly to the fact that the procedure has epistemic value that is publicly recognizable.

This gives something of the structure of epistemic proceduralism's account of democratic authority. We need to say more, though, about why we should think that a procedure with these features does have authority, the moral power to require action.

DEMOCRATIC AUTHORITY WITHOUT CONSENT

A traditional view says that there is no authority without consent. The state is not in a position to lay obligations on me unless I voluntarily and knowingly agree to their having that moral power. The main weakness of this approach is that it does not seem to account for the state's authority over very many people, since most people never consent to the authority of their state. Locke argued that a person consents merely by enjoying the benefits of the state, but this seems to make hash out of the idea of consent. Since you could benefit from the state without realizing you were consenting, you could consent without realizing it. But I would have thought that the whole point of requiring consent is to let the person decide whether to be under the authority or not. If you could consent to authority without realizing it, then being under the authority would not be under your control. So we should not accept that you consent by receiving benefits. You cannot consent to something without realizing it. So, even though consent might be able to establish authority, some other basis of authority would be required to explain a state's authority over most or all of its citizens.

If we look more closely at consent theory, it normally includes some conditions under which apparent acts of consent are null—without the effect of proper consent. This is a familiar idea: if I threaten to kill you unless you agree to let me use your car, you might say, "OK, take the car." But under that kind of duress the consent has no moral effect. It doesn't permit me to take the car. We could even say that it is not consent at all. In any case it is morally null. But notice what consent theory says about non-consent. Non-consent has a moral force too, of course. For example, if I don't consent to your touching me, then you are not permitted to touch me. But while according to consent theory there are conditions that can disqualify consent, there are apparently no conditions that disqualify non-consent. Non-consent is never null. If there were some conditions that nullified non-consent, the result would be morally equivalent to consent.

This looks worth exploring. What conditions might plausibly be thought to nullify non-consent? Perhaps if the non-consent is morally wrong it should be without moral effect. This isn't plausible in some

9

contexts. If I refuse to let you use my car, then even if I am wrong to refuse, you still may not use my car. But perhaps things are different with authority, the moral power to require action. Authority is not a form of interference with a person, their body, or their property. It is simply the ability to put them under obligations. So, suppose I propose for you to agree to work under my direction to help clean my garage—a proposal to put you under my authority in this context. And suppose you would be wrong not to agree to it, possibly because I have given you lots of help lately, in addition to really needing your help now. Should we think that you can escape the obligations of authority by violating this obligation to agree to the authority? We might say, instead, that you are under my authority because you would be morally wrong to refuse to consent—call this normative consent. It is hypothetical: you would have consented if you acted morally correctly when offered the chance to consent. This would simply mean that you would be obligated to do what I asked of you. It would not mean that I could coerce you to do it, but only that you would be obligated to help, under my authority, even though you haven't consented to that authority. I find it difficult to see what moral reason there would be for thinking that you could escape the obligations to obey me by immorally refusing to consent to my authority. I will suppose, then, that normative consent is a basis for authority.

The Jury Analogy and the Commitment Task

Using the framework of normative consent in order to explain democratic authority (all within the structure of epistemic proceduralism) gives us the following question: would people be morally obligated to consent to the authority of an epistemic proceduralist democratic political system? If so, why? We noticed that a jury trial nicely illustrates the epistemic proceduralist structure of authority. I want to appeal to the jury trial again now, for a slightly different purpose. If we can see why people would be obligated to consent to the authority of a jury system, I believe that a strikingly analogous argument suggests itself for thinking that people would be obligated to consent to epistemic proceduralist democracy.

Authority is the moral power to require or forbid action. How does a system of jury trials have that kind of authority? When there is an adequate public system of justice, private punishment is forbidden, whereas in the absence of such a system at least some punishments for some wrongs would be permitted. Vigilante justice is commonly assumed to be morally wrong once there is an adequate public justice system. Why would it be wrong for someone, if asked, to refuse to consent to a jury system's having authority?

The absence of public criminal justice, the world over, would be a great humanitarian problem, a problem on the scale of, say, world poverty. We all have obligations to help solve these problems. It isn't clear how much this demands of us, but few will doubt that we are required to do something. It is plausible to think that the best, or at least a good, solution to the problem of public criminal justice is one in which people are covered by local justice systems—in districts, so to speak. Each is obligated by the commands of the local district, say one's state, but the obligation stems from this being a sensible solution to the larger global humanitarian need for public justice.

Even if we were persuaded that there were obligations to promote a districted public justice system of this kind, that wouldn't yet yield an obligation to do as you're told by your district. I want to grant that authority of this kind raises a special burden for justification: there must be some link to the obligated person's will.

The key is to distinguish between two pressing tasks: the one we have mentioned, which is the need for an adequate and effective public system of justice; the other is one we haven't yet mentioned, what I take to be the pressing task of having people committed to obeying the public justice system. Their being committed to obeying isn't the same as their obeying, but it is a separate important task, something highly valuable in its own right. We often want something morally committed to us even apart from whether that will help us obtain it. Wedding vows might be like this, or promises to repay debts to friends. The commitment task, the task of having people obligated to obey their district for the administration of public justice, is an important task in its own right, important enough that each of us would be wrong to refuse to commit if offered the chance. Consenting to the authority of that system would be required, and so there is normative consent. Normative consent, then, establishes the system's authority. After that, the duty to obey is not directly based on its being a contribution to any important task, but stems simply from the obligation to obey the criminal justice system's verdicts.

The parallels between the jury case and the larger democratic case are very strong. The essential elements of the argument for the authority of the jury system are all present in a democratic system of government. First, there is a very great value, one that no qualified point of view could deny, to having laws and policies that are substantively just. Second, a proper democratic procedure, like a jury, is (or can be) demographically neutral, blocking the qualified objections that would be possible to any invidious comparisons as between the supposedly wiser and less wise citizens. Third, a democratic procedure involves many citizens thinking together, potentially reaping the epistemic benefits this can bring, and promoting substantively just decisions better than a random procedure. So, fourth, I conjecture there is no nondemocratic arrangement that all qualified points of view could agree would serve substantive justice better. In light of all this, citizens would be morally required to consent to the new authority of such a democratic arrangement if they were offered that choice. Non-consent would be null, and so the fact that no such consent is normally asked or given makes no moral difference, and so any existing democratic arrangement that meets these conditions has authority over each citizen just as if they had established its authority by actual consent.

UTOPOPHOBIA

Thinkers about politics are, for some reason, more concerned with "realism" than are thinkers in moral philosophy generally. In an effort to avoid "utopianism," it is very common to see fundamental normative standards adjusted so that there is some reasonable likelihood that they will be met in practice, and no similar tendency to dumb down moral principles. Moral philosophers know that people are likely to lie more than they morally should, but this doesn't move many theorists to revise their views about when lying is wrong. Things are often different in political philosophy. So, for example, many democratic theorists think that standards of political legitimacy should not depend on citizens doing much more than looking out for their own interests in a pretty casual way, and they often think this precisely because they think that is how people are likely to act.

Epistemic proceduralism, of course, suggests that the casual pursuit of self-interest would not be enough. Just as the jury system would lack the epistemic value on which its authority depends if jurors devoted little effort to reaching good verdicts, no democratic system made up of predominantly selfish uninformed voters would have the epistemic features I have been saying their authority is based on. Does this mean epistemic proceduralism is objectionably unrealistic? If the charge is that practice is not likely to live up to the asserted moral standard, then there are three natural ways to reply.

First, there is the familiar charge that voters are and always will be woefully ignorant and selfish. Great portions of the electorate are ignorant of basic facts about the political system, who holds important offices, which candidates would favor the same things they favor, and so on. It helps in putting this kind of data in context to know that parents, when polled about important matters pertaining to raising healthy and educated children, perform pretty poorly. There are good questions about how they could make good decisions without being able to do well on questionnaires, but this is hardly an absurd possibility. What about voters? There's no reason to be complacent about the state of voter competence, but we should be reluctant to infer from voters failing these quizzes to the conclusion that they are incapable of making good decisions.

Consider, next, the possibility that the moral standards should be weakened to accord better with what can be reasonably expected in practice. I treat this together with the third gambit, the suggestion that it is no flaw in a theory to have standards that are unlikely to be met in practice. To weaken what we take to be the appropriate moral standard we would need a moral argument. "That standard is not likely to be met," does not invoke any moral consideration at all against the standard's truth. Why should it make us think that legitimacy or authority require less than we had first thought?

Suppose the challenge were sharper. What about, "It is not a standard people are capable of meeting"? There is a very tempting but unwarranted slide that often happens from "You and I both know that will never happen," to "That's impossible." It is plausible that if people are incapable of doing something then they are not responsible for not doing it, but the mere improbability of your doing something does not insulate you from responsibility in the way your being unable to do it would. Some things that we all know you will never do are, nevertheless, not impossible, and not even the least bit difficult. It is pretty easy to dance like a chicken in front of your boss. Put your hands up under your arms, thrust your head forward rhythmically, and so on. It is easy, but you and I both know you will almost certainly never do it. The same goes for certain things that might be morally required. Maybe you and I both know that you will not tell your mother that you love her. But that

13

does not show that you can't do it, or that it is so difficult that you are not responsible for it if you fail. You could certainly do it, you just are not likely to. That fact, that you are unlikely to, is not even the beginning of an excuse.

I want to pause to say, loud and clear, that I am not conceding that what is needed by epistemic proceduralism is highly unlikely, much less certain never to happen. I am just unsure about that. Rather, I want to ask, what if that were so? Would it be a devastating objection to epistemic proceduralism? It would not. If utopianism is the defense of political standards that are very unlikely ever to be met, it is hard to see why it would be a vice, or why political theorists should be so in the grip of what we might call *utopophobia*—the fear of normative standards for politics that are unlikely ever to be met. (There's no similar epithet in moral theory generally, is there?) Normative standards that people are incapable of meeting are much more dubious, so what the critics of supposedly "unrealistic" normative theories need to show is not that "you and I both know it will never happen." That's no objection to a moral theory of politics. They would need to show that not only will it never happen, it is not something people *could* do (or, at least, not without more effort or sacrifice than it's appropriate to require). Maybe epistemic proceduralism asks more of voters than they will ever deliver, maybe not. Either way, this is no deficiency in the theory whatsoever.

We will treat the charge of voter selfishness only very briefly. The first point is that empirical studies of the question have had a hard time verifying the widespread view that voters are largely moved by their own perceived interests rather than by more agent-neutral values.[4] A little folk experiment is suggestive here. I often ask my students two questions. First, which is it: do most people vote selfishly, or more for the common good? Overwhelmingly they say people vote selfishly. Then I ask, what about you? Overwhelmingly, they say they vote for the common good. Are they being dishonest? They have little to fear from being honest. I do not take their names when they raise their hands to answer. Are they deluding themselves? I see no reason to think so. Is this an artifact of the narrow sample—college students? I doubt that, but I invite you to try it on other groups. Are they biased in favor of themselves without knowing it? Well, I think they probably do know it. We all know that, and so self-interest and other less-than-impartial concerns play an important role. But this simple experiment should shake up any easy confidence that voters are overwhelmingly out for themselves. Hardly any voters see their own motives in that way.

Realism is a vague and dubious constraint when the question is a moral one, when the question at hand is what is right, or just, or legitimate. Obviously, we want to avoid falsehoods. But this includes falsehoods about what bearing people's likely behavior has on what moral standards apply to them.

POOLING WISDOM?

If you have 1,000 coins, with each one slightly weighted to turn up heads—say with a 51 percent chance—what is the chance that at least a majority of them will turn up heads? With that many coins, we know that very nearly 51 percent of them will turn up heads, and so it is quite likely indeed that more than 50 percent will. So now, suppose that, rather than coins, it is 1,000 people, facing a true/false question. And suppose that each person has about a 51 percent chance of getting the right answer (suppose, if you like, that the question is drawn from a pile of which each knows exactly 51 percent of the answers). What is the chance that at least a majority of them will get the right answer? Again, the likelihood is very high, because it is almost certain that about 51 percent will get the right answer, and even more certain that at least 50 percent will. So, under those conditions, the group under majority rule is almost certain to get the right answer. The mathematical fact behind this fascinating scenario was first proven by Condorcet in 1785; it is known as the *jury theorem*, since he was using examples about the likelihood of juries getting the right answer in criminal trials. It has undeniable interest for democratic theory.

If voters are only a little better than random, and choices are between two alternatives, then majority rule would be nearly infallible. Is this the epistemic engine that a theory like epistemic proceduralism needs? I'm afraid that it is not. Consider just a few points.

First, political choices are not always binary, but often take place between several or many alternatives. There will still be some important binary choices: this candidate or that, to build the school or not, and so on. But even if the best choice is likely to be made in those cases, there might be no reason to think that the final two alternatives are the best among the many that were really available. There are some interesting extensions of the jury theorem to more than two alternatives, but the results are not as striking as they are in the binary case.

Second, the jury theorem gives majority rule a high score for accuracy only if individuals are better than random to some significant

15

degree, not just barely. Our example used 51 percent accuracy for 1,000 individuals, and it wouldn't have worked with only 50.00000001 percent individual accuracy. It's true that the margin above 50 percent that is needed for very high group competence is less if the number of voters is higher, but still, it isn't easy to say what level above random we are entitled to assume. Indeed, and this is the next point, I doubt that we can simply assume that they are better than random at all.

So, third, if you were to ask, "How could a person be dumber than a coin flip?" the answer would be "easily." People have more or less systematic views about many issues. If their system is bad, so to speak, then they could easily be wrong all the time. If, for example, people in some time and place were systematically racist, or sexist, or both, it would not be surprising if their political decisions were worse than the performance of a coin flip would be on political matters involving race or sex. Who knows what other important biases or errors people might have in their systematic thinking on issues?

For these and other reasons, the jury theorem looks like it will not support the kinds of epistemic claims that epistemic proceduralism requires for political legitimacy and authority. There's a second approach, very different but also influential, which we might call the democracy/contractualism analogy. Contractualism, briefly, is a family of views that understand justice or rightness as constituted by facts about what would be agreed to in a certain imaginary collective choice situation. What it is for a law to be just (to give a simplified example) is for it to be permitted by principles that could not be objected to by anyone in an imaginary choice situation in which all participants promoted their own personal (not necessarily selfish) reasons, but no one presses their interests at the unreasonable cost of others. It is not that these imaginary participants take a view about justice, but they do have a limited moral reasonableness to their motives. Justice (or rightness, or whatever—it varies with the theory) is whatever no such person would object to in such an imaginary situation of choice. The results constitute what is right.

If this infallible (because constitutive) procedure is simply imaginary, how is this approach of any use to democratic theory? The reason is that it has seemed to many that actual democratic procedures could look enough like the hypothetical contractual procedure that it might tend to produce the same decisions. The results would not be guaranteed to be just, but a real procedure that resembled the hypothetical procedure might have considerable epistemic value.

The problem with this analogy stems from two facts, one about democracy and one about contractualism. The important fact about democracy is that a unanimity rule is not only impracticable but probably morally inappropriate in any case. Letting a single individual veto proposals that are up for democratic decisions would give too much scope to unreasonable obstructionism, favoring the status quo regardless of whether it was more just than the proposed change. This fact about democracy marks a crucial difference from the hypothetical contractualist situation, whose moral center depends on the veto power. In that morally fundamental imaginary situation, a single victim of a cruel proposal has the power to block it, and if he did not, the contractual approach would not generate plausible moral implications.

That first disanalogy, based on the veto power, might be thought not to be so serious if participants are reasonable in a sufficiently full-blooded way. If each voter, for example, looks out not only for herself but also for others, then the single victim of a cruel proposal might be able to muster enough support to block the proposal even without having the veto power. This will not solve the problem, however, because of a crucial fact about contractualism. Since it is an analysis or explication of the foundations of morality, it would be circular and useless if the imaginary participants themselves already had motives that incorporate answers to the very moral question the contractual situation is meant to provide the answer to, such as "What is right?" or "What is just?" Contractualist theorists recognize this, and they assume the hypothetical participants are addressing some more partial question, such as their own interests, or at least reasons from their own point of view but not from an impartial point of view. What this means is that if actual democratic procedures are going to be analogous, then voters should address some narrow or partial question as well. But if they do, since there is no veto power in real democratic procedures, there is no systematic guarantee that the single victim of a cruel proposal won't ever, or even often, be left out in the cold.

If actual democratic procedures are to have any tendency to produce just decisions it seems likely that this is because participants will have some significant tendency to aim for justice, and not only for some narrower personal ends. Now, a procedure like that might superficially resemble the hypothetical contractual procedure, but it really has no necessary connection to contractualism at all. Whether justice is understood contractually or in some other way entirely, there is some

17

reason to think that people cooperatively pursuing it might hope to meet with some success. There may be the rudiments of an epistemic approach to democracy in these points, but it owes nothing to a democracy/contractualism analogy.

How Democracy Could Know

Epistemic proceduralism does not need democratic procedures to be highly accurate. This is an easy point to miss, because a natural alternative epistemic approach might say that laws are legitimate and authoritative when they are actually just or correct. Then the general run of laws will only be legitimate and authoritative if the general run of laws is correct—that is, only if the procedure is highly accurate in that sense. Epistemic proceduralism is importantly different. It says that a modestly epistemic procedure gives legitimacy and authority to the general run of laws, even the mistaken ones. The analogy to keep in mind here is the jury trial, since its epistemic value is a crucial reason we think that even erroneous verdicts have authority. That, too, is an epistemic proceduralist structure. The point here is that we are not looking for a source of extremely high accuracy for democratic procedures (though that would be nice). Something quite modest will serve the needs of the theory.

We can start with the very influential idea in recent deliberative democracy theory, that it seems possible to construct an imaginary forum for collective deliberation about political issues in such a way that it would have a strong tendency to make just decisions—to get right answers, so to speak. If there is some feature of actual deliberations that would block this accuracy, we remove it from the imaginary ideal. There are certain familiar features that many think will serve this purpose: all have equal time and power in the deliberation, all address the common good rather than merely some partial interests, all have certain capacities to recognize good arguments against their proposals and others, and so on.

One use of an ideal deliberative situation is to let it actually constitute the truth about rightness or justice. A different use of an imaginary ideal deliberative situation, and the one I propose to rely on, is to treat it as an ideal epistemic situation, not as constituting the truth. That is, this sort of ideal imagines deliberators for whom there are independent facts about what ought to be done. As a consequence, even the ideal epistemic deliberation can make mistakes. While a morally constitutive ideal deliberation would have to include the veto power, vitiating any serious analogy with democratic arrangements, an epistemic model deliberation has no such need.

This improves the prospects for an analogy between the ideal and actual deliberations, but we should still regard any close resemblance as hopeless. For example, actual political deliberations could not possibly give everyone equal, much less unlimited, time, nor could their rational capacities be what they should be in the ideal. Unlike so many democratic theories that employ a hypothetical ideal (constitutive or epistemic) deliberative situation, the aim here would not be to shape actual institutions and practices in order to structurally resemble the ideal arrangement. If close resemblance were possible that would be fine, but if not there is a "problem of second best": once certain ideal conditions are violated, it no longer makes sense to think that the other ones are still parts of the second-best scenario. If, for example, one side in a political dispute credibly threatens violence in order to coerce a settlement more to its liking (an epistemically distorting move, to put it politely), what would the goal of mirroring the ideal structure tell us to do? First, of course, it would say to remove that element of force. But suppose that is simply not possible. The choice is either for the other side to threaten some countervailing force, or to stand pat and continue deliberating rationally as it gets politically crushed. Which of these is more likely to produce the same results as the force-free epistemically ideal deliberative situation? In many cases the insertion of additional force is more likely to restore the results to what the model deliberation would have arrived at. This kind of countervailing deviation departs only further from any structural resemblance to the ideal, but since the aim is epistemic there is no reason to seek such resemblance for its own sake.

This model of countervailing deviation from the ideal epistemic deliberation promises to give a more plausible account of what is morally appropriate political behavior—as is too often said, it is not a college seminar. Details about what kinds of political practice would be called for by this model are too sensitive to the complexities of specific contexts to say much useful about in a philosophical treatment. This brings us full circle from our opening disclaimer about the limits of a philosophical framework. I have willfully proceeded at a fairly high level of abstraction, since I believe that this is where many of the most important problems in democratic theory reside. Still, is there no concrete vision of politics that emerges from the distinctive features of epistemic proceduralism? I conclude with some impressions of my own about implications the view might have in practice, emphasizing that these are not propositions for which I have argued.

First, if points of view get their influence on public conclusions by virtue of the wealth they have at their disposal, public reasoning will be seriously distorted unless this irrational element of power can somehow be countervailed in creative political practice.

Second, legal and social protection for the ability to dissent from orthodoxies and majority positions is not (at least not merely) some right owed to the dissenter, but a crucial ingredient in a healthy public life, one in which there is a basis for hope that the public view might discover and remedy its errors over time and move progressively toward sounder views.

Third, equality in political matters is also not some natural right, even if a certain kind of equal regard is. Political equality depends on, and finds its limits in, what sorts of arrangements will allow the promotion of justice and common good in a way that can be justified to the broad range of points of view that are owed acceptable justifications for the coercive political arrangements under which they live. Inequality of various kinds is bound to pass this test, but I have argued that the overall system seems bound to be recognizably democratic in its procedures for making law and policy. Finally, where epistemic proceduralism's aspirations are met—which might be unlikely, but is hardly impossible—there is an obligation to obey the law. Not just any law, since some could be too unjust or unjust in the wrong way, but including many laws that are indeed unjust. Legitimate politics involves authority, and there is no getting around it. We cannot collectively live as we ought to live and still be under only our own authority. Perhaps this is still all fairly abstract, and, even as far as it goes it is hardly an original vision of politics in modern times. But originality and detail at the level of institutions and concrete practices are not the areas where I have tried to make my contribution. What I offer instead is a philosophical framework.

Truth and Despotism

TRUTH AS DESPOTISM

Hannah Arendt observes that "from the viewpoint of politics, truth has a despotic character."[1] Some speak of truth, or appeals to truth, as apolitical, or antipolitical, or evasions of the political, but they seem really to mean that these lean toward a despotic kind of politics. Their language exhibits a certain commitment about what it would take to make politics morally superior to despotism. The anxiety about truth is that it is thought to foreclose dispute, disagreement, and deliberation (three different things). Arendt worries that truth "precludes debate, and debate constitutes the very essence of political life."[2] If politics ought to be essentially a realm of contestation, then it must not recognize anything as true beyond contestation. The point of this view is not mainly that certain avenues of contestation must be socially open or even legally protected. It is the deeper claim that for purposes of political discourse truth is not an appropriate category, since politics must not begin with conclusions. Nor, of course, should it ever end, and so it ought not to involve conclusions (as distinct from decisions) at all. It is an especially radical suggestion with respect to what Arendt calls factual truth (an example of hers is, "Germany invaded Belgium in August 1914").[3]

Arendt resists this line of thought, ending her essay "Truth and Politics" by concluding that

> [the political] sphere, its greatness notwithstanding, is limited. . . . [I]t does not encompass the whole of man's and the world's existence. It is limited by those things which men cannot change at will. And it is only by respecting its own borders that this realm, where we are free to act and to change, can remain intact and keep its own integrity and its own promises. Conceptually, we may call truth what we cannot change; metaphorically, it is the ground on which we stand and the sky that stretches above us.[4]

On the other hand, she contends, "philosophic truths," including ethical propositions about justice or human equality, have no legitimate place in politics as truths. That would "violat[e] the rules of the political realm" in which such matters depend "on free agreement and consent . . . discursive, representative thinking . . . persuasion and dissuasion."[5] Deep normative truths could only rule as despots—that is, illegitimately.

There is another source of anxiety about truth in politics, one that doesn't depend on the idea that politics is about conflict or opposition, even of a deliberative kind. This other anxiety is that one person's having the truth does not, by itself, warrant their political authority over those who do not. The Platonic conception—of political authority as expertise—would need to be considered, for its truth, on its own. It seems, at least initially, to confuse experts with bosses. For convenience, we can call it the *expert/boss fallacy*. (Of course, I haven't yet shown that it is a fallacy, but I argue this in chapter 3, "An Acceptability Requirement.") This second anxiety about truth in politics—the one that thinks that the Platonic move from expert to boss is a fallacy—worries that anyone who thinks (as very many are bound to) that their own views are true and their opponents' view are not, will fallaciously and oppressively conclude that their opponents ought to be under their political authority. Against this we might hold, as John Rawls writes, that "since political power is the coercive power of free and equal citizens as a corporate body, this power should be exercised . . . only in ways that all citizens can reasonably be expected to endorse in the light of their common human reason."[6] Where truth cannot meet this condition, it has no political authority.

The first anxiety about truth in politics—the insulation of politics from conclusions—has a very different motivation from this separation of authority from truth. Conclusions are kept out of politics, on the first view, because they are thought to preempt contestation. This second view, in which truths are kept away from claims to authority, assumes rather that appeals to truth are divisive and too deeply contestable for political purposes. On this view, contestation may be the occasion of politics, but the essence of normatively sound politics is, in some form, the moderation or accommodation—or even avoidance—of these contests, disputes, and disagreements. Politics ought to avoid appeal to ultimate truths, on this view, not because they would shut down debate and contestation, but because they would provoke too much debate, contestation, and division. Rawls writes, "Holding a political conception as true, and for that reason alone the one suitable basis of public reason, is exclusive, even sectarian, and so likely to foster political division."[7] (Why and when political division is to be avoided is a further matter, and social peace is certainly not the guiding value in Rawls's view, nor in mine.)

If conflict (even of only an argumentative kind) is placed at the center of the political values, there is a predictable ambivalence about appeals to truth in political discourse. Even though, as we have seen, the appeal to truth is criticized as antipolitical, this latter Rawlsian avoidance of truth is also called antipolitical insofar as it shrinks from the especially deep contestation among competing views on the most deeply held matters. The view of such critics often seems to be that citizens ought to feel free to appeal to the truth in the political sphere and to engage in the ensuing contestation about truth. Political theorists, on the other hand, must not appeal to the truth, since this would be to proceed as if politics ought to begin with conclusions.

It will be important for my purposes in this book to resist both prongs. Against the idea that the truth, as such, must play no role in normative political theory, I will argue that a standard of general acceptability must be put forward as a true standard, not just a generally acceptable one. So the charge that any such appeal to truth is contrary to the spirit of sound politics must be confronted early on. On the other hand, the idea that citizens ought to enter their deepest convictions about what is true into the political forum, since the ensuing contestation is of the essence of sound politics, cannot be supported by any adequate view of political legitimacy and authority. This bracketing of truths for certain political purposes is central to the argument I will mount for a democratic basis of political authority, especially against the ancient view that those who know best ought to rule and be obeyed.

In calling my account of democratic authority "epistemic," it may seem that truth enters the story in a further way, as the standard against which political decisions are judged, with democracy performing best. This would be a misunderstanding, however. As we will see in later chapters, the substantive standards of correctness by which political decisions are judged do not rise to this role by being true, but by being generally acceptable in a certain way. At that stage, in other words, the question of the real truth about, say, substantive justice is bracketed. Beyond that important point, however, there is a parallel line of thought, insofar as I resist the idea that questions of normative substance can be put aside in favor of less controversial questions of process or procedure. Just as a standard of general acceptability is not a self-sufficient substitute for appeals to the normative truths, similarly, the standard of democratic approval is not normatively adequate without some appeal to substantive standards by which democratic decisions ought to be evaluated. This general dissatisfaction with overly procedural approaches to politics will be treated in more detail in chapters 4 and 5. For now it is important to see that despite this abstract point, the substantial standards by which democratic decisions are to be evaluated are not, on the view developed here, standards of truth, or of true justice as such.

I have spoken about normative truths, but that terminology needs a little explaining. Normativity in general comprises evaluative or prescriptive matters of many kinds, including logic, morality, law, roles, etiquette, and others. When I speak of standards for the evaluation of political decisions, I mean a certain kind of moral evaluation, unless I specify otherwise. But it could be misleading simply to speak of moral standards, since the overall argument will contend that the whole moral truth about political decisions is not admissible in political justification. The standards that are used must be generally acceptable in a suitable sense. The result is a qualified sort of moral normativity. The general acceptability requirement is, of course, a moral requirement in its own right. Then, according to it, the standards that apply to the evaluation of political decisions do not apply as moral truths but as generally acceptable standards. I will refer to them as normative standards to avoid the danger of suggesting that they are applicable as moral truths. Still, the normativity these standards possess is certainly of the moral variety rather than some other kind of normativity altogether.

Making Truth Safe for Democracy

The allegedly despotic character of truth would be undercut in a deep way if there were no truth of the matter after all—no truth about what a political community should do. On the other hand, this kind of skepticism has costs, and I hope to show that they are not worth incurring. The costs are too high partly because the existence of normative political truths needn't lead in any despotic direction. If political truth led inexorably to the legitimacy of dictatorship by experts (roughly Plato's view), then we should suspect that something in the argument has gone wrong, possibly the idea that there are political truths at all. I want to argue that there are philosophical costs to denying political truth, and, anyway, they do not justify dictatorship.

It will be helpful to consider some costs of holding that there are no truths about what ought, politically, to be done. As a preliminary, however, we should distinguish two broad kinds of skepticism about such truth, only one of which is germane. The less germane skepticism holds that moral or evaluative statements merely express attitudes of a kind distinct from belief, such as emotions or commitments. On views of this kind (generally called versions of "noncognitivism," in denying that moral statements have cognitive, or truth-evaluable, content), statements such as "murder is wrong" are not true or false, any more than the emotions or commitments they express are true or false. So, in a political debate about whether affirmative action is or is not just, this view about moral statements says that neither side has a true or false view of the matter. But this metaethical position, whatever its merits, is not germane to the question of truth's despotism over politics. Those who hope to undercut the despotic power of truth in politics do so by denying that affirmative action is either just or unjust in any way that is prior to and independent of appropriate political decisions on the matter. But the noncognitivist metaethical view doesn't imply this at all. Noncognitivism is simply a view about the supposed difference between this kind of "holding," on one hand, and belief in truth-evaluable propositions, on the other. That issue is quite separate from the view that affirmative action is neither just nor unjust independently of democratic decisions. Noncognitivism is not necessarily skeptical at this normative level.

To help keep disputes about noncognitivism off to the side, it will be useful to admit a "minimal" kind of truth (even if noncognitivists themselves might not always like the term). Let us say that a statement that "x is F" is true in at least the minimal sense if and only if x is indeed F. This formula allows us to say that noncognitivists hold that "affirmative action is unjust" is true in at least the minimal sense just so long as they hold (as they perfectly well might) that affirmative action is unjust. So now we see that the attempt to block the despotic power of political truth, by denying that there is such truth, would involve denying that statements about what ought, politically, to be done are true or false even in the minimal sense. Noncognitivism is not committed to this, and would be no support for it. I will call the idea that there are no appropriate standards (not even minimally true ones) by which to judge political decisions *political nihilism*. Noncognitivism does not imply political nihilism, and so the assumption that there are truths about justice (at least in the minimal sense) takes no stand for or against noncognitivism.

The costs of political nihilism—an attempt to cut off truth's despotism at the deepest possible level—are now apparent. On this view it will be difficult to make much sense of important components of political processes. One standard motive in political activity is to promote collective decisions that one holds to be normatively good, or right, or otherwise in the public interest. Activists fighting for racially equitable laws protecting civil rights appear often to have motives of this kind, for example. On the political nihilist view, this kind of motive is deeply confused, presupposing, as it does, that the political process is under the authority of some higher normative standard.

The familiarity of this motive is not a decisive objection to the nihilist view, of course. Perhaps public-interested voting is deeply confused in that way. But there is a cost here worth keeping track of: a normative theory of politics should be able to recommend admiration for aspects of politics that are, on reflection, admirable. The nihilist view seems bound to regard many of the central motives—motives (broadly described) of public interest—in what appear to most people to be admirable political activity as deeply deficient, since, so it holds, there is no public interest or any other (potentially despotic) normative standard by which political choices could be better or worse.

There is an influential school of democratic theory that is undeterred by this cost. Schumpeter leads these ranks with the frank declaration that there is no such thing as the common good, or public interest.[8] Voters who previously harbored those fantasies would do well to put their energy more simply behind promoting the satisfaction of their "preferences." If there is a normative account of politics at all here (a serious question in the case of many Schumpeterians), it holds that the only political values are procedural. The value of democracy lies simply in its subjecting important matters to political control, not in any particular tendency of this to lead to supposedly good or just decisions. The revolutionary field of social choice theory owes much to this point of view.[9] Founding authors in this tradition typically begin by denying that there is any standard for evaluating social decisions that is independent of individual values or preferences. Then the question arises— the driving question of social choice theory—of what standard there might be which *is* dependent on, or a "function" of, individual values or preferences. Arrow's impossibility theorem and related results then engender a second tier of skepticism: there is also no standard (of common good, or social preference, or collective will) that is any intuitively acceptable function of individual values or preferences. So, many conclude, there is no preference-independent standard, and no preference-dependent standard, and so no standard at all for the evaluation of social choices. The challenge for this view, then, is to find any reasoned basis of normative support for one form of politics over another.

The two major recent developments in democratic theory—social choice theory, and deliberative accounts of legitimacy—are deeply opposed to each other in important ways, but there is a striking convergence in the shared denial that political decisions are properly subject to prior normative standards (a topic for chapter 5, "The Flight from Substance"). Just as we saw social choice theory resorting to supposedly purely procedural standards for aggregating individual preferences or choices, deliberative democratic theory claims to employ only purely procedural standards for the public employment of reason. Habermas leads the way, exerting important influence on others. "The notion of a higher law," Habermas urges, "belongs to the premodern world."[10] There are no standards that loom over the political process, policing its decisions, not even any standard of reason itself. "We need not confront reason as an alien authority residing somewhere beyond political communication."[11] The only normative standards that apply to political decisions are noninstrumental evaluations of the procedures that produced them—in particular, standards of "procedural rationality" based on the power of reason in public political discourse. Any imposition (in theory or practice) of substantive political standards would preempt the ultimately dialogical basis upon which Habermas thinks political normativity must rest. There is an echo of Arendt here: politics is the site of discursive contestation, so politics cannot begin with conclusions.

Here is where the price of the nihilist view is evidently too high to pay, or so I will argue. No appeal to good outcomes is permitted on this view, there supposedly being no such thing. The only alternative is an appeal to purely procedural values. Perhaps there are purely procedural values; procedural fairness is one salient candidate, standards of rational discussion another. The view developed here, epistemic proceduralism, is proceduralist in an important way. The question, however, is whether procedural values alone can ground a normative account of politics that recommends admiration for politics that are, on reflection, admirable. In particular, these theorists typically want to recommend democratic political forms on such a purely procedural basis. This stratagem will be criticized in detail in chapter 4, "The Limits of Fair Procedure." To anticipate that discussion, no adequate distinction between

27

purely procedural values, on one hand, and substantive values, on the other, can explain on a purely procedural basis why political outcomes ought to answer to citizens' interests or values or choices at all. One cost, then, of resorting to the nihilist view in order to block truth's despotic associations is that one then needs to find some basis for a normative view of politics, if any is to be offered at all, without any appeal to standards of better or worse outcomes or decisions. I have not shown here that this debt cannot be paid, though I will try to show it later. Here I simply register the debt this view incurs.

If the price of the nihilist view looks high, it is important to know whether there are strong reasons for taking it in the first place. The guiding anxiety is the supposedly despotic nature of political truth. It is a political version of a worry that can arise about the existence of moral standards more generally. If we are morally bound by standards external to our will, then are we not bound rather than free? John Rawls, in his doctoral dissertation, objects to the appeal to "exalted entities" such as God, the state, the course of nature, ethical realism, essential human nature, and the real self, as sources of moral authority. He characterizes any such theory as "authoritarian," though he might as well have said "despotic."[12] There is an analogy between this rejection of exalted entities and the view that no independent standards constrain political choices. But despite the analogy, the former is no support for the latter. Even if all moral values are somehow products of the wills of moral agents, there might yet be moral values that apply to political outcomes independently of political choices. The Rawlsian school, indeed, holds that political outcomes might violate applicable principles of justice even if they are produced by proper political procedures. In *A Theory of Justice*,[13] the view was ambiguous between saying that these principles of justice were simply true and saying, with his later *Political Liberalism*,[14] that they are appropriate principles for judging political decisions whether or not they are true, on the basis of their being, in a certain sense, a reasonable political conception of justice. This takes us into the idea of an acceptability criterion, the subject of chapter 3. In any case, on a Rawlsian view the principles of justice normatively constrain political decisions, and that's all that's needed to raise the fears we've seen about truth's despotism.

This use of the ideas of despotism and authoritarianism is metaphorical, and it is worth comparing metaphorical to real despotism in order to get some perspective. Even if there is nothing degrading or objectionable about being under the authority of moral standards that were not produced by my own will, being under the authority of another person's will is open to additional objections. For one thing, whether one person has authority over another must itself be settled by the content of morality. It could be objectionable on moral grounds. By contrast, the supposed authority of morality itself could not be. It is, initially at least, more difficult to see what evaluative standpoint might be adopted from which to criticize the very possibility of authoritative moral requirements. The standpoint of reason is one time-honored possibility. At any rate, there is, in the case of political authority, the standpoint of morality itself. There are more familiar moral resources from which to draw in objecting to someone's claim to rule another person. One reason for noting this is to keep in mind that even if morality is authoritative over us, it is not a boss. Morality's claim to rule moral agents is not the same thing as one person's claim to rule another, and it cannot be assumed that the two different claims ought to be judged by similar criteria. A second reason for noting the difference is that even if independent standards for political decisions are admitted not to be intrinsically (though in any case metaphorically) despotic or authoritarian, it is natural to worry that their existence would lend support to literally despotic or authoritarian ideologies.

It is possible to motivate Habermas's deep proceduralism—his version of the no-truth argument—in terms of this looming threat of superior expertise.[15] The Habermasian concern about the "monological" preempting by political philosophers of genuine political choice is, at root, an objection to the privileging of any particular citizen's normative perspective. In a free society of equals, the philosopher's claim to expertise is and ought to be politically contestable rather than a conclusion from which politics must begin. And yet, if there were genuine procedure-independent standards of justice, it is hard to believe that no one would be any more expert than anyone else. How could that be? Whether or not philosophers have a claim to special knowledge, surely some citizens will be better than others (for, surely some are worse) on any matter about which some opinions are correct and others mistaken. The idea of procedure-independent standards of political decisions may seem to lead inexorably, then, to the legitimacy of rule by the genuine experts, whomever they may be. The choice can seem to be between *epistocracy*,[16] or rule by the wise, on the one hand, and *deep proceduralism*, the denial that such independent standards exist, on the other. If only it can be established that there is no genuine substance in the first place, then the proceduralist flight from substance is complete.

29

Deliberative democracies are then existentially free and self-determining. The value of democratic deliberation is vindicated by making democratic deliberation itself the final political value.

The theory of deliberative democracy, however, is deeply ambivalent. It hopes to explain why deliberation is required in addition to merely fair procedures of voting, but it hopes to do so in a way that never appeals to the existence of any procedure-independent standard for better or worse political decisions. The task for deliberative democratic theory, then, has become the odd one of explaining the central importance of substantive public discussion of the procedure-independent merits of possible political decisions, without ever granting that there actually are any procedure-independent standards. This odd tangle, in which democratic deliberation is valorized at the same time as its content is debunked, is, I think, an embarrassment for the dominant strand of deliberative democratic political philosophy. The more minimal conception of democratic participation to which social choice theory inclines at least avoids this debunking (since voters are seen as promoting their own interests), but only by straining to imagine an admirable politics where citizens (contrary to fact, of course) would not advocate and pursue competing substantive conceptions of justice or the common good.

There is, indeed, a natural association between the ideas of *truth* and *knowledge,* on the one hand, and, on the other hand, the ideas of *expertise* and *authority.* Socrates even argued, in an explicitly political context, that knowledge *is* power.[17] He also held the distinct view that knowledge justifies power—that the wise have a special claim to rule.[18] Unlike Plato, Socrates was no authoritarian, because he denied that anyone was wise in the requisite way.[19] Consider, though, the authoritarian position, which I shall call *epistocracy,* that is barely kept at bay by Socrates' doubts about moral expertise. It includes the following three tenets:

1. *The Truth Tenet*: there are true (at least in the minimal sense)[20] procedure-independent normative standards by which political decisions ought to be judged.

2. *The Knowledge Tenet*: some (relatively few) people know those normative standards better than others.[21]

3. *The Authority Tenet*: The normative political knowledge of those who know better is a warrant for their having political authority over others.

I will treat the idea of authority more fully later, in chapters 7 and 8, but for now we may take it to stand for the moral power of one agent to require action of another. The authority of the state would be its power, at least sometimes, to create moral obligations of obedience by issuing laws.

Epistocracy is authoritarian, not metaphorically but literally, in advocating a form of elite rule. Advocates of democracy, and other enemies of despotism, will want to resist the case for epistocracy. We have looked briefly at some ways of denying the truth tenet, noting how that view owes us some account of how to think normatively about politics without resorting to any normative standards, other than purely procedural ones, for evaluating political decisions. But epistocracy could also be resisted by rejecting either or both of the other two tenets. Even if the Truth Tenet is granted, we might wish to deny the knowledge tenet and argue that the relevant normative political knowledge is not unequally distributed in any significant way. Since there are no experts of this kind, the authority tenet would be shorn of any epistocratic implications. Epistocracy could be rejected without needing to consider the merits of the Authority Tenet, the supposed appropriateness of rule by the wise.

For simplicity I will speak of knowledge and of the wise in a way that ignores the possibility of bad faith or weakness of will. I assume for now that those who knew best what to do and how to do it, would also do it as well as possible. Of course, this is unrealistic. It might seem that the argument requires a good faith tenet, and that this is yet another place to locate a way to resist the argument for epistocracy. I do not posit an additional tenet because the argument does not require the knowers to have "better faith" than ordinary citizens. So long as they have as good faith as the typical citizen and this typical character leans to the good rather than to the bad, the superior knowledge of the knowers would promote the good. Later, in chapter 11 ("Why Not an Epistocracy of the Educated?"), I consider the suggestion that the rulers, even if they are knowers, would have especially bad faith, but I argue that no such premise is available.

I think the knowledge tenet is very difficult to deny. Many reasons for denying it that seem initially plausible turn out to rest on misunderstandings. For example, virtually everyone will deny that some elite has privileged infallible access to a Platonic realm of absolute truths. The knowledge tenet, though, does not claim that anyone has perfect knowledge, but only that some have significantly more than others. Accordingly, the authority tenet doesn't require some high degree of knowledge, but only some degree of superiority in knowledge.

31

Some resist the view that anyone has better knowledge of political justice simply on the basis of their conviction that there is not enough difference to warrant differential political authority. But the knowledge tenet doesn't make any claim about political authority, and so that objection is jumping ahead to the authority tenet. Leaving aside any claims about political authority, on what ground can it be denied that while there are (as we grant now for the sake of argument) normative political truths, no one knows them better than anyone else?

Could the knowledge tenet be resisted by resorting to a noncognitivist account of normative statements? On many analyses of the idea of knowledge, only truths can be known, and so if normative statements are neither true nor false, then they could not be known. But this is not a robust way of resisting the knowledge tenet, since just as we have specified a minimal sense of truth, we could specify a minimal sense of knowledge. To have normative knowledge in the minimal sense we could require that it be true in the minimal sense ("x is F" is true in the minimal sense if and only if x is indeed F). Then a noncognitivist could hold that some few have the normative convictions that are, in that minimal sense, true (plus whatever further conditions they might place on the conviction's being knowledge-like). The point is that if, as a noncognitivist can perfectly well hold, some things ought to be done and others not done politically, then it might yet be that some elite has the right convictions and dispositions so as to be more likely to do what ought to be done.[22]

Another confused reason for denying such differences in knowledge holds that any proposed example of a "knower" will be enormously controversial. No doubt this is correct, and it is a point I will make heavy use of, but it does not address the knowledge tenet, which says nothing about general agreement on who the better knowers are. It says only that there are some, not that any two people would agree about who they are. General agreement turns out, as I will argue, to be important when claims about political authority are at stake, but this would be jumping the gun.

There is some temptation to think that granting that some have more of this kind of moral, practical, political wisdom than others is incompatible with the moral equality of all people. These are very different ideas, however. Indeed, the moral equality of all people is not one single clear thesis, but several (not necessarily clear) theses. Most often it stands for the idea that in some respects (needing to be specified) all people are morally owed equal respect. There are various accounts of the basis of this kind of equality—accounts of which features of people account for this equal right. But the gap between this thesis of equality and the claim that people differ in normative political wisdom can be seen without going philosophically deep. The view that people are owed equal respect, however exactly it is interpreted, is never meant to deny that people's ability to judge of good and bad, right and wrong, can be differentially affected by upbringing, education, social environment, and so on. The right to equal respect is said to be owed to people in spite of the differences in capacity for good moral judgment produced by these factors. The knowledge tenet, on the other hand, gains support from these differences. It doesn't claim that some people are innately better equipped for normative political wisdom than others. It can perfectly well say that whatever features of people might ground a right to equal respect, still there are differences in normative political wisdom. It is true that one important strand of thought in the tradition of a right to equal moral respect places some emphasis on the claim that all people have an equal capacity for virtue, that it is not the province of some special subset of people. Seneca's early formulation held that "virtue closes the door to no man."[23] But this is different in several ways. First, an equal capacity for virtue is not equal virtue. Second, even if all were equally virtuous or even if all had an equal capacity for moral wisdom, some might have greater actual normative political wisdom than others. The knowledge tenet does not apparently conflict with any of the traditional grounds for the thesis of the equality of persons.

The knowledge tenet ought to be granted. For present purposes it can at least be granted for the sake of argument. The reason is that even if it is true, along with the truth tenet, I propose to reject the case for epistocracy by rejecting the third tenet, the authority tenet.

No Invidious Comparisons

Even if there are true standards of better and worse political decisions, there may also be a true general acceptability criterion that brackets the use of the true standards. This would be a part of the nature of justified political authority. To state a rough version: no one has authority or legitimate coercive power over another without a justification that could be accepted by all qualified points of view. The idea of general acceptability can be construed to yield importantly different versions. One simple version requires that all actual subjects would accept the proposition in question. A more complex, and more influential, version holds that not just any ground of objection is, as it is usually put, "reasonable," or as I will put the idea more generally, "qualified." This version owes some account of which grounds of rejection are qualified and which are not, and an account of why. I abstract from the more specific possible versions for now. In this version, political authority must be justifiable in terms that are beyond qualified rejection, though not necessarily beyond all actual rejection. This conception of political legitimacy will concern us throughout the book, and especially in chapter 3 ("An Acceptability Requirement"), but this initial sketch is enough to set up the present issues.

Even standards that meet the general acceptability criterion would subordinate political procedures to these standards in a certain way. The real truth, so to speak, can be bracketed by an acceptability criterion, but that would not free politics from the supposed despotism of prior normative standards for political decisions. So standards of this less metaphysically ambitious kind might be denied for their despotic tendencies. The rejection of the existence of such standards remains a version of the "no truth" view, albeit a variation. The debt incurred by the nihilist view was an obligation to ground a normative account of politics on purely procedural values, since supposedly no nonprocedural or substantive standards for outcomes exist. In the present variant, even if true standards of outcomes exist, these are bracketed in favor of generally acceptable, but still nonprocedural, standards for decisions. The denial that these exist is the denial that any substantive standards for decisions can meet the appropriate general acceptability criterion. Different versions of this skepticism are generated by different versions of the general acceptability criterion itself, on which the boundary between qualified and disqualified grounds of rejection is drawn in different ways. Wherever it is drawn, there is a possible skeptic holding that there are no substantive standards of outcomes that are immune to qualified objection. '

The dialectical situation this presents is familiar. We can substitute "acceptable standards" for "truth" in the three-step case for epistocracy. The new version of the truth tenet becomes the claim that there are standards (the acceptable ones) for evaluating political decisions. The knowledge tenet now holds that some know better than others which decisions meet the acceptable standards. The authority tenet now says that the differential knowledge warrants the authority of those who know better than others. It remains a case for a literally authoritarian view: an epistocratic account of political authority—epistocracy without truth.

One thing that changes in this version built on general acceptability is that the new version of the truth tenet might seem easier to doubt. Granting for now that there is some appropriate general acceptability criterion, it is philosophically easier to doubt that any standard can meet that criterion than it is to doubt that there is any true standard. The simple reason is that it is entirely possible that some true standard yet fails to be beyond qualified rejection. Nevertheless, we have noted an imposing debt incurred by the nihilist view, and it would be incurred equally by the version of the nihilist view that asserts that there are no generally acceptable substantive standards of political decisions. In both cases, any normative account of politics would have to proceed without the supposedly missing substantive standards, with the salient alternative being to appeal only to purely procedural values. We have not refuted this possibility, which is embraced by normatively inclined social choice theorists, and also by many democratic theorists who, whether or not they subscribe to the social choice theory agenda, retreat from substantive evaluation of political decisions to the purely procedural value of, specifically, fairness. Here it is enough to note the reliance of the nihilist view, even in its "no acceptable standards" version, on pure proceduralism. Later, as I have said, I will argue against the kind of proceduralism required, leaving the no-truth and no-acceptable-standards views without any evident source for a normative political theory.

The introduction of a general acceptability criterion, then, has not materially affected the case against epistocracy. Supposing there are some acceptable substantive standards, there might be experts on those. The denial of such experts is no more plausible here than before, and so the question is how to block this new case for epistocracy.

This leaves the revised authority tenet. It says roughly that the experts, if any, ought to rule. This takes account of the general acceptability criterion in one way so long as the experts in question are experts not on true, but on acceptable standards of political decisions. But it seems to ignore the requirement of acceptability in another way by supposing that so long as there really are such experts then they are entitled to rule. But a justification proceeding from the fact—or truth—that someone is an expert is not yet admissible according to the acceptability criterion. In addition, his status as an expert must be beyond qualified rejection. Here, then, is a way to block the new case for epistocracy without denying that there are generally acceptable standards of political decisions, and without denying that some could rule more wisely than others by those very standards: argue that any particular person or group who might be put forward as such an expert would be subject to controversy, and qualified controversy in particular. No invidious comparisons among citizens with respect to their normative political wisdom can pass the appropriate general acceptability criterion (yet to be specified) of political legitimacy. This move is stated only schematically so far, and it will need some filling in. For convenience, call this general kind of move *no invidious comparisons*.

We have not specified which points of view should count as qualified for this purpose, nor will we do so in any complete way. For now we simply assume that not all possible points of view are qualified, and that many points of view are qualified even though they are mistaken on important matters. Finally, the category is not to be defined with the aim of guaranteeing that there will be any justifications acceptable to all qualified points of view. As the argument proceeds we will draw the line between qualified and disqualified views on particular matters as the argument requires.

Is Democracy Rejectable Too?

In asserting that no invidious comparisons enfranchising some adults and not others is acceptable to all qualified points of view, I have made it clear that a lot of disagreement is to be counted as qualified. No one is so obviously better at these things that there isn't some qualified point of view that denies it. This raises the following question about the structure of my argument against epistocracy. Even if all invidious comparisons—claims that some are wiser than others and that letting them rule would lead to better decisions—are open to qualified disagreement, isn't it also contestable among qualified points of view whether majority rule is the epistemically best arrangement? That is, couldn't there be qualified disagreement all around? If so, no epistemic approach to political justification would be able to meet the qualified acceptability requirement. My argument seems to treat universal suffrage as a default, with a presumption against any deviation from it. Deviations are subjected to a general acceptability requirement, whereas universal suffrage itself does not need to meet it. This would seem to assume that democracy is the best arrangement, or at least to erect a presumption in its favor, without argument. I am hoping, to the contrary, to provide arguments in favor of democracy based on principles that do not assume its superiority.

This challenge can be met if, as I will argue, the advantage that universal suffrage has over invidious comparisons derives not from any democratic principle, but from the deeper principle that I am calling the qualified acceptability requirement itself. It places a special burden of justification on proposed relations of authority or legitimate coercive power. When the burden is not discharged, it asserts that the default condition is the absence of authority or legitimate power. Invidious comparisons purport to establish the authority and legitimate power of some over others in a way that universal suffrage does not, and so invidious comparisons must meet a burden of justification that universal suffrage need not. This is the outline of my reply to the challenge at hand, but it requires some explanation.

I don't mean that democratic arrangements involving universal suffrage are free of the qualified acceptability requirement. Democracy involves some ruling others. Roughly, the majority on any decision rules over the minority. Some views, deriving mainly from Rousseau, try to show, to the contrary, that in a proper democracy, each "obeys no one but himself."[24] I do not accept these arguments, and don't mean to rely on any such thing here. The argument of the book, taken as a whole, is that democracy can meet the burdens of justification incurred by proposals to subject some to the rule of others. However, there is something additional present in the case of invidious comparisons used to justify epistocratic arrangements. Here, not only is each minority voter in each decision subject to rule by the majority in that single case. Under unequal suffrage, some people are formally and permanently subjected to the rule of certain others. This is a ruling relationship that is not present under majority rule, even though majority rule is also a ruling relationship of a kind. As such, this additional element is itself subject to an extra burden of justification that universal suffrage does not incur, and if it can't meet it, the default is the absence of that particular ruling relation.

I said that my aim is to justify the legitimacy and authority of certain democratic arrangements on the basis of principles that do not simply assume the value or superiority of democracy. The main principle (or schema of a principle) that I rely on is a qualified acceptability requirement. This can seem like a democratic principle of sorts. It subjects justifications to the scrutiny of all qualified points of view, and they fail if they are rejected in this process. Of course, the "process" never really takes place, and the principle doesn't require any actual process. If a proposed justification is rejectable from any qualified point of view, the justification fails. In later chapters, I discuss and criticize at some length the tendency of much recent democratic theory to locate the democratic credentials of their accounts in hypothetical procedures such as this one.[25] It is important not to let the issue become merely terminological. However one person or another might like to use the term *democracy* for her own theoretical purposes, that won't make her account suitable for my theoretical purposes. What I will mean by *democracy* is the actual collective authorization of laws and policies by the people subject to them. That is the sort of authority and legitimacy of laws that I want to explain by reference to principles that do not simply assume it. The qualified acceptability requirement, since it makes no reference at all to the actual means of authorizing laws or policies, makes no reference to democracy, in that sense, at all, and so does not prejudge the question of its value or justification. The principle leaves open whether nondemocratic arrangements might be justifiable to all qualified points of view. It takes further argument to try to show that they cannot.

The presumption against invidious comparisons, and favoring universal suffrage, is warranted by the qualified acceptability requirement, and this does not beg the question in favor of democracy. This vindicates my suggestion that universal suffrage achieves a certain default status, not subject to the same burden of justification that invidious comparisons are.

Conclusion

In this chapter I have set up two of the main tasks of the remainder of the book, both having to do with the role of truth in democratic theory. One is to critique the pure proceduralist strategy that is so common in contemporary democratic theory, and to propose an alternative. This will require showing how procedure-independent standards for evaluating political decisions can and must play a role in accounts of the authority and legitimacy of those decisions. This requires us to consider the question of political authority generally, the infirmity of purely procedural approaches associated with social choice theory on one side and deliberative democracy on the other, and the development of an alternative that avoids these criticisms.

A second task we have set up is to show why the existence of procedure-independent normative standards for democratic decisions does not support the rule of the wiser citizens. The strategy, as I have suggested, will be to appeal to a requirement that political authority be justifiable to those subject to it in ways they can accept. A requirement of general acceptability cannot plausibly count just any objection as decisive, and so a distinction must be drawn and defended between qualified and disqualified grounds of objection. With the idea of an acceptability criterion in hand, the aim will be to show that justifications that appeal to the greater political wisdom of some subset of citizens will generally be open to qualified objection and so unavailable in political justification. So far, truth is largely kept out of political justification even without denying that it exists.

Boiling my approach down even further, we might say this: I hope to vindicate a democratic account of political authority by reconciling two fundamental ideas. First, since political choices can be made well or badly, the justification of political institutions must rest, at least partly, on the substantive quality of its decisions. Second, the move from expertise to authority is a fallacy, and so the epistemic value of political arrangements must be assessed in terms acceptable to the wide range of qualified points of view. The reasons for avoiding truth in politics are not reasons to avoid addressing the epistemic value of political arrangements. An epistemic approach to politics, morally constrained by a general acceptability requirement, generates a philosophically adequate and recognizably democratic basis for political authority. This, in the most basic terms, is the thesis of this book.

An Acceptability Requirement

WHY NOT EPISTOCRACY? That is a central question throughout this book. As we have seen (in chapter 2, "Truth and Despotism"), the only way to answer such a challenge, since it is certain that there are subsets of citizens that are wiser than the group as a whole, is to appeal to some principle that shows that even though they have these superior abilities, this does not necessarily ground their having authority. After all, from the fact, even granting that it is a fact, that you know better than the rest of us what should be done, it certainly does not follow in any obvious way that you may rule, or that anyone has a duty to obey you. I call this the *expert/boss fallacy*, inferring illicitly from "S would rule better" to "S is a legitimate or authoritative ruler." To the person who knows better, the other might hope to say, "You might be right, but who made you boss?"

The question is, what kind of principle might explain why experts are not necessarily entitled to be bosses? In certain respects, obviously, they are the most qualified for the job. In this chapter I will argue that there is a very attractive family of principles, which I call *acceptability requirements*, that will tend to block the expert/boss inference, and so tend to stand in the way of the usual manner of defending epistocracy. I will mainly defend a family of principles against objections to the whole family. This will leave lots of possible variations, and only some of them will actually do the work that my larger argument requires: especially, blocking epistocracy but not blocking epistemic arguments for democracy. Toward the end of the chapter I will describe a way of proceeding without defending any very specific version of an acceptability requirement. After laying out the structure of the view in chapter 6, "Epistemic Proceduralism," in chapter 11, "Why Not an Epistocracy of the Educated?," I try to meet what I think is the most formidable epistocratic proposal, John Stuart Mill's argument that those who are better educated should have more votes.

There are two main parts to this chapter. In the first part, I defend the abstract idea of a qualified acceptability requirement, leaving it open who should count as qualified. I defend it by rebutting the twin charges that it includes too much, and that it excludes too much. The second part argues that, contrary to many readings of Rawls, a qualified acceptability requirement cannot suffice without appealing to the truth. I support this by noting some consequences of the fact of self-application: that such a requirement is itself among the doctrines to which it applies.

LEGITIMACY VERSUS AUTHORITY

Among other things the state does, it issues commands through the law. When it does, it normally threatens a sanction such as jail or a fine if one is caught disobeying. Two profound and difficult questions concern, first, whether such commands create any moral obligation to obey, and second, whether the state acts permissibly in threatening and carrying out coercive sanctions. The relation between these questions—the state's authority and its legitimacy, as I will use those terms—is a deeply unsettled matter.

I want to argue, in this chapter, for a constraint on successful political justification, but the idea of justification is ambiguous.[1] One thing it would mean for a political justification to be successful is that the commanded citizen has an obligation to obey. What is justified in that case is the state's claim that it ought to be obeyed—its claim to have authority. Another thing political justification might mean would be that the state is permitted to issue and coercively enforce certain commands. What is justified in this case is the use of coercive power. I will say that a state's uses of power are legitimate if and only if they are morally permitted owing to the political process that produced them.

I offer an account of authority later (in chapters 7 and 8). Here I want to offer a partial view of legitimacy, of when the state is permitted to enforce (certain of its) commands. I defend a certain sort of necessary condition on the legitimate exercise of political power: that it be justifiable in terms acceptable to all qualified points of view (where "qualified" will be filled in by "reasonable" or some such thing). Later, I will argue that the acceptability requirement applies only to legitimacy and not to authority, though there is a weaker counterpart there.[2] For now, though, it will suffice to briefly explain the distinction between legitimacy and authority, leaving bigger questions about authority for later.

I will use the term *legitimacy* primarily as applying to acts and threats of coercive enforcement. In a derivative use of the term, I will speak of a legitimate law. This just means that the law is such that the state would, owing to the law's procedural source, be permitted to enforce it coercively.

By *authority* I will mean the condition in which a command is issued by one agent to another and the issuing of the command creates a moral requirement (of some weight or other) to comply. The term *requirement* suggests necessity, but it is meant here as admitting of different weights. I might be under requirements that ostensibly conflict, but where some outweigh others all things considered. The fact that one person's commands would be authoritative over another person in this way does not, according to this definition, yet say anything about whether it is permissible to exercise the authority, to issue the authoritative command. Also, the authority of a command (and even its permissibility)—its power to create a requirement to obey—is conceptually separate from its legitimacy (the question of whether coercive enforcement would be permissible).

It is helpful to limit the question of legitimacy to the permissibility of (threats of) violence or incarceration. These cover the main modes of legal sanction that we are ultimately interested in. Of course, states impose fines too, which do not count as either violence or incarceration. But if you fail to pay the fine, normally, violence or incarceration is threatened.

WHICH EPISTOCRACY?

We have mentioned serious difficulties for a variety of approaches to democratic authority and legitimacy that try to avoid any appeal to democracy's ability to perform well by independent standards. One motivation behind those approaches has been to avoid philosophical difficulties about the nature of the independent standards. Another motivation has surely been the traditional worry that under universal suffrage the average quality of political decision making is poor. So if performance matters, then democracy is likely to lose out to more elitist or authoritarian forms of government.

My argument in this book is not that some democratic form of government would be epistemically better than every alternative. Rather, it is that democracy will be the best epistemic strategy from among those that are defensible in terms that are generally acceptable. If there are epistemically better methods, they are too controversial—among qualified points of view, not just any points of view—to ground legitimately imposed law. A requirement of acceptability, then, plays a crucial role in the argument for epistemic proceduralism. I want to explicate the idea in a somewhat more general way than is usually done in order to high-light what I take to be the strongest arguments in its favor. Issues re-main about how, exactly, the criterion is to be formulated, but some of the most important questions about an acceptability requirement con-cern the very idea of such a thing, and hinge less on exactly which ver-sion we adopt. I will have something to say as well about the idea of specifying the criterion further.

THE IDEA OF ACCEPTABILITY

Liberalism has long been identified with the protection of certain areas of life from the claims of collective authority. Central to the cluster of liberal protections has been a guarantee of freedom of speech, thought, and con-science. Citizens could not legitimately be compelled to acknowledge, for example, the tenets of any particular creed or religion. John Rawls and others have recently extended the liberal concern for freedom of con-science in a natural direction, with Rawls calling the view "political lib-eralism." Political liberalism asserts bold principles of philosophical tol-eration in the realm of political justification. The moral and philosophical principles and doctrines used in political justification need not be true. Indeed, even true doctrines are inadmissible unless they are acceptable to all reasonable citizens without contradicting any of the wide range of reasonable moral and philosophical worldviews likely to persist in a just and open society. Political liberalism, Rawls says, "need not go beyond its conception of a reasonable judgment and may leave the concept of a true moral judgment to comprehensive doctrines."[3] Accordingly, he adopts what he calls the liberal principle of legitimacy: "Our exercise of political power is fully proper only when it is exercised in accordance with a con-stitution[4] the essentials of which all citizens as free and equal may rea-sonably be expected to endorse in the light of principles and ideals ac-ceptable to their common human reason."[5]

Truth is held to be neither necessary nor sufficient for a doctrine's ad-missibility. The moral idea behind this principle is that no person can legitimately be coerced to abide by legal rules and arrangements unless sufficient reasons can be given that do not violate that person's reason-able moral and philosophical convictions, true or false, right or wrong. An apparently new extension of the Western liberal tradition of tolera-tion, it is a philosophical doctrine that "applies the principle of toleration to philosophy itself."[6] It would be a kind of intolerance to think that

43

any doctrines could form a part of political justification even if some citizens conscientiously held reasonable moral, religious, or philosophical views that conflicted with them.

I use the term *doctrine* to cover a wide variety: factual statements, principles, practical proposals, moral judgments, and so forth. Thus, an acceptability requirement is itself a doctrine. "Admissibility" of a doctrine (or a conjunction of doctrines) consists in its not failing any of the criteria for inclusion in a fully valid political justification, whatever they are. The idea of justification must remain largely unanalyzed here. This much will suffice: a fully valid political justification lays out reasons that establish the moral permissibility of the enforcement of legal commands, even coercively.

Different "stages of justification" are individuated by what is being justified: principles of justice, constitutional provisions or interpretation, laws, administrative policies, and so forth. To say justification at every stage is constrained by reasonable acceptability of all justificatory premises is not to say that public discourse in all the corresponding forums is similarly constrained. That is a separate question. Rawls holds that a similar constraint applies to public discussion at least in certain forums, at least on certain matters. However, that question is not addressed here.

Rawls's liberal criterion of legitimacy attempts to put political justification beyond the reach of certain controversies, such as those about religion, the nature of value, or the meaning of life. It does, however, take a controversial stand in distinguishing between reasonable and unreasonable points of view. Rather than engage the debates about where to draw that line, let us look more generally at this kind of approach—not the approach that puts a lot of weight on reasonableness in particular, but at the approach that says legitimacy requires justification in terms that are acceptable, even as it does not require that it is acceptable to every point of view. To avoid any controversial associations with the idea of reasonableness itself, we should speak generically of a distinction between qualified and disqualified points of view, saying nothing yet about the content of the distinction, or about what it might have to do with reason, or reasonableness.

Neither Over- nor Underinclusive

One objection to a qualified acceptability requirement is that it is objectionably exclusive: the theorist takes it upon herself, this objection goes, to put some points of view outside the circle of qualified points of view arbitrarily, and only offers justifications that can be accepted by points of view that are (again, arbitrarily) inside that circle. Call this the *overexclusion objection*. The objection seems to advocate a version of an acceptability requirement that says the terms of justification must be acceptable to all who are subject to the political authority in question, not just to those who are in some way qualified. Call this opposing position the *unqualified acceptability requirement*. By contrast, the approach that somehow distinguishes qualified from disqualified points of view and says that justification need only be acceptable to qualified points of view adopts what I will call a *qualified acceptability requirement*.

The overexclusion objection says that any qualified acceptability requirement is too exclusive. There is another important line of objection from the opposite direction. The *overinclusion objection* argues that too many objections are being honored. The fact that some point of view conflicts with a doctrine that is being used in political justification (for example, a religious premise) should not be thought to defeat that justification unless the conflicting point of view is true or correct. According to this objection, by including (as we will assume it does) a range of incompatible, and so often false, views inside the circle of qualified and decisive objections, the qualified acceptability requirement is too inclusive.

If both the overinclusion and the overexclusion objections can be defeated, this would be strong support for the qualified acceptability approach. Let us start with the overexclusion objection, which holds that any qualified acceptability requirement wrongly excludes some points of view. This evidently means that every point of view should be counted as qualified, where that in turn means that an objection based on any point of view decisively defeats a proposed justification of some use of political power. The overexclusion objection is committed to a highly inclusive view of which objections have the power to defeat a proposed justification: all of them. Let us test the plausibility of this with an example. Consider the legal provision of universal adult suffrage, to be enforced by the threat of violence or incarceration if necessary to protect legally recognized voters against interference. According to the overexclusion objection, if someone objects to a justification of this measure on the ground, say, that the offered justification conflicts with their view that blacks or women are inferior beings of a lesser moral status, that bigoted objection defeats the justification, and the measure extending the vote is illegitimate. Indeed, suppose that the objection stems from the view that blacks are a hostile alien race from another planet. The overexclusion objection, pressed against the very idea of a qualified acceptability requirement, holds that the bigoted objection defeats the justification premised on the equality and freedom of all people.

The overexclusion objection entails what I will call the *actual acceptance view*: political justifications must be acceptable to all. This is not, apparently, a view about what objections are possible, but about actual objections. If it were about possible objections, then it would hold that justifications must be acceptable to all possible points of view, logically guaranteeing that any justification with any content at all is therefore too controversial, in principle, to be sound. That is, I suppose, a possible view, but it is absurd. I interpret the overexclusion objection to say that justifications must be acceptable to all those over whom the power in question is supposedly permissible. This could sometimes be met. It is not quite a requirement of unanimous consent. A person does not give consent to something simply because he has not raised an objection, except in special circumstances that are not typical of the political case (such as being explicitly asked if you have any objections in conditions where silence will be a way of communicating the intention to consent).

The actual acceptance view is a radical and skeptical one. Since there are actual objections to almost everything in politics, the actual acceptance view would imply that almost no law is ever legitimate. This is hardly a decisive objection to it, however. Some radical and skeptical views are true. Moreover, it would be a weak argument to say that not all actual objections are decisive defeaters because some objections are morally or rationally very defective. Indeed, some are, but that is not enough to show that they are powerless to defeat justifications. In some contexts, the moral or rational qualifications of an objection are irrelevant and any objection at all succeeds in morally prohibiting action. For example, sexual contact with someone is normally forbidden if he does not consent. It does not matter whether he is moral or rational in not consenting, the non-consent settles the matter: contact is prohibited. The analogy can be made more like the legal cases we are interested in, where legal commands are issued to a lot of people at once. Imagine a legal order commanding all citizens to submit to sexual advances by police officers. Still, obviously, the police are not permitted to initiate sex without consent merely on the ground that the refusal of consent was, in certain cases, morally or rationally defective. Any basis for withholding consent to sexual contact is decisive, whether or not it is rational, and whether or not it is morally permissible.

The analogy with sexual consent poses a challenge to the thought that legal coercion is permissible, even if some of those subject to it object, so long as the objections are unreasonable or in some other way disqualified. The sex context shows that we cannot assume without argument that there is anything that would disqualify someone's objection to an instance of coercive enforcement. The analogy hardly shows that the actual acceptance view is correct, and I do not mean to suggest that. But it is not immediately defeated by noticing that some actual objections are irrational or immoral. It is harder to defeat than that.

This might look like a very general challenge to the qualified acceptability view, the view I am defending. Here's why: the actual acceptance view is inclusive and does not disqualify any objections; it says they are all decisive justification defeaters. By contrast, the qualified acceptability view does count some views as disqualified, even though it counts many views, including mistaken ones, as nevertheless qualified. So, it might look as though they are incompatible views. But, as I said, I am defending a necessary condition on legitimacy. So let us first construe each of these views as only a necessary condition: actual acceptance says, radically, that there is only legitimacy if there is no actual objection (a condition that is rarely met, of course). Qualified acceptability says there is only legitimacy if there is no possible qualified objection. These are perfectly compatible. Each view says that certain things are justification defeaters. But neither says that nothing else is a justification defeater, and so each is compatible with the other. Together they would imply that there is no legitimacy unless there is neither any actual objection nor any qualified possible objection. If all our argument needs from the qualified acceptability requirement is a necessary condition of this kind, then we can simply avoid the difficult question about whether all actual objections defeat justifications for coercive enforcement—whether, as in the sex case, it is morally false to count any objection as disqualified. This is, indeed, the formulation of the qualified acceptability requirement that I want to defend: whatever other justification defeaters there might be, any possible qualified objection is a justification defeater.

If the actual acceptance view were interpreted as both a necessary and a sufficient condition for legitimacy, then it would conflict with the qualified acceptability requirement. The reason is that it would then say that there is legitimacy so long as there is no actual objection. This denies that there are any further necessary conditions beyond the absence of actual objections, such as an absence of any possible qualified objections. That is, it denies the qualified acceptability requirement. We have no particular reason to believe that actual acceptance is the only constraint on legitimacy, and I will be denying it. The version of the actual acceptance requirement that I will not be denying (or accepting) is the weaker claim that actual objections are decisive justification defeaters—the view that the absence of actual objections is a necessary (but maybe not sufficient) condition for legitimacy.

If the qualified acceptability view were interpreted as both necessary and sufficient for legitimacy, then it would say that there is legitimacy so long as there is no possible qualified objection. That would mean that, even if there happen to be some actual objections, if there are no possible qualified objections then the measure is legitimate. I will not be taking this stronger view, since I wish to avoid contradicting (or endorsing) the actual acceptance view. This maneuver of circumvention will have to be kept in mind. So let me emphasize: as I am construing the qualified acceptability requirement, meeting the requirement would not yet establish legitimacy. It would only show that one necessary condition on legitimacy is met. Accordingly, my central uses of the qualified acceptability requirement in the overall argument are meant not to establish the legitimacy of laws produced in certain democratic ways, but to show that they can meet a requirement of legitimacy that certain other important views cannot. Arguments for epistocracy, for example, will be shown to be open to possible qualified objections and so to fail in a way that democracy need not.

Any view of legitimacy must, at some point, face the question of why coercive enforcement is ever permitted against someone's will—what justifies punishment. That is a big and difficult question, but not one that plagues my view any more than it plagues any other approach to the question of when coercive enforcement of commands is morally permissible. I do not intend to take it up.

Before turning to the objection from the other direction, the overinclusion objection, I want to summarize the discussion of the overexclusion objection to the qualified acceptability requirement. The overexclusion objection complains about treating any objections as disqualified. But we need to distinguish between actual objections and merely possible objections. It would be absurd to say that no possible objection should be disqualified. Since every political measure is necessarily, and as a matter of logic, open to some possible objection, this view would not only imply that none are legitimate (which is not yet so absurd) but that none are legitimate simply because it would be possible, however crazily, to object to them. That is absurd. So the overexclusion objection should be interpreted as the actual acceptance requirement: any actual objection is decisive, and none is disqualified. This still has radical anti-legitimacy implications in the real political world, since there is almost always disagreement about political measures. But it is not absurd to say that actual objections are decisive. In some moral contexts, such as the power to refuse to consent to sexual contact, this is just what we say: consent is required, and it makes no difference if it is withheld for bad reasons. So the actual acceptance view is not easily dismissed. Fortunately, it is compatible with the qualified acceptability requirement, which states only that (whether or not actual objections are also justification defeaters) a political measure is illegitimate if there are possible qualified objections to it—that is, if there is no justification for it that is not open to any qualified objection. (Actual laws can be legitimate even if there are qualified objections to the laws—as the minority will often and correctly believe—on the ground that there is also a justification for the law that is beyond qualified objection, such as its source in a certain procedure.) The overexclusion objection loses much of its force when we see that the qualified acceptability requirement does not take any stand on whether any actual objections should be disqualified, and when we notice that it would be absurd to be "inclusive" with respect to all *possible* objections. One could still quarrel with any particular version about whether the line between qualified and disqualified possible views is drawn in the right place. But a sweeping objection to all qualified acceptability requirements on the grounds that they count too many views as disqualified looks very weak.

We can turn, now, to the other objection: is the very idea of a qualified acceptability requirement overinclusive by letting some objections be decisive even though they are themselves based on false doctrines? To see the motivation behind this objection, suppose that Christianity, broadly speaking, is true: roughly, there is a single all-powerful and loving creator with a son who took human form, was crucified and resurrected, and whose teachings, along with those of certain others, represent God's will and the moral truth. Next, consider a proposal to institute Bible study in public schools as a constitutional requirement. Non-Christians, of course, must reject any argument for this plan that was premised on the truth of Christianity, a premise they believe to be false. A qualified acceptability requirement might well count this objection to the plan as decisive. Some versions will draw the line between qualified and disqualified views in such a place that the rejection of Christianity, whether or not it is true, is qualified. That means that such objections are decisive justification defeaters. The question, in general terms, is this: Why should objections based on false doctrines be thought to defeat justifications that employ true premises and sound reasoning? This is the overinclusion objection, and it amounts to the assertion of an exclusive approach to justification: false views are excluded from counting as decisive objections, contrary to the view of the qualified acceptability requirement that false views might yet be decisive objections if they are qualified.

Let us try to put the objection less as a rhetorical question and more as a positive claim. The objection must say that justifications based on true premises and sound reasoning are successful, that they establish the legitimacy of the political power in question, regardless of who might (falsely, we must assume) object. Looked at in a certain way, this must be correct. If the conclusion of an argument is a claim that a certain law, if passed, may permissibly be enforced, and the premises are true and the reasoning sound, then the conclusion is true and the enforcement is legitimate. That is not the issue. We need to look more closely at what it would mean to hold a qualified acceptability requirement—and one that counts even some false views as qualified—even though true premises and sound reasoning must be granted to establish true conclusions even if they are about legitimate enforcement.

Consider an argument for constitutionally mandating Bible study:

1. Christianity is a truth of the utmost importance.
2. Truths of the utmost importance ought to be taught in public schools, a policy backed up with state force.
3. Therefore, Christianity ought to be taught in public schools, a policy backed up with state force.

If the first two premises are true, then the conclusion must be true. So where does the non-Christian object? The non-Christian obviously rejects (1). But, assuming (1) is true nevertheless, that will not prevent (1) and (2) from proving (3). So, even though the non-Christian will not accept (3) on this basis, if it is nevertheless true, then Bible study may permissibly be enforced. The non-Christian's objection, by itself, can only block that conclusion if it shows either (1) or (2) to be false, not just controversial. But it does not.

We are supposing, for the sake of discussion, that (1), which asserts Christianity as an important truth, is itself true, albeit controversial. Since the reasoning from the premises to the conclusion seems to be valid, the only remaining way to deny (3) is to deny (2). At this point, it does not matter whether the non-Christian denies (2) or not. If it is not true, then the argument for (3) fails.

We should pause to remember what our question is, before looking at (2) more closely. The question is whether the overinclusion objection would be vindicated if we were to accept that valid arguments from true premises concluding in claims about legitimate enforcement establish the truth of those legitimacy claims regardless of who might object or disagree. I grant that (3) follows from (1) and (2), regardless of who might disagree, if (1) and (2) are true. Does this establish the overinclusion objection, which denies that non-Christian objections to (1)'s assertion of Christianity could defeat this justification so long as (1) is true?

The answer is plainly "no." Even if (1) is true, that leaves (2), the claim that something's being an important truth is a sufficient basis for coercively including it in public school teaching. What if that is not true? Then the argument for (3) fails, and it fails for reasons entirely independent of any facts about reasonable or qualified disagreement about it. The argument fails because it has a false premise. The dispute between the advocate of a qualified acceptability requirement and the advocate of the overinclusion objection is not about whether valid arguments from true premises establish their conclusions: both sides can accept that they do. The dispute is over the truth about legitimacy. Premise (2) makes a claim about legitimacy that is not obvious, and is denied by the qualified acceptability requirement. It does not somehow fail because it is controversial. The question is about whether it is true. Any argument concluding in a claim about permissible enforcement will need premises about permissible enforcement. The question is what is true about permissible enforcement.

I have not yet argued that (2) is false. My aim is more modest. The overinclusion objection seems to appeal to many people because it seems to be the view you should take if you love the truth. If it is the truth that matters, then it might seem that objections based on false views should not be allowed to defeat political justifications. Call this the *true objection view*: the only qualified objections should be true ones. This line of reasoning, however, is fallacious. If you love the truth, then you want to know what account of legitimate coercion is true. One possibility, the view taken by the qualified acceptability requirement, is that the true view says that political justifications are specious if they appeal to doctrines that are not acceptable to all qualified, even if mistaken, points of view. In a certain sense, this view still says that justifications are successful if they rely on true premises. But it denies the truth of any premise that says that state enforcement power may permissibly be put behind true doctrines even if they are not acceptable. Premise (2), above, is such a premise.

Christianity might be true. But even if it is, there will also be other truths about how doctrines such as Christianity may figure in our justifications of political power. These would be truths about how we are to treat each other in certain ways. One view is that no one's objections to Christianity affect the state's legitimate enforcement powers so long as Christianity is true. Another view, still a view as to the truth of this matter, says that some objections to Christianity, even if they are mistaken, are qualified to defeat any justification that relied on the truth of Christianity. Loving the truth should lead us to consider which of these is true. It does not somehow directly favor the view that only true objections are qualified.

Let us admit that the true objection view values truth in certain ways that a qualified objection view does not. Both put themselves forward as truths about political legitimacy, and so neither is indifferent to the truth. But the true objection view goes further, saying that true objections are uniquely qualified as justification defeaters. Still, we should not grant that someone who holds the true objection view somehow cares more about the truth than one who holds a qualified objection view, at least not in any way that should appear as an advantage. If the qualified objection view is true, then even a boundless concern for the truth would not obviously move one to violate this true principle by counting only true objections as decisive.

Nothing I have said shows that the qualified acceptability requirement, rather than the exclusive view, is true. My aim is only to point out that it, too, would be a truth. The exclusive view is not entitled to any advantage derived from the idea of loving the truth. Without that advantage the question becomes what basis there is for thinking that people are permitted to treat each other in that way: to coercively enforce laws even when one's only basis for doing so concerns matters about which people can reasonably disagree. That is a possible view, but it is not obviously true.

Applying the Acceptability Requirement to Itself

The acceptability requirement has a logically interesting feature. It says that political justifications cannot appeal to doctrines that are not acceptable to all qualified points of view, and it is itself a doctrine appealed to in political justification. It says, then, that even it cannot be used unless it is acceptable in that way. The acceptability requirement, I will assume, must take some specific form that includes the statement of which views count as qualified and which ones do not. Call these the qualifications. The qualifications, then, must themselves be acceptable to all qualified points of view.

This might look suspicious. How can there already be a category of qualified people before the qualifications have themselves passed muster? This can make the situation look puzzling or paradoxical. But really there is nothing amiss. In general, some requirements apply to themselves. Suppose there is a rule that says that all rules must be publicly posted. There is no logical problem about this. It meets the requirement that it states if it is publicly posted, and otherwise not. In our case, a doctrine used in justification says doctrines used in justification must be acceptable to certain points of view. It applies to itself, and it meets the requirement that it states if and only if it is acceptable to those points of view—the qualified points of view. There is no problem in this, nothing that should count against the coherence or plausibility of the qualified acceptability requirement.

Still, it raises a further question. Do the qualified points of view get to say what count as the qualified points of view? If the qualified acceptance approach had that consequence, it would be fatally flawed. I want to argue that the qualified acceptability approach can avoid this problem. I start, though, by explaining the problem.

The Insularity of the Qualified

Consider the following principle in schematic form:[7]

AN (for "acceptance necessary"): No doctrine is admissible as a premise in any stage of political justification unless it is acceptable to a certain range of (real or hypothetical) citizens, C, and no one else's acceptance is required.

C is usually specified, in versions of political liberalism, as the set of "reasonable" citizens. But in order to emphasize that the points in this section do not depend on anything in the idea of reasonableness, I consider the principle in its more abstract form, calling C the set of qualified citizens. What I will call its different "instances" are constituted by different specifications of C; in one family of instances C is the set of reasonable people somehow specified. AN states only a necessary condition, not a sufficient condition for admissibility. In saying that no one's acceptance is required unless they are in C, it is still left open whether there are conditions other than acceptability conditions on admissibility.

As we have seen, doctrine AN apparently applies to itself as one part of political justification. Under some conditions, therefore, it excludes itself. If an instance of AN is not acceptable to the set of people it specifies as C, then it fails its own test. It is *self-excluding* when not acceptable to C, which is one way in which a doctrine can be excluded. The distinction is similar to that between a view's being defeated and its being *self-defeating*. The latter consists in a view's implying its own falsity, so it is false if true, and so false either way. Self-defeatingness is, of course, a defect in a doctrine. A doctrine's self-exclusion is no defect in the doctrine, but is obviously trouble for any attempt to include it in political justification. The merely conditional fact that since AN applies to itself, it would be self-excluding when not acceptable to C is not even a general problem of this kind for AN, however, since in other circumstances it allows itself into political justification. Suppose that some instance of AN is accepted by C.[8] In that case it is not self-excluding. It is capable of passing its own test. It places no obstacles in the way of its own introduction into political justification.

Some standards apply to themselves, and then they either meet the standard or they do not. For an example of this in another context consider the doctrine that says that the U.S. Constitution should only be interpreted or applied according to doctrines found in the original Constitution. David Lyons points out, "It is by no means clear that originalist theory can be found within the 'original' Constitution."[9] The originalist doctrine applies to itself, and apparently fails its own test. But if the original Constitution had included originalist doctrine, the standard would have succeeded; it would have met its own standard. A standard's self-application is no flaw in the standard. Depending on how C is specified, an instance of AN might meet its own standard. AN applies to itself, though that is not yet an objection to it or its inclusion in political justification.

THE INSULARITY REQUIREMENT

There is a restriction on the specification of C stemming from AN's application to itself, however, and it will lead to trouble. Suppose C is the set of all redheads. To avoid excluding itself, recall, an instance of AN must be acceptable to all members of C. So, this version of AN, which makes C the set of redheads, must be acceptable to all redheads. This is more demanding than it might seem. Many redheads would probably reject AN in this version even though they themselves are included in the *authoritative group* (as I shall sometimes call any specification of C). They may or may not object to their own inclusion, but many would object to making acceptance by all redheads necessary for the admissibility of a doctrine into political justification for the same reasons the rest of us would. In that case not all members of C would accept that instance of AN, and it would disqualify itself. To avoid being self-excluding, AN must specify C so that its members accept that specification.

Each member of C, then, in order to accept AN, must think that acceptance by all and only the members of C is necessary for a doctrine's admissibility, since that is what AN says. This amounts to a requirement that C be an insular group in the following sense.

> *Insularity requirement*: Each member of C must recognize the rejection rights of all and only the members of C.

(An individual has rejection rights over a doctrine if and only if its acceptability to her is necessary for the doctrine's admissibility into political justification. And recall that only members of C have rejection rights according to AN.) Insularity is not here required on any moral or other basis of its own. It is a logical consequence of AN's application to itself. And clearly it does not depend on C's being specified as reasonable citizens, and so it is not due to any feature of the idea of reasonableness. Adjusting that idea or substituting other authoritative groups would not avoid the insularity requirement.

THE IMPERVIOUS PLURALITY OF INSULAR GROUPS

Insularity is a severe constraint, and yet there are potentially infinitely many specifications of insular groups, those whose members recognize the rejection rights of all and only each other. Suppose the Branch

Davidians were insular, for example.[10] Still, we might say, they are not morally plausible as the authoritative group C. The question is, plausible to whom? They are, by assumption, a plausible candidate to each other; each Branch Davidian may well think the Branch Davidians are the perfect way to specify C, the group of people with rejection rights in political justification. On what grounds may one specification be chosen over another?

The specification of C must be acceptable to C, and so insular. AN, however, does not say that acceptability to C is enough for admissibility, and we might hope that further requirements will uniquely qualify one insular group. However, as many people interpret political liberalism (Rawls's own position on the question is unclear to me), the truth of a doctrine is never required for its admissibility. Truth is said to be left entirely aside in order to avoid reasonable controversy (call this principle the "irrelevance of truth"). Acceptability to reasonable (or qualified) points of view is the only standard. With that move, the view loses any way to select among the plurality of insular groups, since the true specification of the set of reasonable or qualified points of view is not privileged. This impervious plurality of insular groups would render the qualified acceptability approach (which is absolutely central to "political liberalism") untenable. Here is why. When a particular version of C is put forward in versions of AN, then, according to the supposed irrelevance of truth, it must not be claimed to be the true or correct version of C, the one that makes AN true. All that can matter about AN and its version of C is whether it is admissible, but its truth is held not to bear on that question.[11]

On one reading of AN, it is pointing to the version's acceptability to *its own* version of C, whatever it is: any specification of the qualified points of view must be acceptable to those points of view. This is precisely the insularity of C. Insularity is indeed a requirement for the coherence of any version of AN. If there were only one insular version, then this would be a fine answer to the question what makes C the admissible version for AN, as we have seen. But, as we have also seen, there are alternative insular versions because there are multiple insular groups, such as, perhaps, the Branch Davidians, and the set of reasonable citizens. Thus, to the question why C is the admissible version rather than alternative insular versions, its self-acceptability is no answer at all. That is something possessed by every insular version of C.

So, it is a problem if *each* insular group is equally admissible, but at most one of them can be admitted. Could the problem be avoided by somehow admitting them all? This is plainly inconsistent with the insularity of each group; by definition, the members of each insular group deny the rejection rights of all others, so at most one insular group could be admissible.

The principle of the irrelevance of truth implies that no set of points of view (or hypothetical qualified citizens) is available to authorize an admissible version of the acceptance criterion. Any insular group meets all the available criteria. There is no way to choose one specification of the qualified over any other insular specification. Of course, one of them might *be* the sole admissible version, but that is a matter of the truth about admissibility, a consideration that is held to be irrelevant.

It seems that political liberalism must find some way to penetrate this plurality of insular groups. This is where it must appeal to the truth and not to reasonableness alone. The difficulty cannot be avoided by saying that "we the reasonable" should just carry on, and ignore the other views about the authoritative group rather than insisting that they are false and risking rancor and division. Whatever practical value tact may have, as a philosophical matter our view must be that the other views are mistaken. For if they were not mistaken, then they would be the ones with rejection rights and we would not. The question is not how often or how loudly we should say this, but whether we can or cannot suspend judgment on it. We cannot, since suspending judgment would leave us with a plurality of insular groups, none evidently having a better claim to be authoritative than any other.

We can briefly summarize the argument so far before taking up two final objections to it. We might distinguish three possible versions of political liberalism and its foundations: a *wholly procedural* version avoids appealing to any standard of truth or correctness outside of acceptability to reasonable citizens. A version that appeals to the truth of the acceptance criterion regardless of its acceptability to reasonable citizens would be a *dogmatic substantive* political liberalism. These ought both to be rejected in favor of an *undogmatic substantive* political liberalism in which *no* doctrine is available in justification unless it is acceptable to reasonable citizens, not even this doctrine itself (this makes it undogmatic), because such an acceptability criterion is true or correct independently of such acceptability (this makes it substantive). As Rawls "applies the principle of toleration to philosophy itself," we might say that the preferred version of political liberalism applies the principle of toleration *to itself*. It must be put forward as true, but it must also pass the same test it applies to all other doctrines that are used in political justification. In doing so political liberalism must assert the requirements of toleration not merely as authorized by the principle of toleration, but as also true. Thus, political liberalism must be, in this sense, both undogmatic and substantive.

Authorization Yet Again?

What is to prevent the adherents of a reasonable (or otherwise qualified) comprehensive doctrine from denying that the acceptance criterion is true, but accepting that it is authorized by a higher-order principle in their philosophical system? Presumably, its acceptance of it as authorized is all the acceptability that is needed for legitimacy and an overlapping consensus. So why cannot the acceptance criterion be put forward as authorized whether or not it is true? It could be put forward as either true or authorized by some higher-order doctrine. This would avoid asserting it as true.

It might seem as though claiming that it is true is unnecessarily controversial. If it is possible for a qualified point of view to hold the acceptance criterion as authorized but not true, then adding the truth claim that I recommend would exclude such qualified views, and thus violate the acceptance criterion and its requirement of acceptability to all qualified views. Thus, it may seem that political liberalism can and must avoid the truth claim, but rest content with the claim that the acceptance criterion is either true or authorized by some higher-order doctrine.

The first thing to note about this point is that it would leave much, though not all, of my argument intact.[12] Much of my argument is devoted to showing that the acceptance criterion cannot be authorized in the same way as the other doctrines in political liberalism and justice as fairness: whereas they are authorized by it, it must be authorized by something other than itself. This has the further consequence that political liberalism must assert that the acceptance criterion has a certain status *in the best comprehensive conception (whatever it might be)*. It must step outside of the nest of doctrines authorized by reasonable acceptance and make a partially comprehensive assertion. That much would remain, even if this objection were to succeed. Still, the objection denies another central claim I make, that the acceptability criterion must be put forward as true. I believe the objection fails, and the reason depends on a somewhat surprising feature of what I will call *authorizing* and *authorized* doctrines. This requires some explanation.

We can illustrate the idea of an authorized doctrine with the example of the so-called facts in a criminal trial. They need not be held as true in order to be appropriately treated as if they were true for purposes of trial and sentencing. That example can be used to bring out the feature I am after. Consider the proposition,

Alibi: The defendant was far from the scene of the crime earlier in the day of the crime.

Suppose, first, that there is some evidence from witnesses that Alibi is true. But suppose the police have discovered a cash machine receipt in his desk that places him near the crime scene at the time in question. However, they have discovered this through a grossly improper and warrantless search. The judge may exclude this evidence from the trial, and both sides may come to stipulate that Alibi is true. The judge and attorneys for both sides know that it is false, and yet there is higher-order doctrine (an authorizing doctrine) that authorizes proceeding for legal purposes as if it were true (turning Alibi into an authorized doctrine). Alibi would then be a false doctrine that is, nevertheless, authorized. It would become one of the "facts" of the case.

Even supposing the prosecutor accepts the authorization for Alibi without believing it to be true, suppose we ask whether the prosecutor accepts the following proposition as true:

Stipulation: The supposition that the defendant was far from the scene (etc.) is appropriate in the context of this trial, and the verdict is no less legitimate for the falsity of this supposition.

Apparently the prosecutor does believe this to be *true*. This is guaranteed by his accepting Alibi to be authorized. Now, and here is the important point, suppose someone said that we should not assume that the prosecutor believes even Stipulation to be true, since he might only believe it to be authorized by some higher-order doctrine. But how could a proposition such as Stipulation be authorized without being true? It seems rather that if Stipulation is so much as authorized, then the supposition of Alibi *is* appropriate for purposes of the trial, and so forth. But that is what Stipulation says. So if Stipulation is authorized, then it must also be true.

I take this to militate in favor of the following suggestion:

True authorization: Statements of authorization cannot themselves be authorized without being true.

Now, I believe the acceptance criterion itself is a statement of authorization. It asserts that doctrines that are acceptable to all qualified people are appropriate in political justification in the sense that normative conclusions from those doctrines are no less legitimate for the falsity of any of the doctrines. If it is itself a statement of authorization, then it cannot be held to be authorized but not true. If it is so much as authorized, then what it claims must be true, namely, that the derivation of principles of justice and legitimacy from the doctrines in question does genuinely morally warrant, say, coercive enforcement and/or duties to comply. So the suggestion that the criterion might be put forward not as true but merely as authorized turns out to be mistaken.

COULD QUALIFIED PEOPLE REJECT THE TRUTH ABOUT QUALIFICATIONS?

I argue that the qualified acceptance criterion requires that the specified group of qualified citizens be insular: each much accept all and only the others as having rejection rights. Otherwise some qualified people would reject that very criterion, and so it would be self-excluding. This means that there cannot be any qualified disagreement about who is qualified, since then the qualified group would not be insular. Of course, the specification of the qualified is partly meant to include a wide variety of points of view, including many false ones, because a wide variety of views seem not to disqualify their owners from being owed acceptable reasons to justify state coercion. Doesn't it seem extremely likely, then, that there is qualified disagreement about who is qualified? In that case, the acceptance criterion is bound to be self-excluding.

If the criterion for qualified points of view is too broad, of course, the members will not all accept the criterion. In that case, the acceptability requirement would be self-excluding: if it is true, it forbids its own use in political justification. Notice that this seems bound to be the case with what I have called the actual acceptance view, to which the overexclusion objection is committed.[13] It says that no doctrine is admissible in political justification if anyone actually rejects it. This is itself a doctrine, of course, and so it falls under its own strictures. But since there is bound to be some actual point of view that rejects such a broad definition of qualified points of view (just for one example, I reject it), the actual acceptance view is self-excluding. This does not bear on whether it is true or not, and if it is, then political justification would evidently be impossible. As I have said before, I shrink from the task of arguing against this radically skeptical position, preferring to assume, without argument, that it is false.

Is the true criterion of reasonableness or qualification subject to qualified disagreement, and so self-excluding in this same way? The problem is avoided if we say, as I shall, that one feature that a person must have in order to count as qualified is to accept the acceptance criterion including its correct account of qualified people. This would guarantee that there would be no qualified disagreement about who is reasonable, and the acceptance criterion would not be self-excluding. We count a person as disqualified if he does not accept the correct acceptance criterion. He does not ascribe rejection rights to all and only qualified people (even though he may think he does). This sounds morally significant.

Still, it might be said that we are being inconsistent. Elsewhere, the mere fact of someone's holding a mistaken view is not enough to count him as disqualified, but here it is. This is not really so. We do not count someone as disqualified just because his comprehensive doctrine is false, but we do count people as unreasonable for failing to hold *certain* views, such as, perhaps, that all people are morally free and equal, that even reasonable people can disagree, and so on. Here is one more thing they must accept: a certain view of who counts as reasonable or qualified. We assert its moral significance simply by saying that if you don't accept this view of who is qualified, then you are not qualified.

The objection to this move is most compelling when we use the term *reasonable*, because a person who we ordinarily regard as reasonable is not guaranteed to accept this arcane view about qualified acceptability and legitimacy. But this is why it can be helpful to avoid that terminology of reasonableness. It carries connotations from ordinary language that are no part of its meaning in the theory. It is a term of art for a certain theoretical role, and we cannot learn everything we need to know about it by reflecting on the meaning of the word *reasonable*, or by studying the people we might ordinarily call reasonable. The term *qualified* is a bit sterile, but, in a way, that is its virtue.

Conclusion

Joseph Raz has argued that Rawls's political liberalism is incoherent unless it puts itself forth as true.[14] Raz argues that the theory must present itself not only as true, but as bundled with a comprehensive moral and philosophical view. Thus he thinks Rawls must throw over his "epistemic abstinence" for epistemic indulgence. Raz's conclusion is much less congenial to political liberalism than the conclusion of the present chapter, and I believe the argument for it fails. It is worth concluding by criticizing Raz's argument, if only to highlight its difference from the argument presented here. The crux of Raz's criticism comes in this short paragraph:

> My argument is simple. A theory of justice can deserve that name simply because it deals with . . . matters that a true theory of justice deals with. . . . To recommend one as a theory of justice for our societies is to recommend it as a just theory of justice, that is, as a true, or reasonable, or valid theory of justice. If it is argued that what makes it *the* theory of justice for us is that it is built on an overlapping consensus and therefore secures stability and unity, then consensus-based stability and unity are the values that a theory of justice, for our society, is assumed to depend on. Their achievement—that is, the fact that endorsing the theory leads to their achievement—makes the theory true, sound, valid, and so forth. This at least is what such a theory is committed to. There can be no justice without truth.[15]

Raz wonders how a certain theory of justice could be "the one for us," actually grounding obligations and warranting coercive enforcement in our society, without thereby *counting* as "true, or reasonable, or valid" or "sound." His point is strongest where his conclusion is this weak one, with four choices. The argument is, I believe, even conclusive if he means (as he does) true, or reasonable, or valid, or sound, *or some such thing.* For there must be some such word for this kind of, shall we say, *normative success* of the theory—its actually grounding obligations and/or warranting coercive enforcement. (I take these to follow from its being "the theory for us.") I propose to mark this with the name *success.* A theory of justice counts, by definition, as successful for a polity if it accounts for obligations of citizens normally to comply with laws and policies that accord with the theory, and/or if it justifies coercive enforcement of such laws in certain ways. So a theory of justice cannot be "the theory for us" without being successful.

Raz, however, lumps the concepts of truth, reasonableness, validity, and soundness all together as so many different ways of calling a normative proposition "true." There is a substantial question that Raz's terminology prevents us from asking: could a theory of justice be successful apart from whether it is true? Raz does not see this as a substantial question, since he suggests that there is nothing to the truth of a theory of justice except precisely what I have called success.

But truth and success are different. It is not a conceptual confusion to think that obligations can sometimes be grounded, not in true justice, but in a conception which, whether or not it is true, is authoritative for other reasons, such as that it is the only conception that is acceptable to all reasonable citizens. In that case, the theory of success would be saying that the false conception of justice ought to be obeyed as if it were true. One need not accept this particular theory of success in order to see that Raz's objection fails, for it is a counterexample to Raz's argument claiming that, as a conceptual matter, our being obligated to do what a theory of justice purports to obligate us to do is simply the truth of that theory. It is conceptually coherent, at the very least, to allow that a theory of success might point to a theory of justice and tell us, for certain reasons, to obey it whether or not it is true. Analogously, one could be morally obligated to obey a false set of moral rules in a classroom if that were the only set of rules all reasonable students could accept, and they were not too far from the truth, and the teacher said to do so. This does not make them the true moral rules, and yet there is a moral obligation to obey them as if they were. There may be an authorizing doctrine that gives them this status.

Raz is quite right to point out that "there can be no justice without truth," by which I take him to mean that a society cannot count as truly just by conforming to a theory of justice that is not true. This is quite right, and important. But it is not, I think, an objection to Rawlsian political philosophy properly understood, since it neglects the possibility that political rights, powers, and obligations are determined by the *success* of a theory of justice, not by its truth. Thus, Rawls must admit that a society that is well-ordered in accordance with justice as fairness may or may not be truly just, but it may yet be just in the only sense of justice that can legitimately be brought to bear in the fixing of political obligations and state powers, that is, being well-ordered according to a conception of justice that is acceptable to all reasonable citizens.

To conclude this chapter, I should be clear that I will not be laying out a principle of reasonableness or a substantive criterion for which points of view count as qualified. Rather, at certain points in the ensuing argument I will need to assume that certain points of view are qualified and others are not. I will be asserting, in those cases, that those views do or do not have what it takes to ground the demand that they be accommodated in political justifications. The plausibility of those claims will have to arise in context, and will not be shown to derive from some general account of the boundaries of reasonableness or qualification. It would be good to have a precise general account for some purposes, but it would not make much difference for my purposes. We could never arrive at a general principle of this kind without resting much of our case for it on its matching a number of less general plausible convictions. If our aim were to interrogate those convictions in order to arrive at a general account of qualified points of view, we certainly could not take all of our intuitive views of the matter as fixed starting points. But I am not seeking a general account of the content of reasonableness or qualification. I avail myself of this moral idea, and so I have devoted this chapter to understanding the idea and the role it plays in the larger view. A general account of its content would be a further task, but the lack of such an account does not necessarily weaken the case for epistemic proceduralism.

The Limits of Fair Procedure

IN PLATO'S DIALOGUE *EUTHYPHRO*, the question is raised whether something is pious because it is loved by the gods, or whether the gods love it because it is pious. The "Euthyphro question" has a form that crops up all over philosophy, and democratic theory is no exception. Many people today think that, at least under certain conditions, good political decisions are those that are democratically made. We do not have to accept the old slogan that *vox populi, vox dei* (the voice of the people is the voice of God) to see the parallel to the Euthyphro question: are good (or just, or legitimate) democratic outcomes good because they are democratically chosen, or are they democratically chosen because they are good? I want to display and criticize the widespread sympathy in recent democratic theory for the former answer, the view (in its simplest form) that the value of democratic decisions is entirely a matter of their being democratic.

I assume that the core of the idea of democracy is, or at least includes, the idea of citizens collectively authorizing laws by voting for them, and/or for officeholders who make them.[1] We should normally understand someone, then, who rests some claim on the value of democracy to be resting it on the value of this procedural arrangement: the collective authorization of the laws by voting.[2] It is not merely the emphasis on procedure, then, that is notable in recent democratic theory. The notable thing is the claim to explain the value of democratic procedures without appealing to any other (extrademocratic) values of democratic decisions, such as a tendency to be right or just or good on independent grounds.

I will consider three influential versions of this flight from substance in democratic theory. First, in this chapter, I will criticize fair proceduralism, the view that democratic arrangements are justified by being procedurally fair to participants, and not by any tendency of democratic procedures to produce good decisions. Second, partly in this chapter, and partly in chapter 5, I will consider what I call "normative social choice theory," normative democratic theory that is primarily based on insights derived from social choice theory of the kind pioneered by Kenneth Arrow. Third, in chapter 5, I consider what I call "deep deliberative democracy." In all three cases we will see that, though eschewed by these schools of thought in the name of proceduralism, procedure-independent outcome standards are present in those views and indispensable.

Democracy, the authorization of laws collectively by the people who are subject to them, is inseparable from voting. People are normally held to authorize laws by voting on the laws themselves or, more commonly, by electing representative legislators. What is it about voting that has this moral significance, the power to render the resulting laws legitimate and authoritative? One popular and simple answer is that voting is a fair procedure for making decisions when people disagree. Each person gets an equal say, and the result, whether it is good or just by any other standards, has at least this to be said for it: everyone had an equal role in determining the outcome. The outcome is fair in the sense that it was produced by a fair procedure. Let us call this view about how democracy renders laws legitimate and authoritative *fair proceduralism*.

Fair proceduralism avoids appealing to any supposed ability of democratic procedures to make substantively good decisions, and we should admit that this is a selling point. If fair proceduralism succeeds, it allows us to avoid potentially messy questions about which independent standards should be used to judge outcomes. It is also less embarrassed than some other approaches if voters are irrational, selfish, badly informed, or all three. A procedure can be fair to participants whether or not they are smart, or well informed, or virtuous. Fair proceduralism, then, would be an elegant and philosophically chaste way of accounting for the moral significance of democratic authorization of laws.

My purpose in this chapter is to show that fair proceduralism is subject to serious problems. In brief, the central problem is that procedural fairness, properly conceived, is a very thin and occasional value. Democratic procedures (some of them anyway) might indeed be fair, but this will turn out to be morally too small a matter to support an account of authority and legitimacy. Procedural fairness alone also cannot explain most of the features of democratic institutions that we are likely to feel are crucial. To anticipate my argument with a one-liner, if what we want is a procedure that is fair to all, why not flip a coin? That is, why not choose a law or policy randomly?

Epistemic proceduralism, the approach I will be developing and defending throughout the book, gives little or no role to procedural fairness, and so its defense does not depend on details about what fairness is. However, rejecting fair proceduralism on the grounds that fairness is too thin for our purposes does require an account of what procedural fairness is in order to support these deflationary claims about its importance. Fair proceduralism is sufficiently attractive and influential that it is worth devoting some time to understanding where it goes wrong. So that is what I set out to do in this chapter: I develop a theory of procedural fairness in order to show that it will not do what democratic theory needs done.

The work of this chapter is more than just an argument against a competing approach. The account of procedural fairness is also an important part of a fuller understanding of the different roles that procedural thinking might play in democratic theory. Epistemic proceduralism gives an important role to procedure, and so much of the discussion of fair proceduralism has a positive value for explaining and defending epistemic proceduralism, as well as for refuting its most important competitor, fair proceduralism.

AN OCCASIONAL VALUE

It will be useful to turn away from the specific context of democracy, in order to look at the idea of procedural fairness more generally. Fair proceduralism appeals to this more general idea, procedural fairness, and that is the idea we want to get a handle on.[3]

It can sometimes seem as if everything should be fair. The hegemony of fairness is partly owed to an unfortunate linguistic habit, in which anything that is not fair, but could have been fair, is called unfair. Since unfairness is, as the language works, so obviously a moral failing, it would follow that everything ought to be fair if it can be. But there seems to be a legitimate question about this, which we should not let linguistic habits settle. For example, to defend my choice to save my son from drowning rather than saving the stranger next to him, it is not obvious that I should need to show that doing so conforms to some appropriate standard of fairness. Or consider my giving five dollars to one beggar and nothing to the next. Is it obvious that this is only permissible if it is, in some way, fair? It is obviously not fair, but is it unfair? (We might call this the *non/un issue*.)

The problem is not handled by saying that fairness yields only *pro tanto* or defeasible obligations. This might seem to help, since it would allow us to say that certain choices or procedures are permissible even if they are not fair because the value of fairness is outweighed or overridden. But this suggestion still clings to the assumption that even if these choices are permissible, they are nevertheless unfair and that this still counts against them.[4] This ignores the possibility that some things that could have been fair, but are not, do not have any vice or deficiency owing to their deviation from fairness. This would make fairness an *occasional* value rather than (though perhaps in addition to) being a defeasible one. On this view to say that something is fair is not yet to say that it conforms to any moral requirement of fairness; rather, its fairness is one thing, and the question of whether it is required to be fair, or whether it is good in any way insofar as it is fair, are always further questions.

Conceptually, fairness is very close to impartiality. If we are drawn to the idea that morality is, at root, a certain kind of impartiality, then this might seem to support the idea that fairness is of overriding and sweeping importance after all. For the sake of argument, suppose morality is ultimately a form of impartiality, requiring a fair regard for every individual.[5] It would still not follow that everything that can be fair should be, since there are very many ways for things to be fair beyond merely being justified from an impartial morality. That is, even if everything that's morally permitted is, in one way, fair in virtue of morality's impartiality (say, the impartiality of counting each person's happiness equally, or the impartiality of a universalizable maxim of action) many things could be fair in further senses in addition. This is what I think is not always required, and not always valuable. So, suppose impartial morality can explain why it is permitted to save your drowning family member rather than the stranger, or to give to one beggar but not the other. I would interpret this as meaning that the fair regard for all individuals required by the moral point of view is often compatible with acting contrary to what fairness would involve in particular contexts. For example, you are not required to distribute your pocket change among beggars by a fair procedure, even though this would be possible. And recall, I am suggesting not only that it isn't always required on balance, but that it isn't always even a value to go into the balance.[6] That is clearest, I think, from the drowning example.[7]

So I won't assume here that everything that can be fair should be, since fairness seems to have only an occasional value. I will have more to say about the relevant occasions.

Roots and Branches of Fairness

In this section, I want to argue that among the various ideas of fairness there is an intrinsically procedural kind. Just to have a convenient example in which various issues of fairness might arise, consider a law banning bikes from public roads, passed by a majority of well-informed citizens. Someone might say that this law is unfair to cyclists. An outcome or arrangement is often said to be fair in one way when no one has more or less of certain goods than they ought to have (whatever standard might be used for determining this). In this sense, the law banning bikes might be held to be unfair to cyclists simply on the ground that they ought to have access to public roads. To reflect the point that this kind of fairness or unfairness is independent of any procedures that might have produced the arrangement, call this,

> *Substantive fairness*: When each (relevant) individual has no more or less (of the relevant goods) than he or she ought to have, or is due.

A traditional formula for justice has it rendering to each his due. Echoing that formula, I will use the terms *substantive justice* and *substantive fairness* interchangeably.[8]

There is also a second idea of the fairness of an arrangement, a kind that derives from facts about the procedure that produced the arrangement (call this the *parent procedure*) rather than any other facts about what the outcome should have been. (I will not define "procedure" here; let it range very broadly for now as any causally explanatory antecedents.) In this sense, an outcome is often said to be fair owing to the fairness of the procedure that produced it (Rawls would call it pure procedural fairness). So the law banning bikes might be fair in this sense if the political process that produced it was fair. This kind of fairness of an outcome is, in an obvious way, *retrospective*. The law restricting cyclists can be said to be fair in this retrospective sense, whether or not it is substantively fair, so long as the procedure that produced it—majority rule—is fair. Whether retrospective fairness is also substantively fair—whether such a procedure is itself a way of giving each what they ought to have—is an additional question, and no answer is implied simply by making this distinction.

The idea of an outcome's retrospective fairness directs our attention to a third idea of fairness: the idea of a fair procedure. One thing that is often meant by calling a procedure fair, but which will not serve the

69

present purpose, is that the procedure tends to produce outcomes that are substantively fair, in which each gets what he ought to get. A procedure can, in this way, be *prospectively* fair.[9] A dictatorship could be a fair procedure in this sense if the dictator produces substantively fair or just laws and policies—giving each what he should have.

We still need a different idea of the fairness of a procedure in order to capture ordinary ideas of retrospective or pure procedural fairness. The remaining idea would be of a procedure's nonprospective and nonretrospective fairness—its *intrinsic* procedural fairness. There seem to be two main kinds here. The first kind can be put aside, the kind that applies when a procedure is conducted according to the rules that constitute it, as in the idea of a fair play of the game. Call this *noncheating* fairness. The outcome of a game of chess can be said to be fair in a certain way when the game was played according to the rules. This idea of procedural fairness does not address whether the procedure or game is a fair one or not.[10] Procedures can be constituted by various rules, but some procedures, we might say, are unfair, even when they are run according to their rules such as a political procedure in which only men can vote.

This leads us to the second notion of intrinsic procedural fairness, the one that will be my main topic. A procedure can be fair or not, and then, in either case, it can be fairly run or not. I will not have any more to say about the noncheating sense of procedural fairness, and so I will use the term *intrinsic procedural fairness* to refer to the other sort:

> *Intrinsic procedural fairness*: the nonretrospective nonprospective fairness of the procedure whether or not it is properly run.

Whether intrinsically fair procedures are also substantively fair or just is left open by this definition. That is, the definition does not settle whether, in any particular circumstance, it would be unfair not to have a fair procedure. Recall the non/un issue: just because it would be nonfair in a certain way not to have a fair procedure does not settle whether it would be unfair. And I have not yet said in any detail what would make a procedure fair in the intrinsic procedural sense.

Fairness as Retreat

All we have so far is the idea of a kind of fairness a procedure can possess that is not a matter of its being the outcome of a certain kind of procedure, nor a matter of the kinds of outcomes it tends to produce. I want to propose an account of what we might call the dynamic of fairness, an account I will call *fairness as retreat*, an account of how fairness gets its value. This dynamic of retreat would then also help explain the moral thinness of fairness as well.

We can put procedural fairness into a familiar kind of rudimentary puzzle. Why think that it matters what procedure is the source of an outcome, since what should matter is simply whether it is the right or best outcome? It is an important fact, I think, that the idea of a fair procedure would not even arise if it were common knowledge that everyone agreed about what the correct decision is.[11] In that case no one would have any decent objection to simply doing it rather than substituting a procedure whose outcome might be uncertain. This reflects a certain intuitive priority of substance over procedure.

There are at least two ways in which that sort of consensus about ends can be lacking: first, there might be disagreement about what ought to be done. This might matter for moral reasons, or it might simply be a de facto obstacle, a practical challenge. Second, everyone might agree that there is no procedure-independent standard of what we should do. It might be simply a matter of arbitrary decision. The only question would be whose decision it is to make.

Disagreement about what ought to be done, or skepticism about any independent criteria, raises the question of how the group should determine what gets done, the question of a decision procedure. This is a retreat from substantive outcome standards, based on disagreement or skepticism.

This retreat does not yet get us to the idea of a fair decision procedure. Suppose it is clear to everyone who the experts among us are. Then, presumably, the experts should decide. If there is no disagreement about who they are, or about whether they are very expert, then no one would have any case for a fair procedure rather than the expert one. But, again, there might be disagreement about the experts, or a general belief that none are experts to any significant degree. This would raise the question of how we will determine what gets done without any presumptions about what the correct thing to do is, *or* about anybody's special expertise. We would be forced to a further retreat.

Suppose next that everyone can see that a certain way of proceeding, a certain procedure, would tend to lead to good decisions (though at this stage of retreat we do not know or cannot agree on what makes them good). In a very simple case, suppose we want to know whether our large group should hike to the other side of the island. Without any generally agreed experts, we might yet agree that it would make sense to send a few scouts. We might not even agree on what the criteria are, but we might yet agree that we will make a smart decision once we have heard what is there and the nature of the route. It looks as though the idea of a fair decision procedure would still be out of the picture, and that there would be no decent objection to employing the agreed effective procedure, so long, that is, as everyone acknowledges its effectiveness. Of course, depending on the nature of the case, there might not be any procedure that is generally acknowledged to have that kind of instrumental or epistemic value. Now what should we do? We would have to retreat again.

Perhaps there are other detours available in some cases, but suppose there is no longer any agreed or available way to try to make the independently correct decision. One thing this does is raise the question of what procedure we should use to determine what gets done. Another question it raises is what answer to that first question is itself agreeable or available. So the question becomes this, after a series of strategic retreats: what procedure for determining what gets done can be generally agreed upon without relying on procedure-independent criteria of correct decisions, or on the special expertise of any subset of the group to make the correct decision, or on any tendency of any particular procedure to perform well by independent standards? What *intrinsically procedural* standards might we yet agree upon? Here, I suggest, is where intrinsic procedural fairness finds its voice. If we want to decide whether to hike across the island, but we have neither any available standard for whether that is the substantively best decision, nor any available standard for how to make the substantively best decision, we seem to be left with only intrinsically procedural standards by which to judge our decision. This, too, might turn out to be unavailable—either unknown or too controversial. But it might not. If intrinsic procedural fairness lies at the end of this sort of retreat, we can begin to see why it is only an occasional value.

Fairness as Anonymity

This specifies a sort of function for fairness, but we have yet to consider what it might amount to in its content. Of course, as I said, any particular conception of intrinsic procedural fairness might itself be too controversial. So the idea of fairness as retreat needs to show that intrinsic procedural fairness could remain uncontroversial—could stem the retreat—despite controversy on every means for making independently correct decisions. The resort to fair procedure is still a resort to something, not to nothing—it is not a retreat to the law of the jungle, or a complete throwing up of our hands. It is an appeal to a moral conception of intrinsic procedural fairness. So it is only possible if certain things remain widely agreeable, despite disagreement about any way of meeting procedure-independent standards.

Intrinsic procedural fairness becomes a value, then, in a context where despite the absence of any agreed way to promote independently good decisions, there is agreement, on either moral or merely pragmatic grounds, about affirming the equal importance of each individual.

One common view of a fair collective decision procedure is that it should fairly promote individuals' interests. Note the two distinct elements in that view: (1) promotion of parties' ends, and (2) procedurally equal treatment of the parties. This second element I will refer to as a procedure's *anonymity*, its operating on the parties as if they were entirely interchangeable. The first element, that the individual parties' ends or preferences or interests are collectively to be promoted, is one version of what I will call *aggregativity*. I define these two ideas more carefully below. I want to argue that the idea of a full retreat from substantive matters would press all the way toward anonymity, leaving behind even aggregativity. The upshot is that fair proceduralism is an exceedingly weak foundation for the legitimacy or authority of democratic outcomes. Nonprocedural values must be brought in, and indeed they usually are. Doing so, however, goes beyond fairness and into the realm of procedure-independent standards.

Excluding Aggregativity

Let us define aggregativity very broadly as follows:

A collective decision procedure is aggregative if and only if for any set of ends, aims, or choices of the individual parties to the procedure, and any given outcome of the procedure, there is some change in the individual ends, aims, or choices that would have resulted in a different outcome. (More briefly, the procedure is sensitive to changes in aims or is *aim-sensitive*.)

For example, in any given application of majority rule, if some people had voted differently, the outcome would have been different. So it counts as aggregative. By contrast, a random choice of outcome, being completely insensitive to people's ends, is not aggregative. I want to argue that aggregativity should not be included in the idea of procedural fairness, though it does not necessarily violate fairness either.

The most familiar kind of aggregativity would more specifically require some sort of positive responsiveness to individual ends, in order to favor collective choices that are favored by individuals. One common view, as I have said, is that a fair procedure fairly promotes people's interests. But other requirements such as merely nonnegative responsiveness, or even (oddly) that the response *be* negative, count as aggregative on my very general construal. I define it very broadly to emphasize the strong claim I want to make: no aggregative standard, even construing that idea this broadly, is a part of intrinsic procedural fairness, because none is an intrinsically procedural matter.

This flies in the face of many interpretations of social choice theory, where aggregativity of various kinds is standardly described as a procedural matter, often even as a matter of procedural fairness.[12] In this section I want to argue that doing so is a mistake. Social choice theory would be, I think, the best case for showing how aggregativity can be seen as a procedural matter, and so an important challenge to my contrary view. Its failure in this sense is instructive.

Social choice theory studies the formal properties of mathematical functions or rules aggregating multiple individual preference rankings into a single collective preference ranking. Social choice theory is often said to study social choice procedures, among them voting procedures. However, it is well known that individuals' votes might not reflect their preferences over the social alternatives, even if they are instrumentally rational. Voters only reliably express their preferences as between ways of voting, since that is the choice they are given. But there is a very imperfect connection between preferred ways of voting and preferred social outcomes; the best way to promote one's preferred outcome is often to vote for something else (say, because you have a better chance of helping it to win).

It is not individual votes or choices, then, that social choice theory is primarily interested in, but individuals' underlying preferences over the social alternatives. Social choice theory evaluates *rules of aggregation* from individual orderings to collective orderings, not *actual procedures*, which might or might not conform to those rules. (From here on I will call social choice functions *rules* rather than *procedures*, letting the latter always be actual temporal procedures.) But it is the actual temporal procedures and not the abstract rules to which the retrospective sense of fairness looks. The point is important: the standards studied by social choice theory are, insofar as they are aggregative, really substantive standards applied to outcomes of possible temporal procedures. They are substantive standards in that they are logically independent of any actual temporal procedure that might have produced them. Social choice theory is not really about pure or retrospective procedural values at all.

What about mathematical rules operating on actual temporal inputs like votes? Mere conformity of an outcome to a rule aggregating votes still does not capture the idea of retrospective fairness. That idea requires a causal relation between the votes (or other inputs) and the outcome. To see this, suppose that the ruling dictatorial powers have decided that cyclists shall be banned from all automobile roads. As it happens, a vote (or call it a poll; it does not matter) has also been taken on this matter out of idle curiosity, and the rule banning bikes received a majority. In this case, the law conforms to the abstract rule requiring that laws must be logically or mathematically related to actual votes in a certain way: a majority of votes support the law. This is an abstract rule linking certain temporal individual inputs to certain social decisions by a mathematical relation. Should we regard this as a temporal procedure, the outcomes of which could be fair retrospectively? No: the decision to ban the bikers was not the outcome of any procedure that aggregated individual votes.[13]

I believe this temporal kind of proceduralism is part of our ordinary idea of retrospective (or "pure procedural") justice or fairness. The outcome of a fair coin flip, for example, is retrospectively fair only if the outcome is produced by the coin flip in the right way. Suppose my uncle will take my watch whether or not I win the flip on which I have staked it. I lose the bet, though my uncle never actually bothers to discover this, and he takes the watch as he had planned in any case. His having the watch conforms to an abstract rule relating the result of the coin flip with the post-flip facts about possession of the watch. But it is not retrospectively fair, not the outcome of the fair procedure. The reason is that my uncle's having the watch is not an outcome, an effect, of the application of the rule about how bets can legitimate outcomes.

This shows that in order to explain the idea of retrospective fairness it is crucial to distinguish temporal procedures from abstract aggregative rules. Doing so shows that social choice rules are not procedures in the sense that matters for retrospective fairness. The aggregativity or responsiveness that is usually assumed to characterize those rules is part of a procedure-independent standard. To suppose it is available is to suppose that its superiority over the other contenders is knowable and not too controversial. My point is not to deny this, but only to point out that this is no retreat to procedural fairness after all. Aggregativity goes beyond intrinsic procedural values, and so beyond intrinsic procedural fairness.

Do as We Say, Not as We Want

A familiar puzzle asks whether there would be anything wrong (or, alternatively, anything undemocratic) about using electrodes or some less invasive technology to ascertain individual attitudes without their voting, and then proceeding the way democracy typically handles real votes. If a majority prefer Jones, then Jones wins, and so on. If the attraction of democracy is simply its ability to force policy to track people's attitudes, then highly accurate polls might be as good as votes.

One question is whether the concept of democracy is fully satisfied by tracking. For what it is worth, it seems clear that rule by the people is something different from rule in accordance with the people's views.[14] Even if some mechanism forces or guarantees that people's views are tracked, putting their views "in control" in a certain way, that is not the same as *people* being in control.[15] This is not yet to decide whether this is a morally important distinction, but if it is arguably present in the idea of democracy, we will be interested to ask whether it is a morally crucial ingredient.

In some nonpolitical contexts it is clear that merely tracking someone's preferences is not good enough. Suppose you ask me to dinner, not because the idea of dinner with me appeals to you but because you know I would like you to ask me. But suppose I have explicitly asked you never to invite me to dinner for that reason. Have you treated me appropriately? I do want you to ask me to dinner, and you have done so. It might even be that I secretly want you to ask even if it is just because I want to be asked, despite what I have said to you. (Maybe this is because I would prefer that we pretend that it was not your reason for asking.) So you have done what I want, because I want it. Still, you have not done as I asked, and this seems potentially morally important. This might be a context where you are morally bound to do as I say, not as I want. It is easy to think of contexts that are like that. Sometimes "no" means "no." That is, sometimes my having said "no" is decisive, morally preempting any speculation about whether "no" reflects what I really want. Tracking a person's preferences, then, is not always all that is required in order to treat them appropriately.

What, then, about democracy? Is it enough for people's preferences or other attitudes to be in control, or is it important that, in addition, the people themselves be in control (so to speak)? I believe tracking is not enough. To see why, it helps to reflect on how I might be offended by your want-tracking dinner invitation. One thing to object to is that you have taken it upon yourself to guess what I want rather than taking my word for it. Of course, you may have gotten it right, and maybe you even tend to get it right reliably, but I can still sensibly be offended by your presumptuousness.

In the political context, suppose you have taken it upon yourself to guess the people's attitudes rather than doing what they say. You might be very good at this, just as some people (candidate epistocrats) might be very good at knowing what the just political decision would be, without any detour into what the people say *or* want. But even if you are good at one of these things, that does not mean that your skill will be agreed by all qualified points of view. You might be correct, but what makes you boss? In other words, the requirement that justifications be acceptable to all qualified points of view rules out claims about who knows better than whom what is just, and, for the same reasons, about who knows better than whom what the people's views are. Assuming here that doing what the people think should be done is the best generally acceptable epistemic route to doing what really should be done (a claim I argue for throughout the book), I contend that doing what the people *say* to do is the best generally acceptable epistemic route to doing what they really *think* should be done. There might be epistemically better routes, such as some special ability certain people have to know such things, but they (I claim) are controversial among qualified points of view. It would follow that doing as the people say (rather than necessarily doing as they actually think should be done) is the best generally acceptable route to doing what really should be done. This, at any rate, would explain why we might require more than that the people's views be tracked by policy, requiring instead that their decisions be honored.

Doing as the people say, rather than as they might want, might seem to commit us to an idea of a corporate or collective agent which says something. We could use the idea of a collective intention or action if necessary, but since there are active philosophical problems about that idea, it would be best to steer clear if possible. I think it is possible. An individual vote is an intentional contribution to the procedure every bit as much as an individual shot fired by a member of a firing squad, even if the agent knows that the effects of her action might be overdetermined or preempted. The agent intends to effect the execution or the election in the event that circumstances unfold so as to make things hang on her own action. Heeding votes is different, then, from tracking the voters' views or preferences. It is doing as they say, not merely as they want, even though no use is made of the idea of a corporate entity with a will of its own. It is doing as the people—a majority of them, individually—say to do, which is, as I have argued, different from merely ascertaining and tracking their views.

DEFINING ANONYMITY

There is an idea of equal treatment that might be generally acceptable even when all routes to substantive correctness (including aggregativity) are unavailable, namely, the idea of treating each person, in the operation of the decision process, just as anyone else is treated. I propose to interpret this as anonymity. This is importantly different from ideas of anonymity often used in social choice theory and related contexts, but the usual ideas of procedural anonymity will not suit our purposes. For example, social choice theory often employs a certain anonymity condition on aggregation rules. Call it,

> *Preference anonymity*: A rule is anonymous if and only if no difference is made in the collective ordering if the identity of the owner of the preference ranking is changed.

It is not absolutely clear that a person's identity can survive a dramatic change in their preference ranking, so it is not clear how to interpret the counterfactual that preference anonymity involves. But even if that idea were unproblematic, that kind of anonymity is compatible with allocating goods to individuals according to their preferences. It is not, in that way, fully anonymous (even leaving aside whether or not full anonymity is normatively a good thing). Its divergence from full anonymity can only be explained by a kind of aggregativity, which is a procedure-independent value—a positive valuation of preference-satisfaction—and so ought not to be built into the idea of intrinsic procedural fairness.

Letting people's preferences affect the outcome while treating each person's preferences like any other's conjoins a kind of anonymity with a kind of non-anonymity. The non-anonymity aspect consists in the fact that the procedure is influenced differently by the features of different people. For at least some people, if you prefer A to B, the procedure responds in a different way than if you preferred B to A. It notices and responds to this feature of the person, so to speak. It is not indifferent as between people insofar as the people have different preferences from each other. Still, beyond this, it is anonymous to a great extent. It does not respond to facts about who holds a particular preference. It is preference sensitive, but preference-holder insensitive. This is a mixture of anonymity and non-anonymity. The departure from full anonymity amounts to a procedure-independent standard, or part of one, holding that outcomes should vary according to what individual preferences are. My point is not to challenge this standard, aggregativity, on its merits, much less to challenge the use of procedure-independent standards. It is simply to say that this is a procedure-independent standard, and so procedures that incorporate preference-anonymity have not really eschewed procedure-independent standards. They are not in a position, then, to say that they have some advantage of that kind. They might wish to say, instead, that the standard they invoke is a better standard than certain other standards, and I do not prejudge the outcome of that debate. It would simply clarify matters to engage on those terms.

I have just argued that certain procedures that claim to avoid independent standards in favor of mere procedural fairness are actually using the procedure-independent standard of aggregativity. If my way of understanding procedure-independence showed that all possible procedures invoked procedure-independent standards, its usefulness might be doubted (though it would not yet be a devastating objection). To avoid that worry, it is helpful to see that a fuller conception of anonymity is possible.

Accordingly, I propose, contrary to some other uses of the idea of anonymity, that a procedure's full anonymity consists in the outcome being oblivious to any features of individuals. Outcomes would not have been different if any personal features had been different. This, then, is the logical limit of procedural fairness. A random choice from alternative decisions is a procedure that is blind to all features of the individuals in question in this way, as is a procedure linking the outcome to the weather, or any other facts or processes external to the features of the relevant people. Following the preference of one randomly selected person is not a way of being blind to all personal features, of course. Majority rule is obviously sensitive to people's choices and so is not blind to personal features.

> *Full anonymity*: A procedure is fully anonymous if and only if it is blind to personal features: its results would not be different if any features of the relevant people were changed.

This sort of blindness to personal features might, at first, seem not to be about fairness at all, which might be thought to be essentially about taking an appropriate account of each person's interests or choices. If that were right, however, then we should never think of a coin flip, which gives no regard to preferences at all, as a fair way to resolve a dispute, and yet we often do. The account here rejects the association of the core of procedural fairness with a due regard for individual interests or choices of individuals. As we will see, those might be fair things to attend to in some circumstances, but they are not of the essence of procedural fairness.

On this conception of procedural fairness, a procedure that notices people's choices or preferences does not differ, with respect to fairness, from a procedure that notices people's race or gender. Neither is fully or purely fair. Any moral distinction will be made based on evaluation of the non-fairness standard that a given procedure uses. If a procedure attends to race in a morally objectionable way, then it will be unfair—wrongly lacking fairness. This still does not make it any less fair than majority rule, which departs from full anonymity in a formally similar way by attending to people's preferences or choices. If it is not wrong to attend to choices in the way majority rule does, then doing so is not unfair because the departure from fairness is not wrong, but that does not make it more fair. It just means that its departures from fairness are not wrong. It all depends on the moral merits of one kind of feature-sensitivity or another. Sometimes a procedure that attends to race, ethnicity, or gender (and so departs from full procedural fairness) might be morally entirely appropriate. Perhaps the votes of native Americans should be counted more heavily in certain decisions about the governance of reservations. Similarly, in some contexts a procedure that attends to preferences might be morally wrong. For example, a military conscription procedure in which the order of selection is determined by a popular majority vote would normally be deeply unjust. Sensitivity to personal features is a departure from procedural fairness, but that does not tell us whether it is morally appropriate or not.

We should not say that procedures, including majority rule, are not fair simply because they are not fully anonymous. Rather, procedures can mix fairness and other principles, remaining fair, among other things. But the fairness of a procedure is, on my view, to be understood by reference to anonymity, the blindness to personal features. One way for a procedure to retain elements of fairness even without being fully anonymous is to retain a certain kind of blindness to feature changes. It is part of the fairness of majority rule that it treats one person's vote like another's. While it is sensitive to changes in votes, and so not fully anonymous, if votes are held constant and any other personal features are changed, the result will remain the same. The fairness of this is clearest if we put it in terms of possible exchanges of other features between two people. Holding our votes constant, if (so far as possible) I had certain features of you and you took mine, the procedure would still give the same outcome. For example, in simple majority rule your vote does not count more in virtue of your race. This is not necessarily a morally valuable thing; that depends, as we have seen, on the context. In a context where race should matter, we can still ask if, holding our votes and our races constant, the procedure is indifferent to changes in our other features. That would be a measure of a remaining kind of fairness, which might be a morally valuable thing.

We should pause to take stock. Why, you might ask, isn't this just a battle over the word "fairness"? If fairness is not even such an important thing (as I argue), who cares whether true fairness means full anonymity? I think the answer is that appeals to fairness strike us as so attractive precisely because they purport to be fully neutral, not carrying any conception of good ends other than the procedure itself. But only full anonymity, which often has little moral value, actually lives up to that. Anything less than full anonymity imports nonprocedural and potentially controversial values. I am all for that. My approach, epistemic proceduralism, is distinctive partly for insisting on something more than procedural fairness: an appeal to democracy's epistemic value. The point here is that it is just false advertising to say of any procedure that is not fully anonymous that it involves nothing but procedural fairness. If a standard is not fully anonymous, then it cannot lord its supposed substantive chastity over an epistemic theory such as mine. I admit that there might be degrees of promiscuity (epistemic proceduralism is pretty moderate, as we will see), but our first question is what, in these matters, counts as virginity. It turns out not to be an inspiring aspiration. We can see this more clearly by finally applying the analysis to theories of democracy.

Beyond Fairness

It is a common thought about democratic procedures, as I have said, that their moral value consists in their being procedurally fair, and not in anything about the quality of their outcomes. The view is often motivated by the suggestion that procedure-independent standards of good political outcomes are all too controversial to be available in the justification of democracy, but that the procedural value of fairness is sufficiently agreeable. As I will now try to show, a problem for that view is that procedural fairness does not seem sufficient to explain the institutions that democrats would insist upon, not even voting.

Granting that majority rule is, in a certain way, a fair procedure (by virtue of being blind to features other than votes), however, does not grant what fair proceduralism mainly claims—that the justification of majority rule rests on its procedural fairness and not on any procedure-independent standards for outcomes. A close look at procedural fairness has led us to conclude that the value of majority rule cannot be explained without bringing in procedure-independent standards for outcomes. Majority rule is a fair procedure in an important respect: it pays no attention to who casts which vote. But that is also true of a procedure that holds a vote and chooses one person's vote randomly. A random procedure of that kind has all the procedural fairness of majority rule and more, since it is blind to all features, not just some. If procedural fairness were the justification for majority rule, why not go all the way (or, to reverse the simile, why not stay "fully" virginal)? Why not flip a coin from among possible decisions? This would be not only blind to features of people other than their votes, but also blind to all features of people. It is an absurd proposal in most political contexts, of course. A theory of the value of majority rule is only plausible if it is *not* substantively innocent, and so not really based entirely on fairness. There is no interesting divide, then, between fully proceduralist theories of democracy, on the one hand, and impure theories that depart from merely procedural values, on the other. The interesting debates will turn, then, on which nonprocedural values are available or appropriate and which are not. Fair proceduralism, which would be satisfied by flipping a coin, is not a plausible account of the superiority of democratic principles and institutions over coin flips. With an analysis of procedural fairness in hand we have been able to see that it is too thin a thing to support democratic legitimacy and authority. It is true, I have defined procedural fairness in a certain way, and only then did it turn out to be paper-thin. But I mean to offer this as the most adequate analysis of the idea of procedural fairness, at least for purposes of understanding the attempt to ground democracy in an idea of procedural fairness that avoids importing procedure-independent standards.

Suppose fair proceduralism accommodates the points of this chapter, and reasserts itself in new terms. Suppose fair proceduralism granted that only a partial kind of fairness is appropriate—sensitivity to people's votes, but not to their other features. The sensitivity to voter preferences is granted to import a procedure-independent value, the principle that outcomes should reflect what is preferred by more people. The selling point is no longer said to be that fair proceduralism steers clear of all procedure-independent standards. The point of insisting on the importance of procedural fairness is now to emphasize that this attention to voter preferences is a very minimal and uncontroversial substantive standard for outcomes. Approaches to democracy that rely on more robust standards for just outcomes such as principles of justice, or experts or procedures to guide us to good outcomes, are criticized by fair proceduralism not for importing procedure-independent standards, but for importing standards that are too controversial. This, I believe, is the right way to frame the debate. The emphasis shifts to the question of what is too controversial and on what grounds. This is a question I consider at length in other chapters. My conclusion is that there is no basis for thinking that the concern about controversy immediately forces us to adopt the most minimal standards and principles possible. Indeed, if we did that, we would not even allow ourselves the sensitivity to voter preferences that fair proceduralism, on this adjusted presentation of it, accepts. Procedural fairness is a retreat from substance. Substance has primacy, if only it is available. That primacy of substance pulls against the pressure to retreat in the face of disagreement, and we ought to incorporate as much substance as is available. The challenge of political disagreement needs to be taken seriously, but there is no simple route from that observation to the rejection of all procedure-independent standards. Procedural fairness is about the retreat from substance, and the question is when to retreat and when to hold our ground.

Later, in chapter 5, I criticize two related approaches to democratic theory, related in their efforts to restrict themselves to procedural values. Deep deliberative democracy is one, and fair deliberative proceduralism is the other. These are important to consider, since they try to give a central place to public political deliberation in the justification of democracy but, again, without bringing in any tendency to make substantively good or just decisions. We will see that the use of independent standards can hardly be avoided, pointing to the need for an epistemic dimension to democratic authority and legitimacy.[16]

Finally, we can briefly note how epistemic proceduralism claims to stem the retreat to procedural fairness: it claims that certain democratic arrangements are agreeable (among qualified views) as being effective at discerning and implementing substantively good decisions. If so, this ends the retreat that would eventually lead to nothing but procedural fairness. If it were not so, if there were no epistemic account of democracy agreeable to all qualified views, then mere procedural fairness, with all its thinness, might emerge as the best principle for organizing politics. It would not clearly point in a democratic direction, however, since, as we have seen, random choice of policies is as fair as majority voting.

I will be arguing that such a retreat from all substantive ambition is unnecessary. Epistemic proceduralism retreats from some, if not all, substance about what would be a just outcome, and also from all claims for the superior wisdom of any person or group. These are all subject to qualified disagreement. The retreat ends with the assertion that the epistemic value of properly arranged democratic institutions will tend to produce substantive just outcomes (whatever those might be). By retreating to this ground, epistemic proceduralism has incorporated a dimension of fairness. Since no one's expertise is available, the procedure should be blind to a voter's identity (no invidious comparisons). By holding ground with respect to the epistemic value of democratic procedures, the account rejects fair proceduralism's full retreat. The difference this makes is great both in theory and in practice. By holding on to the epistemic dimension that is rejected by fair proceduralism, epistemic proceduralism can explain why it makes sense to have informed public discussion among equally enfranchised voters, whereas fair proceduralism ought to be satisfied with the unimpeachably fair procedure of choosing an outcome by flipping a coin.

The Flight from Substance

FAIR PROCEDURALISM, AS WE SAW IN CHAPTER 4, claims not to use any procedure-independent standards of good political decisions, but is committed to such standards after all. It claims to stay with the values of procedure, but is embroiled in substance in the end. We saw that social choice theory, which has deeply influenced much normative democratic theory, is also often misleadingly portrayed as innocent of substance, relying wholly on procedural values. It turns out that social choice theory evaluates actual temporal voting procedures by the procedure-independent standards embodied in the conditions it imposes on the abstract relation between individual preferences and the social decision. Fair proceduralism and normative social choice theory must be among the best candidates for the status of purely procedural approaches to democracy, and yet they are not purely procedural after all.

Deliberative democracy names a broad approach to democratic theory that opposes itself to mere aggregation of preferences, emphasizing instead the social and political processes of forming preferences and arriving at choices. An emphasis on public deliberation about what is right and just might suggest that procedure-independent standards are more frankly embraced than they are in fair proceduralism or normative social choice theory. It is striking, then, that in the central strand, which I will call *deep deliberative democracy,* they are not. In this chapter I argue that deep deliberative democratic theory represents itself as wholly proceduralist, and as eschewing procedure-independent standards, but that it invokes independent standards after all. Despite many differences, deep deliberative democratic theory and normative social choice theory share this fate: they promise not to go beyond procedural values, and yet they do go beyond them in the end. Keep in mind, I am all for going beyond procedural values. The important lesson of these two chapters is that the leading attempts to avoid independent standards, and the attendant philosophical challenges such standards would bring, need to resort to independent standards after all. This is an important piece of my case for epistemic proceduralism, which openly brings procedure-independent standards into the theory.

As it stands, the terminology we have been using of procedure and substance is too vague for our purposes. Roughly, of course, a substantive value in this context is one that is procedure-independent. One possible strong claim is that normative political theory should not appeal to any procedure-independent values at all—that the only available value is the value of democracy itself. The weaker, more limited claim on which I will focus is only that normative political theory should not appeal to any procedure-independent values *in the evaluation of political outcomes*—for this specific purpose only the value of democracy is available. This weaker view attempts to do without any standards of good political decisions (such as basic rights, or principles of justice, or the common good), except standards based on good ways of making decisions. It emphasizes procedural values in this way. But it might still appeal to nonprocedural values. For example, it might assert the basic equality of persons without claiming that this value is itself based on or derived from the value of any decision procedure. It could be a substantive value in that sense. It might be appealed to as a basis for regarding certain equality-respecting decision procedures as valuable. Still, this is all compatible with the weaker way of avoiding substantive standards—the view that *political outcomes* are only evaluable in terms of the value of certain political decision procedures. Here, then, is the particular kind of flight from substance I will explore and criticize:

> *Intrinsic democratic proceduralism*: Only democratic political arrangements are legitimate, and the value of their being democratic does not depend on any qualities of democratic decisions other than whether they are democratic in two senses: (a) decisions must be made by democratic procedures, and (b) they must also not unduly undermine or threaten the possibility of democratic procedure into the future.

We should pause to note (b), this second way in which a decision can be, or fail to be, democratic: according to whether it protects the conditions for decisions that are democratic in the first sense (retrospectively). For example, if a society with suitably democratic laws and practices votes to disenfranchise women, the decision is undemocratic in this latter sense, undermining the possibility of democratic procedures, even if it were made by a perfectly democratic procedure. Intrinsic democratic proceduralism does not insist on using only retrospective standards for evaluating outcomes; it insists on evaluating outcomes only for whether they are democratic, and this question has both a retrospective and a prospective aspect. The distinguishing feature is that both aspects rely on the intrinsic value of democratic procedures. On this view democratic procedures are to be respected *and promoted* because of their intrinsic value.

The opposing view can be simply read off. Against the claim that appeals to substantive outcome standards (to use a compact phrase) are impermissible in normative democratic theory, the denial would say that such appeals are permissible. What makes this position interesting is the possibility that, in a stronger claim, normative democratic theory will be inadequate unless it avails itself of some standards for the evaluation of political outcomes beyond those that can be derived from the value of democratic procedure itself. I will not argue for this opposing view directly yet. Rather, building on chapter 4's critique of fair proceduralism, I look closely at two additional influential versions of intrinsic democratic proceduralism, versions that I believe underlie quite a bit of contemporary normative democratic theory, in order to raise what I think are serious difficulties.

Deep Deliberative Democracy

In general terms, deliberative democracy names the idea that political authority depends on a healthy application of practical intelligence in reasonably egalitarian public deliberation. It emphasizes the social processes that form individual attitudes, where social choice theory emphasizes rules for aggregating attitudes (i.e., preferences) that are, for purposes of analysis, taken as given. Deliberative democratic theory also distinctively understands practical rationality as including more than an individual's pursuit of her own aims. Certain claims by other agents are assumed to be unreasonable to ignore. There are these philosophical differences between the two schools as well as political differences. But central strands of both schools present themselves as intrinsically proceduralist theories, and I turn now to the critique of this claim in the case of deep deliberative democracy.

The popular turn to deliberative democracy was partly a reaction to the influence of the social choice model in normative political contexts.[1] Social choice theory takes preferences as given and does not ask whether they are wise, or ethically good, or wellconsidered. It can abstain from these matters and simply address the matter of aggregation of whatever set of preferences one wishes to aggregate: predeliberation, postdeliberation, it does not matter.

Critics of social choice theory's model of politics have often targeted the quality of individual preferences themselves and called for more attention to how these preferences are formed.[2] The idea of aggregating individual preferences into a social choice seems misguided, many have thought, when the preferences themselves are the product of misinformation, manipulation, confusion, and ill will. More recently, others have responded to this point simply by arguing that the individual attitudes that should be consulted are those formed under more favorable conditions, such as edifying public political deliberation.

HABERMAS

For Jürgen Habermas, there are no standards that loom over the political process, policing its decisions, not even any standard of reason itself: "We need not confront reason as an alien authority residing somewhere beyond political communication."[3] The only normative standards that apply to political decisions are noninstrumental evaluations of the procedures that produced them—in particular, standards of "procedural rationality"[4] based on the power of reason in public political discourse. Any imposition (in theory or practice) of substantive—that is, procedure-independent—political standards would preempt the ultimately dialogical basis upon which Habermas thinks political normativity must rest.[5] Habermas claims to eschew procedure-independent standards as much as normative social choice theory does. The result is an approach to political theory in which social institutions are evaluated holistically: do they together constitute a rational process for forming public intentions for guidance of law and government?

On the other hand, Habermas believes, the proper political process cannot be understood independently of the guarantee of certain individual liberties, so it must operate so as to maintain these liberties. This allows a certain standard for directly evaluating outcomes after all: destruction of the relevant liberties would be illegitimate even if it had been decided by the proper procedure. Still, this standard is rooted in the noninstrumental value of a procedure of rational political communication—in a procedure's intrinsic value, not derived from the values it produces or aims at. Habermas's account of proper procedures of rational political communication relies, of course, on what he famously calls the "ideal speech situation," a hypothetical scenario in which participants are fully informed and unlimited by time, and where the course of deliberation is guided only by the force of reason, not by any other kind of power or influence.[6] Politics is not meant to resemble such an imaginary situation, but, evidently, it ought to have a tendency to produce the same decisions. On this view, then, outcomes are evaluated partly by standards that are independent of the actual instance or token procedure that produced them. This element of Habermas's view remains proceduralist only in a thinner sense: the prospective standard of protecting basic liberties is meant to be dictated entirely by a conception of political procedures that are to be promoted or maintained. Basic rights or liberties receive their status as constraints on political decisions only in this way, and so are still driven by procedural democratic values in this sense.

A theory could have this sort of constraint on political outcomes but otherwise confine itself to retrospective evaluation of outcomes: did they arise from proper collective decision procedures? But Habermas's theory does not actually have this structure. It is not proceduralist even in that way. The reason is that, according to Habermas, outcomes are legitimate when they *could* have been produced by ideal deliberative procedures.[7] The procedures that set the standard are hypothetical, imaginary. Whether a decision is legitimate or not is always logically independent of the actual procedure that produced it. It is a substantive, procedure-independent standard in this important sense.

The point here is similar to the one I pressed against normative social choice theory's claim to eschew substantive values in favor of intrinsic procedural values only. Recall that once we distinguished between a standard that calls for conformity to an abstract aggregative rule (preference rule) and a standard that calls for decisions to be causally produced by certain actual temporal procedures (voting processes), we saw that it is the former that normative social choice invokes. But then it becomes clear that conformity of outcomes to preference rules is just one among the contending standards by which outcomes might be directly evaluated. Whatever its comparative merits, it is a substantive standard of outcomes, logically independent of their procedural origins.

Deep deliberative democracy judges actual political processes by independent standards, too. The reason is that the use of a hypothetical deliberative procedure as the standard for evaluating actual democratic decisions is one way of holding outcomes to a standard that is logically independent of their actual procedural source. Granted, procedure figures in the ideal standard in a certain way. But it should have been antecedently clear that some standards of just outcomes are contractualist, involving procedural ideas in that way. Rawls's two principles of justice, for example, are defended on certain grounds involving a hypothetical collective choice procedure: the original position. Nevertheless, they are standards by which outcomes can be evaluated quite apart from the outcomes' actual procedural source. As Rawls says: "Justice is not specified procedurally."[8] The tendency of democratic procedures to produce outcomes that meet these standards—the principles of justice—is an instrumental value of those procedures, not an intrinsic value, because the standard is logically independent of the actual procedural source.

Deep deliberative democracy, in effect, puts forward one or another contractualist standard for good political choices. Democratic values— values resting in actual democratic procedures—are not, in the end, fundamental and self-sufficient. Just as with normative social choice theory, a substantive outcome standard is often construed as an intrinsically procedural standard, and (nondemocratic) substance such as justice or common good is thought to be avoided in a salutary way. Whatever the merits of social choice theory's aggregative substantive outcome standards, or deep deliberative democracy's different contractualist substantive outcome standards, they are substantive outcome standards and go beyond intrinsically procedural features of real democratic institutions.

COHEN

Joshua Cohen insists that democratic authority is free and self-determining. It is not under any other authority, not even the "authority" of prior normative standards for better or worse choices. His debt to Habermas is explicit, and both seek to make democratic values the basis of normative political reasoning, not as one set of values among others, but as unrivaled—not in competition with or merely in the service of other, nondemocratic values such as welfare, or the basic human rights familiar in the liberal tradition, or justice. Cohen constructs an ideal deliberative procedure meant to "highlight the properties that democratic institutions should embody, so far as possible." The ideal is "meant to provide a model for institutions to mirror," rather than merely a hypothetical construction in the manner of Rawls's original position.[9]

Ideal deliberation is *free* [partly] in that ... the participants regard themselves as bound only by the results of their deliberation and by the preconditions for that deliberation. Their consideration of proposals is not constrained by the authority of prior norms or requirements.[10]

But there's a wrinkle. Cohen, like Habermas, complicates what looks at first like a clear reliance on the entirely procedural values of ideal democratic deliberation. For Cohen the fundamental tenet of a deliberative account of democratic legitimacy is the principle that coercive political arrangements and decisions are morally illegitimate unless they can be justified in terms that can be accepted by citizens with the wide range of reasonable moral, religious, and philosophical views likely to emerge in any free society. Violations of this principle would leave some reasonable citizens without a justification in terms they could accept. Cohen argues that this is a violation of specifically democratic values. He writes, "There are many ways to exclude individuals and groups from the people, but this surely is one."[11]

Cohen's central claim for our purposes is that this criterion of legitimacy is not some moral right imposed as a constraint on what democracies are morally allowed to do, but rather is itself part and parcel of the democratic ideal. According to Cohen, to impose restrictions on religious liberty under those conditions would be "a failure of democracy";[12] not an instrumental failure (where proper democracy gets improper results), but a constitutive failure—a case of undemocratic politics. Partly to mark this claim, he calls the principle of legitimacy the "principle of deliberative inclusion," putting a more democratic cast over the very same principle Rawls had introduced under the name "the liberal principle of legitimacy."[13] This latter name, Cohen might seem to say, could misleadingly suggest that liberalism might be pitted against, or at least externally constrain, democracy. According to Cohen, democracy is constrained in no such way.

To defend a view of this kind it is necessary to explain what the value of democratic procedures consists in. It seems to hold that the procedures themselves are part of a society's justice or common good, constitutively rather than instrumentally. But then we need an account of why they should be thought to have such intrinsic value or importance. The intended account is still, overall, procedural rather than substantive in the following sense: once all the democratically motivated constraints are fully respected, the value of democratic procedures is held to be intrinsic in some way and not based on any tendency to promote other values such as justice or common good.

I doubt, in any case, that we should accept Cohen's construal of the Rawlsian criterion of legitimacy (could the arrangement be justified in terms acceptable to all reasonable citizens?) as a properly democratic consideration. It is too hypothetical, and so too independent of a decision's actual procedural source. The idea of democracy is being stretched too thin to be recognizable. If acceptability to all reasonable citizens is the core democratic requirement, then too many arguments count as democracy-based. A principle of democracy must surely assert something like inalienable popular sovereignty, the right of citizens actually to authorize their government, not merely to have a government that is justifiable from their point of view. Hobbes accepted a principle of individualized justifiability, which was surely not a democratic principle.[14] The Cohen/Rawls principle of individualized justifiability is different from Hobbes's, and it is probably more supportive of a principle of democracy, but it is not inherently a more democratic principle. It is, rather, a certain liberal ideal of justification, one upon which the justification of a principle of democracy can be held to depend. I do not think this is any deficiency. The point is only that it would be misleading to deny it.[15]

As I defined intrinsic democratic proceduralism, then, Cohen does not accept it. He does not understand democracy as essentially procedural. Cohen stays within the value of democracy only by expanding the boundaries of that concept, not by constraining the menu of values to which he wishes to appeal. This is not an indifferent terminological matter, though. Under his broader conception of the idea of democracy, actual citizens now turn out to be under the authority of standards for better or worse decisions (i.e., are they justifiable in terms acceptable to all reasonable people?), and not "free" in the more radical sense that Cohen, as quoted, seems to suggest. My verdict is the same for Cohen's view as it was for Habermas's: Cohen's view depends for its plausibility on appealing to standards for evaluating political decisions on grounds going beyond whether they stem from or promote actual democratic procedures.

Summing up this section: normative social choice theory and deep deliberative democracy treat democracy as a kind of correspondence between outcomes and certain (reasonable or brute, actual or hypothetical) individual interests of the citizens. They have very different conceptions of this correspondence, but both argue for their own as an interpretation of the idea of democratic procedure. This as-if conformity to a certain pattern of interest satisfaction (or reasonable rejectability, etc.) is a version of collective rule. I assume that democracy must, in some way, involve rule by the people, and that this is not the same as rule by others in accordance with proper utilitarian or contractualist principles of just outcomes. I do not oppose the appeal to these procedure-independent outcome standards. My point is to see them for what they are: values that go beyond the value of democracy, and values upon which the value of democracy itself probably depends. Normative democratic theory, then, cannot be *radically* democratic if this means that political decisions are to be evaluated entirely according to whether or not they are democratic.

An Unstable Hybrid: Fair Deliberative Proceduralism

We have seen that fair proceduralism fails to put democracy on purely procedural grounds. If it were only procedural fairness that mattered, we might as well flip a coin, but that is not a procedure that any democratic theory accepts. This might seem like a cramped conception of fairness, one that defines it into a strange and indefensible form. Why, it might be asked, can't we speak of a broader kind of fairness in a way that makes some sense of why we do not just flip a coin to choose the outcome, or to fairly choose a ruler, but prefer intelligent public discussion culminating in a vote?

For Jeremy Waldron, large assemblies air a wide range of citizens' concerns, and this is important as a form of fairness to citizens whose disagreements run deep. Individual rulers or small boards of regents would air a narrower range of views, unfairly privileging the views of the powerful few. This view of fairness denies that it could be achieved with a coin flip. For Waldron, the point is not the sheer number of views represented, but the institutional effort to let *more of the people* have their views represented, whatever those views might be. It is a kind of respect to take people into account "as active intelligences and consciences."[16] Waldron is clear that he is contrasting the fairness of a large assembly to any emphasis on the epistemic value of such a process. He explicitly puts aside Aristotle's idea that a large number of people can come together to achieve a better understanding than any could have alone. The fairness embodied in large assemblies is, in Waldron's view, an explicitly non-epistemic kind of fairness. It is not his view that a large assembly is fair because the only fair way to come to a decision in circumstances of disagreement is to let all views be heard in order to let the best one rise to the top. That would be an appeal to the epistemic value of the process and is no part of Waldron's argument. The idea must be, instead, that fairness requires giving everyone's view a hearing, and that fairness requires this quite independently of any epistemic value of treating views in this way.[17] I call this sort of theory *fair deliberative proceduralism*, a kind of hybrid between fair proceduralism and deliberative theories. We should look more closely at this kind of fairness to see what its value is if no epistemic value could be assumed.

Certainly, it would be plausible to say that a procedure is unfair if participants have unequally accurate views of their own convictions or interests when the vote is taken, and deliberation before the vote might be held to reduce this kind of unfairness. One problem with this approach is that it has not avoided epistemic claims for the process after all. On this view, a fair majoritarian process is one that aggregates expression of informed preferences, not simply brute preferences, and the process transforms brute preferences to informed ones. More precisely, the process has two phases: deliberation and voting. The deliberation phase is not recommended on grounds of its fairness but on grounds of its ability to transform the inputs in a valued way. The voting phase is one way of giving each person an equal chance of determining the outcome (though not the only way) and could be called fair on this basis. Since Waldron's recommendation of large assemblies on grounds of fairness appeals crucially to the airing of a wide variety of views, the deliberative phase is crucial to his conception of the process. If he explains the value of that phase in terms of people becoming better informed, this is an epistemic function and so not a matter of the kind of non-epistemic fairness that he hopes is a sufficient explanation for large assemblies.

Secondly, though, what is normally troubling about unequally accurate interest views or unequally informed preferences is not mainly the unfairness this might involve. Fairness alone would seem only to require that no one's view of their interests be more accurate than another's; it cannot tell us whether we should rectify the erroneous views, or instead reduce the accuracy of the more accurate. The unfairness of the process, distinguished carefully from any more epistemic or instrumental value, would be removed either way. If pre-vote deliberation is recommended as a way of ensuring that voters' preferences are informed, this is an argument from a certain epistemic value of the process and not an argument from its fairness. Granted, it is not an epistemic value of the process in another sense, that of promoting social decisions that are better in terms of standards that are entirely logically independent of the process that produced them. So far the aggregation by majority rule of informed preferences might be held to be a version of pure procedural justice, employing no further procedure-independent standards. My point is not that the view that deliberation improves inputs to the process has gone over to this stronger kind of epistemic view of democratic deliberation, only that it has decisively extended beyond the idea of procedural fairness. Having pointed this out, though, we might still ask whether a plausible account needs to take that further step and appeal to the epistemic value of the procedure with respect to the quality of the outcomes, rather than (or in addition to) only with respect to the quality of the inputs.

Giving a person the chance to enter her views into public deliberation prior to a majoritarian procedure can certainly be, as Waldron says, a way of expressing a certain kind of respect for the person. And giving everyone something approaching an equal chance of this kind can express a kind of equal respect. This in turn may seem to be more accurately described as a form of fairness than as a device of collective wisdom. The question is whether this strikes us as any valuable form of respect even if we purge the scene of all traces of epistemic value. A thought experiment is useful. To make sure we are not being favorably moved by epistemically valuable elements, let participants have views of no better than random quality (whatever that might mean), and let the process of deliberation produce results just as good or bad, wise or foolish, as if they had been pulled randomly from a hat (or, alternatively, they are no better on average than they would have been without any public deliberation, whatever that would mean). Now ask what is involved in giving each person's view a "fair hearing." Specifically, what kind of respect is present here that would be missing, and missed, if a policy had been chosen simply at random? Do individuals have interests in there being a deliberative process with fair participation even apart from any epistemic value in that process, and beyond the insistence on being treated equally that can be accomplished by a random procedure?

Compare several procedures. A random drawing of the social choice does not give any scope for exercise of any participant's effort or skill, but is fair in the sense of giving each an equal probability of getting what she wants. Majority rule gives each person an equal chance of being decisive, but gives each majority voter a higher chance than a minority voter of getting what she wants. Giving each person the equal chance to influence the votes of others in public discussion gives those who know which buttons to push a higher chance of getting what they want. Letting each person throw darts at a board containing the alternatives, and choosing the alternative receiving the most darts, gives good dart throwers a higher probability of getting what they want than bad dart throwers, ceteris paribus. And yet it gives each person an equal chance to exercise her dart skills toward the end of promoting the alternative she wants.

These are all fair procedures in certain respects, but that plainly does not show that they are equally appropriate in every context. In particular, Waldron's proposal is strikingly like the dart method. Both methods give every participant an equal chance to use certain skills that are unequally possessed to influence the procedure in the direction of what they prefer. (In Waldron's explanation of large assemblies, the participants are the representatives, but the procedure is held to be fair to citizens generally.) Since dart contests can be perfectly fair, the point is not that Waldron's method is unfair simply because it favors people with certain skills (or people with the views advocated by skillful representatives). Rather, the focus moves from fairness to the question of which fair procedure we ought to have. Why, for example, should greater persuasiveness be rewarded in social choice rather than greater dart skills? This is not a matter of determining which procedure is, internally, a more fair procedure. Dart contests are perfectly fair in their way, and so are persuasion contests. It is, rather, a question of what reasons there might be to let collective political choice be a persuasion contest rather than a dart contest, or no contest at all but a random choice? To answer this it is necessary for a theory to bring in other values. The idea of fairness to views is difficult to understand without assuming that the goal is a deliberation or outcome that is more responsive to the genuine balance of applicable reasons.

Fair deliberative proceduralism is an unstable hybrid. Insofar as procedural fairness is really the point, the deliberation is superfluous. Insofar as the deliberation is important to the theory, the view shifts away from procedural values and toward epistemic ones.

Conclusion and Looking Ahead

We have seen a variety of normative approaches to democratic legitimacy or authority that claim to avoid appealing to any tendency of democratic procedures to produce decisions that are better or more just by procedure-independent standards. This flight from substance is, perhaps, the single most characteristic ambition of normative democratic theory of the last several decades. I hope to have cast serious doubt on the proceduralist ambition.

Proceduralism is not the problem, but the effort to rely on nothing but proceduralism is. Democratic authority and legitimacy could never be understood without relying to some extent on the idea of retrospective or purely procedural value in certain ways, and epistemic proceduralism is a form of proceduralism for that reason. It does not limit itself to procedural values but brings in, in addition, a prospective epistemic value to democratic procedure—a tendency to produce decisions that are better or more just by standards that are independent of the actual temporal procedure that produced them.

Having argued that most normative democratic theory is not substantive—or epistemic—enough (at least not admittedly), we need next to worry about a theory's being too substantive or too epistemic. As I have argued in chapter 3, we should accept a constraint on political justification that prevents us from recommending simply the epistemically best method of decision, whatever it might be: political justification is specious if it relies on doctrines that could not be generally accepted by people with the wide variety of reasonable worldviews that will flourish under free conditions. This principle is what prevents the concern with the epistemic value of political decision procedures from recommending epistocracy, or the rule of those who know how to rule best.

Epistemic Proceduralism

ASSUME THAT FOR MANY CHOICES FACED by a political community, some alternatives are better than others by standards that are in some way objective.[1] (For example, suppose that progressive income tax rates are more just than a flat rate, even after considering effects on efficiency.) If so, it must count in favor of a social decision procedure that it tends to produce the better decision. On the other hand, there is wide disagreement about what justice requires, and no citizen is required to defer to the expertise or authority of any other. Thus, as we have seen, normative democratic theory has largely proceeded on the assumption that the most that can be said for a legitimate democratic decision is that it was produced by a procedure that treats voters equally in certain ways. The merits of democratic decisions are held to be entirely in their past.

This contrast between procedural and epistemic virtues ought to be questioned. Certainly, there are strong arguments that some form of proceduralism must be preferable to any theory in which correctness is necessary and sufficient for a decision's legitimacy. Democratic accounts of legitimacy seek to explain the legitimacy of the general run of laws (though not necessarily all of them) under favorable conditions. However, even under good conditions many laws are bound to be incorrect, inferior, or unjust by the appropriate objective standard. If the choice is between proceduralism and correctness theories of legitimacy, proceduralism is vastly more plausible. It should be noted, however, that correctness theories are not the only form available for approaches to democratic legitimacy that emphasize the epistemic value of the democratic process—its tendency to produce outcomes that are correct by independent standards. Epistemic criteria are compatible, at least in principle, with proceduralism. Thus, rather than supposing that the legitimacy of an outcome depends on its correctness, I suggest that it derives, partly, from the epistemic value, even though it is imperfect, of the procedure that produced it. Democratic legitimacy requires that the procedure can be held, in terms acceptable to all qualified points of view, to be epistemically the best (or close to it) among those that are better than random. In this chapter I mainly explain the structure of this kind of approach, what I call *epistemic proceduralism*, and how it can be both epistemic and proceduralist. It will take further argument, reserved for chapter 8, "Original Authority and the Democracy/Jury Analogy," to show just how it accounts for the legitimacy and authority of laws.

Why suppose that there is any kind of legitimacy for a political decision other than whether it meets some independent standard such as justice? Why not say that it is legitimate if correct, and otherwise not? Call this denial of proceduralism *a correctness theory* of legitimacy.

One thing to notice about a correctness theory of legitimacy is that in a diverse community there is bound to be little agreement on whether a decision is legitimate, since there will be little agreement about whether it meets the independent standard of, say, justice. If the decision is made by majority rule, and voters address the question whether the proposal would be independently correct, then at least a majority will accept its correctness. However, nearly half of the voters might deny its correctness, and on a correctness theory they would in turn deny the legitimacy of the decision—deny that it warrants state action, and/or places them under any obligation to comply. Brute disagreement of this kind raises pragmatic questions about how to maintain stability. A morally deeper worry stems from the fact that much of the disagreement might be reasonable, or in our more generic term, qualified. First, there might be qualified disagreement on what counts as just. Second, even if there is an account of justice that is beyond qualified objection, I assume there will be qualified disagreement in many cases about what actual decisions and institutions meet the agreeable principles of justice. If so, correctness theories of legitimacy, those that say that a law is legitimate simply because it meets the independent standards of justice, will not have a justification that is acceptable to all qualified points of view. Correctness theories cannot meet the qualified acceptability requirement. I take this to be conclusive against them. Theories that avoid the epistemic dimension altogether have been rejected already as well. The space is opened up for epistemic proceduralism.

A critical taxonomy will allow the argument for epistemic proceduralism to develop in an orderly way. Let us begin with one more family of views, an important and influential one, and then locate the several different approaches on a chart with respect to the role they give to epistemic value.

Some authors seem to advocate a view that is like fair deliberative proceduralism, which we rejected earlier (in chapter 5, "The Flight from

Substance"), except that the procedure's value is primarily in recognizing good reasons rather than in providing fair access (though fair or equal access would be a natural corollary).[2] We might thus distinguish fair deliberative proceduralism (FD) from *rational deliberative proceduralism* (RD). This view would not claim that the procedure produces outcomes that (tend to) approximate some standard (of, say, justice or common good) that is independent of actual procedures, and does so by recognizing better reasons and giving them greater influence over the outcome (e.g., by way of voters being rationally persuaded). That would be an epistemic view. Instead, RD insists that the only thing to be said for the outcomes is that they were produced by a reason-recognizing procedure; no further claim has to be made about whether the outcomes tend to meet any independent standard of correctness. The process is not held to perform well or badly in this procedure-independent sense. The outcomes are rational only in a procedural sense, and not in any more substantive sense. This claim would be analogous to fair proceduralism's claim that outcomes are fair in a procedural, not a substantive, sense.

This procedural sense of rational outcomes is not clearly available to the advocate of this reason-recognizing procedure, however. If the procedure is held to *recognize* the better reasons, those reasons are being counted as better by procedure-independent standards. Then to say that the outcome reflects the better reasons might only mean that the outcome meets or tends to meet that same procedure-independent standard. (By contrast, in the case of fair proceduralism, the procedure is never held to recognize the more fair individual inputs.) If that were the basis of its claim to fairness, then it too would be an epistemic view. The space held out for a nonepistemic rational deliberative proceduralism would have disappeared.

However, there are two ways RD might resist this dilemma. First, there might be background reasons for thinking that, while deliberation might improve people's grounds, there are other factors influencing their votes, and that these will not often be outweighed. In that case, a better appreciation of the reasons will not often lead a person to a different vote, and yet the better appreciation of the reasons is still a feature of the procedure that might recommend it. Second, even if many people do change their votes in light of their improved view of the reasons, we might have background reasons for thinking that the margin of victory will tend to be too large to be overcome by this effect. I do not know whether these suppositions play a significant role in our thinking about actual politics, but they are available in principle. So, let me turn to a different difficulty for the view, without assuming it is relying on better outcomes after all.

We can see how there is some value even when the outcomes are not improved by thinking of an example of a planning committee for a high school prom.[3] We might have background reasons for thinking either that letting the committee members discuss and decide things for themselves will not much change what they decide, or that even if it does, their decisions will still not tend to be substantively very good. And yet we might let them decide for themselves because many of them will come to appreciate the structure of the reasons for and against the various options, and often to come to a sounder view of the merits of their choices (none of this in the hope of improving the outcomes).[4] There is recognizable value here. But is it weighty enough for us to take the same view when it is not a prom but the laws and policies for a whole society? Granting that it has some value, does it have enough to explain our plausible commitments about the importance of democratic institutions?

We should doubt that it does, for several reasons. First, their coming to appreciate the reasons for and against alternative policies can occur even if they don't vote. If we want them to manifest their improved view of matters by playing a role in making the decision, RD has yet to provide any basis for this part of the decision procedure. Second, while there may be some intrinsic value in people appreciating the relevant reasons, a decision procedure might have lots of intrinsic value. It might be fair, or it might be humorous, or it might be fun or pleasant, or it might be reason-recognizing. If its being reason-recognizing is some especially great value even when there is no claim at all that it will improve decisions, we would want to know what is so valuable about it that requires us to organize our political decision making around it rather than around the other intrinsic values a procedure could have. Why do we want our political decisions to be made by a reason-recognizing procedure rather than by, say, a merely fair procedure (such as a coin flip), unless the reason-recognizing procedure is thought to tend toward better decisions? The intrinsic procedural value emphasized by RD is, like procedural fairness, a fairly thin thing. I do not mean it is thin simply because it does not improve decisions. I mean that it is far from clear how it is any more weighty than lots of intrinsic values a procedure could have, but which everyone would recognize are very thin, such as the intrinsic procedural fairness of choosing policies with a coin flip.

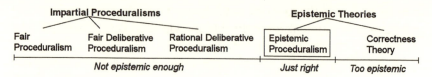

Figure 6.1

I conclude that without any space for the view that democratic outcomes are procedurally, but not substantively, rational, deliberative conceptions of democracy are forced to ground democratic legitimacy either in the infertile soil of an impartial proceduralism or in a rich but combustible appeal to the epistemic value of democratic procedures. Turning, then, to epistemic theories of democratic legitimacy, there is a fork in the road. Three challenges for epistemic theories are helpful in choosing between them: the problem of *deference*, the problem of *demandingness*, and the problem of *invidious comparisons*. Epistemic proceduralism, I will argue, can meet these challenges better than nonproceduralist epistemic approaches, which I am calling *correctness theories*. The latter sort of theory holds that political decisions are legitimate only if they are correct by appropriate procedure-independent standards, and adds the claim that proper democratic procedures are sufficiently accurate to render the general run of laws and policies legitimate under favorable conditions. This was Rousseau's view, and has also been advocated by some contemporary theorists such as Carlos Nino and William Nelson.[5] Having pushed things in an epistemic direction, I now want to prevent things from getting out of hand. Existing epistemic conceptions of democracy are, in a certain sense, too epistemic (see fig. 6.1).

The moral challenge for any epistemic conception of political authority is to let truth be the guide without illegitimately privileging the opinions of any putative experts. As I have argued in chapter 2 ("Truth and Despotism"), experts should not be privileged because qualified citizens will disagree about who counts as an expert. Epistemic proceduralism needs to hold that unlike any supposed expert elite, a proper democratic process taken as a whole can be agreed by all qualified points of view to have epistemic value with respect to political questions. It would be easy to go overboard with this kind of account, asking citizens to take democracy's word for it when they lose to a majority. Epistemic proceduralism does not ask the minority voter to defer, in her judgment, to the democratic process in this way. This feature of the view can be clarified by contrasting it with Rousseau's view, as the classic example of correctness theories of epistemic democracy.

Rousseau argued that properly conducted democratic procedures (in suitably arranged communities) discovered a procedure-independent answer to the moral question, "What should we, as a political community, do?" The correct answer, he held, is whatever is common to the wills of all citizens, this being what he called every citizen's "general will." In this way, citizens under majority rule could still "obey nobody but their own will,"[6] securing autonomy in a way in which under Locke's theory, for example, they could not. (For Locke, the minority simply loses, since the majority determines the direction of the whole group.)[7] For Rousseau, democratic procedures discover the general will when citizens address themselves to the question of the content of the general will, though they often use the process illegitimately to serve more particular ends. The key point for our purposes is that, according to Rousseau, outcomes are legitimate when and because they are correct and not for any procedural reason. When they are incorrect, they are illegitimate, because nothing but the general will can legitimately be politically imposed.

Rousseau, uncharacteristically, asks the citizen to surrender her judgment to the properly conducted democratic process: "When, therefore, the opinion contrary to mine prevails, this proves merely that I was in error, and that what I took to be the general will was not so."[8] The minority voter can, of course, conclude instead that the process was improperly conducted, and that others have not addressed the question that was put to them. But she must decide either that it is not even a legitimate collective decision or that it has correctly ascertained the general will—the morally correct answer. In a well-functioning polity, where she has no grounds to challenge the legitimacy of the procedure, she must not only obey it but also surrender her moral judgment to it. She must say to herself, "While it doesn't *seem* right to me, 'this proves merely that I was in error.'"

One problem with Rousseau's expectation of deference is suggested by a passage in John Rawls's doctoral dissertation. In chastising appeals to exalted entities as morally authoritative, he writes,

The kinds of entities which have been used in such appeals are very numerous indeed. In what follows I shall mention some of them very briefly. The main objection in each case is always the following: how do we know that the entity in question will always behave in accordance with what is right[?] This is a question with [*sic*] which we *always* can ask, and which we always *do* ask, and it shows that we do not, in actual practice, hand over the determination of right and wrong to any other agency whatsoever.[9]

In *A Theory of Justice*, Rawls applies the idea to democratic choice:

Although in given circumstances it is justified that the majority . . . has the constitutional right to make law, this does not imply that the laws enacted are just. . . . [W]hile citizens normally submit their conduct to democratic authority, that is, recognize the outcome of a vote as establishing a binding rule, other things equal, they do not submit their judgment to it.[10]

This is the problem of deference faced by epistemic approaches to democracy. My objection is not to Rousseau's requirement that the outcome be obeyed. I believe that something much like Rousseauian voting can justify this requirement. Rousseau goes wrong, I believe, in resting this case on the fact—when it is a fact—that the outcome is the general will, the morally correct answer to the question faced by the voters.[11]

Here we can see the promise of an epistemic form of proceduralism, one that departs from correctness theories by holding that the outcome is legitimate even when it is incorrect, owing to the epistemic value, albeit imperfect, of the democratic procedure. Such an account would not expect the minority voter to surrender her judgment to the procedure in any way, since she can hold both that the process was properly carried out and that the outcome, while morally binding on citizens for procedural reasons, is morally mistaken.

What if a nonproceduralist theory can support the claim that the majority is overwhelmingly likely to be correct? Wouldn't it be sensible to expect deference to the outcome in that case? Recent discussions of the epistemic approach to democratic authority have usually invoked the striking mathematical result of Rousseau's contemporary Condorcet, known as the *jury theorem*: roughly, if voters are better than chance on some yes/no question (call this their individual competence), then under majority rule the group will be virtually infallible on that question if only the group is not too small. I argue against the value of the jury theorem for democratic theory later.[12] Here I want to make a few points about any device or procedure that might be held to be highly reliable on the questions that political communities must decide. Is any such device or procedure really an instrument to which we can comfortably surrender our moral judgment on certain matters?

Suppose there were no good reason to challenge the overwhelming likelihood that the procedure's outcome is correct. And never mind whether the basis for this likelihood is the jury theorem or something else altogether. Since correctness theories treat outcomes as legitimate because they are correct, the reason for obedience given to the minority voter is the correctness of the outcome, something the minority voter is on record as denying. So correctness theories go on to say to the minority voter that it is overwhelmingly probable that the outcome is correct. Correctness theories need this claim for two reasons: first, to actually supply legitimacy in the vast majority of cases; second, to give the minority voter in any given case reason to change her opinion to match that of the outcome of a majority vote. Correctness theories, then, apparently rely on the following premise:

Probability supports moral judgment: One who accepts that the correctness of a given moral judgment is extremely probable all things considered has good reason to accept the moral judgment.

Epistemic proceduralism does not rely on any such assumption, since it does not rest the minority voter's acceptance of an outcome's legitimacy on the outcome's correctness. This is an advantage for epistemic proceduralism, since the claim that probability supports moral judgment is deeply problematic. It may be false; at least it is not something all reasonable citizens can be expected to accept, as the following thought experiment suggests.

Suppose there is a deck of 1,000 cards, and each has written on it a putative moral statement about which you have no strong opinion either way. Suppose further that you accept on some evidence that exactly 999 of these contain true statements, and 1 is false. Now you cut the deck and the card says, "Physician-assisted suicide is sometimes morally permissible" (or some other moral statement about which you are otherwise uncertain). It is not clear that you have been given very good reason to accept that physician-assisted suicide is sometimes permissible. Of course, you might doubt the reliability of the deck of cards (or the "expert"), but suppose you do not. There is nothing inconsistent in holding that, "While there is almost no chance that this is incorrect, still, that doesn't make physician-assisted suicide *seem* permissible to me, and so I do not accept that it is. The expert is almost certainly correct,

105

and yet I am not prepared to share in the expert's judgment." This attitude may make sense for moral judgments even though it apparently does not for factual judgments.

Rawls prefers to say that we can always rely on our own moral judgment as our basis for denying that the expert is infallible. But why would this be? If we do not say this about physics, why say it about morality? It would normally be epistemically irresponsible to dismiss the trained physicist's judgment about whether, say, there is such a thing as objective simultaneity, merely on the ground that things seem a certain way to us. It might seem to me that there is objective simultaneity, but I should normally take the physicist's word for it if she tells me that there is not. The fact that we can and sometimes do doubt the word of supposedly expert physicists and moralists does not capture the way in which the cases are different. We are permitted to doubt the moralist even though it would be irresponsible to doubt the physicist in parallel circumstances.

I admit, this is all somewhat puzzling. Even if we could assume that the deck of cards were 100 percent reliable, knowing that the card we turn up is certain to be correct still does not give us any idea of what is correct about it, any moral basis for the judgment. And, yet, "P is (certainly) true but I do not believe it" is probably not a sensible stance. I will leave the point here, only to say that there is a puzzle here that raises questions for correctness theories, those that say the minority ought to obey the outcomes of majority rule because this gives them their best evidence about what the substantively correct decision is. Epistemic proceduralism avoids any such difficulties, since it does not say that the democratic outcome is a particularly strong reason for a belief about what the correct outcome would be. The reasons it gives the citizen are moral reasons to comply, not epistemic reasons to believe.

Since the problem about moral deference is puzzling and uncertain, we should notice another way in which correctness theories take on burdens that epistemic proceduralism avoids. Since the reason for enforcement and obedience that correctness theories give stems from the claim that the democratic outcome is substantively correct, then it could only explain the general run of laws being legitimate and binding if it held that the general run of laws are substantively correct. Epistemic proceduralism generates more legitimacy and authority with less demanding epistemic claims. All it claims is that the democratic process has a certain modest epistemic value. Since it can have that modest value even when it is mistaken, it gets more authority and legitimacy out of a given degree of epistemic value of democratic procedures.[13]

What moral reason is there to obey the decisions of the majority, when they meet the criteria of epistemic proceduralism, even if they are incorrect? Begin with a case where it is granted that each individual is under an obligation to abide by the outcome of a fair procedure. The question "What should we do?" is treated as answered by aggregating what each of us wants to do in some impartial way. But now suppose it is known that the choice we make will be morally better or worse, and we do not all agree on which choices are morally better. First, it would be odd to use a procedure that operated solely on our individual interests, ignoring our moral judgments. I have argued that there would be little obligation to obey the outcome of such a procedure despite its procedural fairness. Second, it still seems an insufficient ground of obligation merely to use a procedure that chose the alternative in accord with the moral judgments of a majority for reasons of fairness. There is no point in attending to moral judgments rather than interests (or rather than choosing the outcome randomly) if they are simply to be counted up on the model of procedural fairness. Why should this produce any stronger sort of obligation than the straight procedurally fair aggregation of interests? The reason for moving to the moral judgments could only be to apply intelligence to the moral issue at hand.

I propose, as the counterpart of the idea of procedural fairness in cases where there is an independent moral standard for the outcome, the idea of epistemic proceduralism: procedural impartiality among individuals' opinions, but with a tendency to be correct; the impartial application of intelligence to the moral question at hand.

Why do you have any obligation to obey such a procedure when you firmly believe it is mistaken? The question is sometimes prompted by supposing that the epistemic dimension is meant to make the procedure's outcome also the individual's best guess as to the answer, as if the goal of the procedure were to find epistemic reasons.[14] But, as I have said, that is not the role of the epistemic dimension in epistemic proceduralism. That would be roughly like supposing the role of majority rule in fair proceduralism is to make the outcome conducive to my own interests. Thus, one would ask, why obey a fair procedure when it does not accord with your own best interests? I am taking as a starting assumption that the fairness of the procedure is a fully adequate reason to obey in simple non-epistemic cases. The problem is to stay as close to this model as possible, while making adjustments to fit the case where there is a procedure-independent moral standard for the outcome and there is a generally acceptable way of trying to meet it. In neither case will the reason to obey be based on any substantive feature of the outcome—both are pure proceduralist accounts of the reason or obligation to obey. One looks back to the procedure's fairness, whereas the other, epistemic proceduralism, looks back to the procedure's generally acceptable tendency to make substantively correct decisions. This is retrospective still, since the procedure retains its relevant epistemic features whether or not it gets the right answer in a given case.

Mere procedural fairness, as I have repeatedly argued, is a very weak reason to obey when I believe the outcome is morally mistaken. It may seem, then, that my own moral judgment about the outcome is supreme in my own deliberations. That is not, however, the only reason for thinking procedural fairness is insufficient in such cases. A different reason is that procedural fairness is not equipped to address cognitive issues—it is not a cognitive process. This can be remedied without making my own moral judgment supreme if proceduralism can be adapted to cognitive purposes. There is a moral reason to abide by its decisions quite apart from their substantive merits, just as there is reason to abide by a procedure that fairly adjudicates among competing interests quite apart from whether it serves your interests. Epistemic proceduralism is proposed as a conservative adaptation of the idea of procedural fairness to cases of morally evaluable outcomes. It is conservative in requiring no more epistemic value than necessary (just-better-than-randomness)—while still fitting the cognitive nature of the cases.[15]

This begins to clarify the sort of reason for compliance that epistemic proceduralism is held to generate: it is a moral reason, and one not dependent on the democratic outcome's being the agent's best epistemic guide. You might have more reason to believe your own opinion even when a proper democratic majority disagrees. Epistemic proceduralism holds that in that case you ought, rationally, to believe that the majority is mistaken, but you ought, morally, to obey the mistaken law (within limits, about which more shortly). The structure is similar to what we might naturally say about the authority of a jury's verdict in a criminal trial: the jury system is designed with great attention to its epistemic value (among other things.) When the jury reaches a verdict, its legitimacy and authority do not depend on its correctness, but they do depend on the epistemic value of the procedure.

So far, this is still just a clarification of the structure of the view. In order to show more specifically how epistemic proceduralism yields legitimate and authoritative laws, we will have to engage directly with the relevant general principles. To explain how epistemic proceduralism generates authoritative law we need to argue that procedures conforming to the epistemic proceduralist structure would receive normative consent. I reserve this argument for chapter 8, "Original Authority and the Democracy/Jury Analogy."

Looking at epistemic proceduralism from the standpoint of Rousseau's view, the authority of the public view takes the place of the authority of the general will. The Rousseauian will object that if the general will is replaced in this way, political obedience will no longer be obedience to oneself, and political society cannot be reconciled with freedom. The Rousseauian argument that legitimacy requires correctness is based on a respect for the ultimate authority of the individual will. Only if the political decision is willed by each citizen can required compliance be reconciled with autonomy. The general will is that part of each citizen's will that all have in common, and so only decisions in conformity with the general will can be legitimately required of everyone.

If this were a good argument, then the authority of the majority decision would not depend, as it does in Rousseau, on majority rule having been agreed upon in an original social contract.[16] By positing a previous unanimous authorization of majority rule, Rousseau undermines the idea that majority decisions are legitimate only because they correctly ascertain the general will. If the procedure must be previously authorized, this could only be because obedience to the general will is not straightforwardly obedience to one's own will. This is because a person's general will is not simply the person's will, but the part of his or her will that is also a part of every other citizen's will. The authority of the general will is the authority of all over the behavior of each. Even if this is conceived as compatible in a certain way with freedom, morality is not simply freedom to do as one wills, even on Rousseau's view, since each person's private will is morally subordinated to the general will. Thus, Rousseau thinks the legitimacy of majority rule depends on unanimous contractual acceptance (apparently hypothetical). Once this is admitted, we see that even Rousseauian democracy does not avoid every kind of subjection of the individual to external authority, rhetoric notwithstanding. The question is how this kind of subjection can be justified, not how it can be avoided. It is not as if Rousseauian theory avoids subjection to political authority whereas epistemic proceduralism embraces it. The rhetoric of individual self-rule in the context of political authority places the bar higher than any theory can meet, and epistemic proceduralism proceeds without it. Legitimate and authoritative commands are plainly not compatible with individual self-rule. It is possible to rest your political philosophy on the principle that no one owes obedience to another unless they have actually consented to that authority (or, as with Wolff,[17] not even then). But why is this more plausible than the view that, just as we find ourselves with other moral obligations whether or not we consent to them, we might find ourselves with obligations to obey others in certain cases? For now, let it suffice to say that there is no attempt here to reconcile authority or legitimacy with self-rule or actual consent. I leave the more general accounts of legitimacy and authority to chapters 7 and 8.

Epistemic proceduralism says that even some substantively unjust laws might nevertheless be legitimate or authoritative or both, because they are produced by the right sort of procedure. Correctness theories, which are defined by the contrary view, are rejected. The idea that even unjust law is sometimes legitimate and authoritative is, first of all, consistent with many ordinary convictions. Recall the jury context: the legitimacy and authority of the verdict are not canceled just whenever the jury is mistaken. If they were, then jailers and police officers ought not to carry out the court's judgment, but should rely on their own judgment of the defendant's guilt or innocence. That conclusion would be the striking and heterodox one. Epistemic proceduralism is one of many views that say that so long as proper procedures and guarantees were respected, even erroneous decisions will often have authority and legitimacy.

Still, there must obviously be limits to this. Some verdicts, and some legal commands, must be too unjust or otherwise over the line beyond which legitimacy and/or authority falls away however proper the procedure for making the decision might have been. Of course, this could be denied. It is natural and important to try out the hypothesis that these could always be explained in terms of failures of the procedure: perhaps no really proper procedure would ever generate laws that should not be enforced or obeyed. I know of no argument that lends serious support to such a conjecture. Certainly, actual heinous laws can normally be shown to have been produced by defective procedures, but that may be only because actual procedures are always more or less defective. That would not show that if they had not been procedurally defective they also would not have gone substantively so terribly wrong. There seems to be no reason to believe that. In the end, democratic procedures, however procedurally pristine, will reflect the views of those who vote. And those views might be anything at all, as heinous or as

noble as you please. We are forced to conclude that even a fine procedure, one that normally lends legitimacy and authority to its decisions,
can sometimes generate laws that lack the characteristic legitimacy and
authority that the procedure normally provides. A complete theory,
then, must say something about where these limits lie—about which
laws are over that line even though not all mistaken laws are.[18]

Of course, a complete theory would say something about everything,
and the theory presented here will not be complete. In particular, I will
not offer a theory of where these limits lie, except to make the following
limited points. First, one category of limits seems very likely to stem
from the idea of laws that, while democratically produced, would either
directly or indirectly undermine the possibility of proper democracy in
the future. The classic example of a majority disenfranchising a minority
falls into this category. Ideally, we would want the theory that establishes
the authority and legitimacy of democratic outcomes to also explain why
these cases are exceptions. The authority of democracy does not extend
even to all antidemocratic measures a democracy might pass. But, second,
I do not have any hope of explaining all the exceptions in that way. A law,
passed by proper democratic procedures, that established, as a punishment for anything, being boiled in oil would be neither legitimate nor
authoritative even though it has no real antidemocratic dimension to it.
There is no reason to demand a democratic, or even a political, account of
limits like this. Morality is not exhausted by democratic politics however
perfectly carried out, and there is no reason to think it cannot place limits on democracy's ability to permit enforcement or require obedience.

There will also be the intermediate cases of unjust laws that, while
not so heinous as to silence any suggestion of authority or legitimacy,
warrant disobedience of a conscientious or demonstrative kind. Civil
disobedience and other forms of resistance and noncompliance have
their place as well. Here we should just note that, again, the mere fact
that a democratic decision is in error should not be taken to trigger any
of these forms of resistance or noncompliance. Some errors do, and
some do not. I say more about sharp forms of protest in chapter 10,
"The Real Speech Situation."

Nothing short of a full moral theory could give a full account of the
limits of democratic authority and legitimacy. But we have not left the
field open to all possible views of the matter: some (putative) laws lack
legitimacy and authority simply because they were not produced by a
proper democratic political procedure. Some laws are authoritative and
legitimate even if they are substantively unjust, such as some mistaken

jury verdicts, or laws that are moderately in error on just taxation rates. Some laws with a perfect democratic pedigree would lack legitimacy and authority because they undermine democracy itself in a forward-looking way, such as disenfranchising blacks or women. Yet other laws are neither legitimate nor authoritative despite unexceptionable retrospective and prospective democratic credentials, such as laws punishing any crime with boiling in oil. We will not be able to draw the boundaries of all these categories, but this defines a distinctive kind of view and clarifies the intended structure of epistemic proceduralism.

The general acceptability requirement applies at two places in epistemic proceduralism. First, the proposition that the political procedure has epistemic value must be generally acceptable if it is to figure in political justification. Second, though this is less obvious, it must be a generally acceptable conception of justice or correctness, rather than true justice, that the political process is said to be good at ascertaining. Or, at least, this is probably required. The reason is that there is so much qualified dispute about true justice that public deliberation about what will promote it seems bound to be splintered. Different moral, religious, and philosophical schools would be attending to such different subsidiary questions—the ones they take to be central to the substance of true justice—that the prospects for thinking constructively together would be severely limited. Too much of the dispute would be about the nature of justice itself, and not enough about what justice permits and requires in the real cases at hand. Matters would be improved if there were a public conception of justice, acceptable for practical purposes, to all qualified points of view who still disagree about the whole truth about justice.[19] If it were to turn out that there is no conception of justice acceptable to all qualified points of view, epistemic proceduralism would need to try to make its case with citizens addressing themselves to true justice. We will assume, however, that citizens share, at least roughly, a public conception of justice and take it for granted in their deliberations about what to do. We need it to be generally acceptable that the procedure has a certain tendency to make decisions that are good according to a conception of justice that is, itself, generally acceptable as a public conception of justice.

The Idea of Accuracy

We need to say more specifically what is meant by saying that the political process is accurate, or tends to get things right. To say that democratic decisions tend to get the right answer is ambiguous in the same way as saying that a certain medical test tends to get the right answer.[20] This might mean either that it is sensitive or that it is discriminating, in the following senses:

> Given that x is the right answer it is very likely that the test or decision procedure says x. It rarely gives false negatives. We might call this *sensitivity*.

Or,

> Given that the test or decision procedure says x, it is very likely that x is the right answer. It rarely gives false positives. We might call this *discrimination*.

So we might define the perfectly accurate procedure as having both properties to the maximal degree (substituting "guaranteed" for "very likely"). Any deviation from the perfect procedure will include proneness to one kind of error or the other.

It is easy to avoid false positives by running very few tests, or running the procedure only rarely. Zero decisions means zero false positives. If there are zero decisions (or zero diagnostic tests), the *system* (which we might say sometimes runs a *test* and sometimes does not) produces no false positives but lots of false negatives—indeed it yields all possible false negatives. This could be the case even if the test, once it is run, rarely produces false negatives. Suppose you were connected to a device that was programmed to check you for a virus every so often. Suppose we measured the test's proneness to false positives and false negatives by looking only at the times that it actually checked. But this would not capture the kind of sensitivity that we really want from the device, since on this way of measuring its performance it could perform perfectly by never running a test at all (no false positives, no false negatives), or running a test once and getting it right (say, one correct negative in the course of your life). Rather, we want the device both to detect the virus if it is present and not to falsely report it if it is not present. So the distinction between a test and a system of tests is important.

Suppose, now, that the question is justice, and the system is a political system that makes decisions. In this system suppose that a certain decision procedure, a test, is conducted at certain intervals, say majority rule voting by all citizens, or polling a panel of rulers. The decisions are, by some independent standard, either permitted by justice or not, and if permitted, then they are also either required or not. (I assume all required decisions are permitted.) There are two dimensions here: permitted/not permitted, and required/not required. In addition, there are also the two kinds of error in each case: possible false positives and false negatives with respect to what is permitted, and also with respect to what is required. So far, for our purposes, we can suppose that epistemic proceduralism cares about both sensitivity and discrimination, both for the permission and requirement dimensions, all somehow balanced (though we will modify this assumption shortly).

What about the idea of accuracy that is better than random? Think about a continuous detector, such as an electronic monitor for water on the basement floor. We can define random accuracy in the following way: the probability of water, given that the detector says water, is no higher or lower than the probability of water overall (its unconditional probability). That would be a random level of discrimination. And the probability that the detector says water given that there is water is no higher than the probability that the detector says water overall—a random level of sensitivity. The conjunction of those two features defines random accuracy of a detector.

We can bring this approach together with our distinction between the requirement dimension and the permission dimension of accuracy for a political system. We want democracy to do what justice requires, and not do what justice forbids (leaving aside political supererogation). Start with requirements:

Requirement Sensitivity
Given that legislating x is a requirement of justice, it is very likely that the system legislates x.

And,

Requirement Discrimination
Given that the system legislates x, it is very likely that legislating x is a requirement of justice. (This is equivalent to: Given that x is not a requirement of justice it is very unlikely that the procedure legislates x.)

Requirement discrimination is not as compelling, intuitively, as requirement sensitivity. It does not seem highly important that nothing be legislated unless doing so is required by justice. Some optional things might be positively good to do. On the other hand, there are some natural libertarian qualms about the possibility of too much legislation.

To incorporate permission-justice as well as requirement-justice, it stands out immediately that there is no reason to want the procedure to tend to legislate everything that it would be permissible to legislate. But there is a strong interest in refraining from legislating where doing so is not permitted. Still, let us lay out the two kinds of accuracy in question.

Permission Sensitivity
Given that legislating x is permitted by justice, it is very likely that the procedure legislates x.

And,

Permission Discrimination
Given that the procedure legislates x, it is very likely that legislating x is permitted by justice. (Equivalent to: Given that x is not permitted by justice, it is very unlikely that the procedure legislates x.)

Again, one of these seems more important than the other. In fact, we certainly do not want every permissible law. It appears that it would be natural to want a procedure that was *requirement-sensitive and permission-discriminating*. (This is a simplification, because we would also want a system that did some things that were not required, and this is not measured by our concepts so far.) We can now define a benchmark of random accuracy on these two dimensions (putting aside requirement discrimination and permission sensitivity) as follows:

Random Requirement Sensitivity
The probability, given that legislating x is a requirement of justice, that the procedure legislates x is no different from the unconditional probability that the procedure legislates x.

Random Permission Discrimination
The probability, given that the procedure legislates x, that x is permitted is no different from the unconditional probability that x is permitted. (Equivalent to: The probability, given that x is not permitted, that the procedure legislates x is no different from the unconditional probability that the procedure legislates x.)

For our purposes, then, random accuracy of a democratic procedure would be the combination of random requirement sensitivity and random permission discrimination.

Being *better* than random is a little more complicated. Certainly, if a system is no worse than random in either respect but better in one respect, then it is better than random. But if it is better than random in one respect and worse in the other, there is no simple answer to whether

115

it is, in some sense, better than random overall. A more elaborate account could try to specify how much better it needs to be in one dimension to compensate for shortfalls in the other, but this is more than I will attempt here. We avoid these problems if we try to establish that some democratic system would be better than random in at least one respect, and no worse than random in either respect. This is how my talk of the system being better than random should be understood. Epistemic proceduralism prefers a democratic political system insofar as it performs better than the alternatives, so long as it is better than random. We can now refine this criterion. The question is whether a system (not just a test, such as majority voting) performs better than the alternatives and is better than random with respect to both requirement sensitivity and permission discrimination.

Conclusion

This chapter has laid out the structure of epistemic proceduralism. It is not the view that since (at least improved) democracy almost always gets the right answer citizens ought to take democracy's word for it about what ought to be done. It is the view that partly because democracy has some modest epistemic value (in a way that no qualified point of view can deny), its outcomes are legitimate and authoritative in a purely procedural way. It is a proceduralist view, linking legitimacy and authority of a decision to its procedural source and not to its substantive correctness. Unlike more familiar proceduralist accounts, however, it does rely on the epistemic value of the procedure rather than on some non-epistemic virtue of a procedure such as its fairness to participants or to their points of view.[21] Citizens are not given strong reasons to believe its results are correct. They are, rather, given moral reasons to comply with and enforce those results even, in many cases, when they think they are mistaken. Not in all cases, however, since some decisions (such as ordering criminals to be boiled in oil), however democratic their sources or their consequences, will lack legitimacy or authority for moral reasons having nothing special to do with democracy.

Authority and Normative Consent

EPISTEMIC PROCEDURALISM IS AN ACCOUNT OF, among other things, how democratically produced laws can be authoritative and legitimate. In this chapter I step back from democracy to offer an account of the basis of political authority in general terms. In the next chapter I will link this general account to my epistemic approach to democracy in order to explain the authority of democracy. For now, though, I consider the basic idea of political authority.

Moral obligations can simply befall us. Sometimes we are morally required to help someone in need, or to tell the truth, or to undo some damage we have inadvertently caused, and we are required whether or not we consented to accept these requirements. But it is often held that certain obligations, obligations to do as we are told, can never simply befall us. We are never under the authority of another person unless we have consented to be. This view adds that even if we have consented to authority, we are still not under authority unless the consent meets certain conditions of adequacy, such as being uncoerced, informed, and so forth. Sometimes even consent is null, failing to create any obligation to obey.

Among our moral requirements, there might be moral requirements to consent to authority in certain cases. In those cases, what happens if we do not consent? Can we escape the authority in that way, by abusing our power to refuse consent? Why not say, instead, that just as consent is sometimes null if it fails to meet certain standards, likewise, non-consent can be defective too? I will concentrate on the case of wrongly withheld consent and argue that in some cases this renders the non-consent null. The nullity of non-consent means that the authority situation is just as it would have been if the non-consent had not occurred—that is, just as if consent had occurred.

The result would be a novel form of a hypothetical consent theory of authority, based on what I will call *normative consent*. If this view can be sustained, authority can simply befall us, whether we have consented to it or not. Still, the normative consent approach does not separate authority from issues of consent completely, as some views do. My aim in this chapter is to begin to explore the implications of the idea of normative consent. I begin with actual consent theory and criticize some arguments that have traditionally been offered in support of it. I then develop several points that appear to support normative consent theory. Many questions remain, and I will note some of them in passing. Nevertheless, I hope to show that it is an approach with some promise.

THE LIBERTARIAN NUB OF CONSENT THEORY

Consent is morally important in several contexts. I want to concentrate specifically on consent theories of authority. Much of what I say would have implications for other contexts of consent as well, but I will not be pursuing them. My interest is especially in the authority of political states, but I will not treat that case specially here. I will look at the general case of one person's authority over another, in the hope that a general theory of authority will eventually help us to understand the authority of states. I will also be leaving aside questions of law.

By *authority* I will mean the moral power to require action (borrowing a phrase from Raz).[1] To say you have authority over me on certain matters is to say that on those matters if you tell me to do something, then I am, for that reason, required to do it. There are bound to be limits; no one thinks I could be required to do just whatever you say. But within those limits I can perhaps be required to do some things just because you said so.

The phrase "the moral power to require action" might seem to cover too many things for our purposes. If a petulant child of a brutal dictator whimsically tells the minister to leave the palace, and the dictator will unleash brutality on the masses out of anger if the minister disobeys, then the child's command has created a moral requirement to obey.[2] The child has the moral power to require action, but it sounds wrong to say that she has authority. One way of capturing this is to point out that in this case, when the minister considers what to do, the fact that the child commanded him to leave has no weight of its own. The danger of the dictator's brutality is triggered by the command, but the command itself drops out of the set of reasons for action. In cases of authority the fact that it was commanded is itself a moral reason for action, a reason that requires action unless it is canceled or outweighed. We have not said how commands can be reasons in this way yet, but this is a reasonable constraint on the concept of authority. I will simply build this into the idea of a moral power to require action, assuming this is different from

the moral power to command actions in ways that result in requirements. A moral power to require action, then, is the power of one's
commands to count as moral reasons for action on their own. We would
need to explain how an agent can ever have such a power, but when
someone has it the fact that they command something is a reason to do
it, a reason that will be a moral requirement unless it is canceled or outweighed. This, at any rate, is the sort of moral power that I try to account for in this chapter.

By a *consent theory* of authority I will mean basically (to be refined
later) the view that there is no authority over a person without that person's consenting to be under that authority. On this view no one has the
moral power to require action by me unless, first, I have consented to
their having that moral power.

Consent theory is not distinctive for holding that under the right
conditions consent can establish authority. That is very widely agreed.
In any case, I will assume that it is true for my purposes in this inquiry.
Consent theory, as I am understanding it, is more controversial. Its distinctive claim is that without consent there is no authority.

Consent theory, then, holds that,

> Without consent there is no authority (the *libertarian clause*), but unless
> there are certain nullifying conditions (the *nullity proviso*), consent to
> authority establishes authority (the *authority clause*).

The nub of consent theory, its controversial element, then, is the libertarian clause: if A does not consent to B's authority, then, for that reason, B has no authority over A. Roughly, *no authority without consent*.[3]

SUPPOSED GROUNDS FOR CONSENT THEORY

What is meant by the idea that people are born free, or are naturally
free? This idea is central to modern moral and political thought. In what
sense are we all naturally free? Children are normally treated as exceptions, since they are naturally under the authority of parents. Without
delving into that question, I concentrate on adults only. One thing that
is often meant is that it would be wrong of others to interfere with me
in a certain wide range of activities. This kind of natural freedom will
not concern me here, since it is not about authority as understood here.

Another thing that is often meant by natural freedom is that no
person is born under the authority of anyone else. The authority of

one person over another is, as I have said, simply the moral power to require action. So this thesis of natural freedom is the claim that no one is naturally subject to another's commands in this way. The claim is not that there are no authority relations at all, but only that none are owed to nature. This idea of authority relations being owed to nature is still vague, however. One thing this might mean is that no adult is under the authority of another except by voluntarily accepting his authority. If this is what is meant by natural freedom, then it just asserts that there is no authority without consent. This assertion is just the libertarian clause of consent theory, and so it is no argument against other alleged grounds for authority; it just asserts that they are false. The question I want to consider in this section is what reason there is to accept that there is no authority without consent. The appeal to mankind's natural freedom, in this sense, only begs the question.

Sometimes consent theory is based less on natural freedom than on an appeal to a natural descriptive equality. Hume's version is typical:

> When we consider how nearly equal all men are in their bodily force, and even in their mental powers and faculties, till cultivated by education, we must necessarily allow, that nothing but their own consent could, at first, associate them together, and subject them to any authority.[4]

Descriptive equality really establishes very little about authority. At most, it would refute the claim that *owing to certain descriptive inequalities*, some naturally have authority over others. This leaves the field open to any basis for authority other than descriptive inequalities, and consent is only one possibility.

Consider the idea that the "default" condition is the absence of authority. This might only mean that there is no authority without consent, in which case, again, it begs the question. The idea that non-authority is the "default" might instead mean that there is no authority unless some positive moral case can be made for it. Absent moral considerations in either direction, a person is free from authority. Non-authority requires no reason, on this view, and is the default in precisely that sense. (Nothing is implied, by the way, about what kinds of reasons might establish authority, or how they might weigh up against conflicting reasons.) So understood, I accept the idea that non-authority is the default. As I have argued,[5] the qualified acceptability requirement burdens authority (and legitimate power) with the need for justification in terms acceptable to all qualified points of view. Absent such justification, the default condition is the absence of the authority or legitimate power in question. But this is no particular support for any claim of natural liberty in general or for consent theory in particular. All it implies is that if people are under authority (possibly even "naturally" or apart from any consent), there is a moral basis for it.

Appeals to natural freedom, or to freedom from authority as a default, are no particular support for consent theory. I turn next to a point about consent theory that has a tendency to subvert it: the idea of nullity.

Nullity Goes Both Ways

The nullity proviso in consent theory says that consent does not establish authority when it fails to meet certain standards, with different consent theories specifying different standards. Sometimes it is suggested that under those nullifying conditions (such as duress or coercion) there is, really, no consent after all. Other times, it is said that it is consent but that it fails to have its characteristic moral power. For now, I want only to point out that consent theory includes an account of when (putative) consent is null or disqualified.

When we say that a (putative) act of consent is null or disqualified, we should not assume that the resulting condition is one of non-authority. All that follows is that there is no authority *owed to that (putative) consent*. To assume that this means there is no authority would be illegitimately to assume the libertarian clause: that without consent there is no authority. Even where consent fails, other circumstances might establish the authority relation that is in question. So long as consent theory is held in question, null consent does not entail nonauthority. It only entails that there is no authority stemming from that consent.

There is an interesting *asymmetry* of a sort in consent theory. The authority clause (stating that consent can establish authority) is limited or qualified by the nullity proviso (stating that consent is sometimes null or disqualified). But the libertarian clause (stating that without consent there is no authority) is not subject to any such qualifications. Non-consent establishes non-authority, no questions asked.

We can put the asymmetry this way:

Consent only establishes authority if it meets certain standards, whereas non-consent establishes non-authority without the need to meet any standards at all.

121

Many of the familiar qualifications are aimed at ensuring that an act of consent is not valid unless it genuinely expresses the agent's will. For example, consent might be rendered null if the agent is seriously mistaken in certain ways about the nature of what is being consented to. The details of this are difficult. It is not clear that my consent to your borrowing my car is null if unbeknownst to me you will change the station playing on the radio. But if, unbeknownst to me, you do not have a driver's license, then arguably my consent is simply null. Qualifications on valid consent that preclude certain kinds of coercion and duress have a similar will-expressing function.

One possible version of consent theory, which I will call the *hard-line consent theory*, holds that the only conditions that nullify consent are conditions that serve to promote the accurate expression of the agent's own will. We can contrast this with a more *moderate consent theory*, in which there are some nullifying conditions that have a basis other than accurately tracking the agent's will. The moderate version is perhaps the traditionally more important one, since most major consent theorists held that some rights were "inalienable." The sort of condition that I want to consider applying to non-consent, that the non-consent is (often) null if it is morally wrong, does not aim to promote the accurate expression of the agent's will. So, it would not count as a symmetrical consideration for a hard-liner. The hard-line view, though, has some morally dubious implications. It implies that a person could become a slave, under the complete authority of another person, by consenting to it, so long as this genuinely reflected his or her will. Many people will reject the hard-line view for that kind of reason, and so they think that in some cases consent is null even if it genuinely reflects the will of the agent. They accept a moderate view, accepting what I will call *external normative nullifying conditions*, and not only the *will-tracking nullifying conditions* of the hard-line view. The condition I propose, that non-consent is null if it is wrong, is not will-tracking and so cannot gain any support from the idea of symmetry, on a hard-line view.

But on a moderate view, positive consent is nullified also by some conditions whose point is not the accurate tracking of the will. Consent to slavery, or to having a limb removed for amusement—these are often held to be null even if the person genuinely intends to consent. Exceptions like these might have various kinds of moral basis, and obviously there can be many different moderate views that accept different nullifying conditions. But then moderate views are vulnerable to the question why no nullifying conditions apply to non-consent. A condition such as the one I propose, in which non-consent is null if it is wrong, now has some standing on grounds of symmetry.

In principle, the libertarian clause could be subject to nullifying conditions too. The idea can seem foreign: *what would it mean to say that non-consent is null?* Such a view would be one form of hypothetical consent theory. Since we are modeling the nullity of non-consent on the standard idea of the nullity of consent, we should note a few features of that more familiar idea. For one thing, to say that (putative) consent is, for some reason, null or disqualified seems to be to say that the authority situation is as if the consent had not occurred. (As noted earlier, we are not assuming that this means there is no authority; that is a separate issue.) But now that we have noticed the possibility of *disqualified non-consent*, we see that it would be indeterminate to refer to "the authority condition that non-consent would have produced." Qualified non-consent and disqualified non-consent would produce different moral conditions.

On the other hand, if we wish to model the nullity of non-consent on the nullity of consent, by referring to the authority condition that would have obtained without it, the idea must be that when x is disqualified, the authority condition is as if there had been *qualified* non-x. Otherwise, the "as-if" construction would threaten to bounce back and forth infinitely. This also seems to capture the normative position of consent theory: if consent is disqualified, then the authority condition is as if there had been *qualified* non-consent.

So the nullity of non-consent would come to this: when non-consent is disqualified, the authority condition is as it would have been if there had been *qualified consent*. That authority condition would often have been, as even consent theorists agree, the establishment of authority. This would be a particular version of hypothetical consent theory: even in some cases where you have not consented, you are under authority just as you would have been if you had consented (and not been disqualified).

EXAMPLE

The normative consent theory of authority relies to a great extent on the reasons that would make it wrong not to consent to authority. There need not be any great unity to these reasons across contexts and examples. Clearly, it would be helpful to have examples in which non-consent would be wrong, and in which this wrongness renders it null—cancels what would otherwise be the authority-blocking power of non-consent—with the result being authority.

Consider a flight attendant who, in an effort to help the injured after a crash, says to Joe, "You! I need you to do as I say!" Let us not yet suppose this puts Joe under her authority. Even if it does not, Joe would (I hope you agree) be morally wrong not to agree to do as she says (at least under a significant range of circumstances). Once that is granted, the question remains whether by refusing, wrongly, to agree to do as she says, Joe has escaped the duty to do as she says. Consent theory, with its libertarian clause, draws the libertarian conclusion: Joe may have various obligations in such a terrible scenario, but the flight attendant's instructions have no authority over him.[6] Why? Because, lucky for Joe, he is despicable. If you find consent theory's implication implausible here, as I do, then you think that Joe has not escaped the authority by refusing to consent. So he is under authority even without having consented. In this case, non-consent to authority is null. If this is granted, consent theory must be rejected. Normative consent theory does not jettison considerations of consent completely, and I will return to the comparison with direct theories—those resting authority on something other than actual or hypothetical consent.

It could yet be objected that Joe is not under any obligation to consent to the flight attendant's authority, but only to what we might call her leadership. He has a duty to follow her so long as she leads well under these urgent conditions, but authority is something more. The objector might say, and I am happy to agree, that there is no authority present if the commanded person may simply disobey if he thinks the commands are themselves at all defective. The objection continues, the flight attendant is well positioned and knowledgeable enough to supply the most effective plan to aid the crash victims. But no one is obligated to accept her authority even in cases where she gets it wrong. So what they must agree to is not authority at all.

In reply, it is important to see that authority is rarely if ever absolute, if that means that some commander must be obeyed no matter how erroneous or immoral the commands. The mere presence of exceptions of that kind would not suffice to show that authority was not present at all. We should accept that authority is present to some extent so long as a duty to obey survives in some cases of erroneous or wrongful commands. Those cases of error put into relief the fact that the source of the subject's requirement is the command, not some other goal, requirement, or consideration. That is the characteristic of authority, the moral power to require action by commanding it.

Does the flight attendant have authority, even though, of course, some errors would be too grave for a requirement of obedience to survive? Consider a modest error. Suppose that she were to order Joe to grab the bandages from the remnant of the overhead compartment. Joe correctly believes that it would be wiser to secure whatever fresh water can be found first. Does this exempt Joe from the duty to obey her command? On the contrary, unless the stakes were especially high, it would be wrong for Joe to decline to obey on that ground. The flight attendant may be making a mistake, but she is in charge. This is characteristic of authority, and different from merely following the leader when and only when she is leading correctly.

Certainly the flight attendant's having authority has something to do with her having the training and position to have some tendency to lead well in these conditions. The question, though, is whether the duty to obey runs out whenever she errs. If, as I believe, it does not, authority is present. So, to sum up the point of the example: when she asks Joe to agree to do as she says, it is (new) authority, not merely leadership that Joe would be wrong not to agree to. The result is a duty to obey, which unlike a mere duty to follow, survives some of the commander's errors. Normative consent theory says that you are under authority even if you refuse to consent because, owing to her knowledge and situation, you would be wrong to refuse to consent to her having the power to require actions of you even, sometimes, when she is in error. The duty to consent in this case concerns the potential authority's expertise and capacity to guide under urgent circumstances, but normative consent theory is open to other grounds, in other circumstances, for the duty to agree to authority. As it happens, our use of the normative consent approach (in chapter 7) will rely on the epistemic value of the authority in a similar way.[7]

THE MORAL POWER TO WITHHOLD CONSENT

Appeals to hypothetical consent can seem to miss the point of consent. Often, it is a source of freedom and power to be able to refuse to consent to something and thereby prohibit certain actions of others. This is a value that hypothetical consent theories might be charged with ignoring. Even in a case where it is wrong to refuse consent, it is often one's own choice to make, and the non-consent keeps its moral effect: that which is not consented to remains morally wrong even though the non-consent is also wrong. For an example (not involving authority), if someone asks for your consent to touch you, then even if under the circumstances you are required to consent (suppose, for example, you had promised, or it would do them a world of good), normally they are not permitted to touch you unless you actually do consent. How might you be required to consent? Surely, not all refusals of sex are morally permitted, even if they all are sufficient to forbid sex. Consider a committed sexual relationship. Normally, each partner will have a moral duty to be sexually available to the other to some degree. To simplify, suppose that this was simply promised. When sex is proposed, the partner can still prevent it from being permitted by refusing to consent. If this refusal is too frequent or at the wrong times, it might itself be wrong in light of the promise (an "imperfect duty" not to always say no). Still, it is each partner's moral power, a power that can be rightly or wrongly used, to permit or forbid sexual contact at will. We should have grave doubts, of course, about a view that said sexual contact is permitted so long as the partner was morally required to consent, whether or not he actually did. Hypothetical consent is not enough for that. (We might express this by saying that normative consent is null in this context.) What I have said is only that the refusal of consent can be wrong, not that this permits contact. My whole point is that even if refusal can be wrong, and even if this fact were to generate an obligation to be sexually available, this does not nullify the refusal. It retains its prohibitive moral force.

Why should wrongful non-consent be nullified when authority is proposed rather than sexual contact, as normative consent theory proposes? There is an important difference between the cases. It will be helpful to look at a few examples. We have seen that wrongful non-consent to sex is not null. Here is another example in which wrongful non-consent is not null: in order to get to the movie theater, you ask to borrow my car, for which I have no use at the moment. You have recently let me borrow your car several times. If I refuse to consent to your borrowing the car, this would be wrong, but it would still be morally effective: you may not borrow my car to go to a movie without my consent even if I am wrongly withholding it.

Now consider some cases in which wrongful non-consent is null. Suppose we are roommates, and you never consent to my listening to the stereo. This is wrong of you and, after a certain point, null. I should ask for your consent because, so long as you do not abuse your power, I may not have the stereo on without your consent. But you have a duty not always to say no. Moreover, in this case, if you violate that duty, your non-consent is null. If I were proposing sex rather than music, your non-consent would not be null, and so what makes it null is not simply the fact that it is wrong.

I do not know what the criterion is for when wrongful non-consent is, or is not, null. In the sex and car cases, if non-consent were null, this would permit another to interfere with my person or property. In the stereo case, null non-consent does not have this effect. I doubt that this draws the line finally in the right place, though it might be a relevant distinction. But with this in mind it is notable that the nullity of non-consent to authority does not permit anyone to do anything. It does not even permit anyone to issue commands, since all it does is put someone under a duty to obey them if they are issued. Whether it is permissible to issue the commands is a separate question. Since null non-consent to authority only creates authority, and does not permit any actions, then a fortiori it does not permit interference in my person or property. This is as far as I am prepared to take the matter.

Recall (from chapter 3) that I have chosen to avoid the question whether actual consent is required for legitimate law—law whose enforcement is permissible owing to its procedural source. Maybe law is like sex in this way: even impermissible refusals are successful at forbidding the proposed action. In any case, normative consent is an account of authority, saying nothing about anyone's being permitted to do anything. Normative consent (without actual consent) can establish authority even if it cannot establish legitimacy.

The Opportunity Objection

It can only be wrong for a person to refrain from consenting if that person has had the opportunity to consent. Indeed, unless there is an opportunity, she has *not* refrained. It might seem as though this limits our conclusions a great deal: if, when offered the opportunity to consent to authority, a person wrongly refrains, then (in a certain class of cases) she is under that authority just as if she had consented. But if there is no opportunity to consent, there is no wrongful refraining in the first place, and the point simply fails to apply. Call this the *opportunity objection* to normative consent theory.

It is certainly true that without the opportunity she hasn't wrongly refrained. So her subjection to the putative authority could not rest on this (missing) act or decision. On the other hand, we are not taking for granted that a person only falls under authority owing to voluntary acts of her own. So, the fact that there is no responsibility-anchoring act of refraining in these cases (where there was no opportunity to consent) is not of any clear relevance to the question whether authority exists. The question is whether the presence of that element—that factual difference—makes any moral difference. Here are the two slightly different cases:

> *Case 1:* Jodi is offered an opportunity to consent to some authority, in conditions where refraining would be wrong. And assume this is a case where wrongful refraining is null, leaving the authority situation just as if she had consented.

> *Case 2:* Conditions are just as in Case 1 except that Jodi is not offered the opportunity to consent. Still, if Jodi had been offered the opportunity, she would be bound whether or not she consented.

The opportunity objection must say that even though Jodi's decision whether to consent would make no moral difference with respect to the authority, her being bound depends on whether she is offered the chance to consent or refrain. What moral basis would there be for thinking she escapes it? It is not as if offering her the chance to consent or not would give her a choice between being under the authority and being free of it. We are assuming that she would be under the authority whether she consented or not because non-consent would be null. The opportunity to consent or to refrain presents only a morally trivial choice: whether to consent without moral effect, or refrain without moral effect. There is no clear moral basis, then, for the opportunity objection.

THE DIRECT AUTHORITY OBJECTION

I have said that normative consent theory, the view that results from saying that non-consent is sometimes null, is a version of hypothetical consent theory. Normative consent is present when it is the case that if you had been offered the chance to consent to authority, you morally should have consented, and as a result the authority situation is as it

would have been if you had. There must be some prior moral considerations, then, that make consenting required. In a certain way, this
means that normative consent is never the complete basis of an authority relation. So what is its significance?

Since I am not claiming that normative consent is the only basis of
authority, I want to consider this objection in a particular form:

> *Direct authority objection:* Whenever it would be wrong to consent to
> authority in light of certain facts, those same facts already establish
> authority independently of anything about the duty to consent.

Just because the hypothetical agent looks to certain prior moral considerations does not show that those must already be the very moral
facts—authority facts—that the hypothetical scenario is designed to account for. So, just as Rawlsian contractors look to nonjustice facts, and
Scanlonian contractors look to non-rightness facts, normative consent
theory's hypothetical consenters look to non-authority facts.[8] The person whom we imagine being offered the chance to consent does not address the question whether there is authority present, but a separate
question: "Even if no authority were already present, would I be wrong
to refuse to consent to the proposed new authority?" There will be various non-authority facts that will bear on the answer to this question.

An example might help: suppose you think that there is no authority
without consent. Still, suppose I ask you, a passenger in my car, if you
will do as I ask (within reason) with respect to caring for the car. If you
refuse to consent, the refusal is wrong, or so I hope you will agree. Stop
the story before I try to claim that any authority enters. The important
point is that you are faced with the issue about the permissibility of accepting new authority even if you believe that there is, at least so far, no
authority already present to determine the matter. So the passenger's
reasons are not, as the objection claims, the authority reasons themselves. It might be that it would be extremely rude to refuse, a rudeness
that is bad enough to be morally wrong. Or there might be other considerations that require you to consent to my authority.

A set of facts that guarantees (materially entails) some moral condition might not yet be a sufficient (or any) moral basis for that condition.
The physical facts as stated in the language of physics entail all present
moral conditions, but they are not generally a sufficient moral basis. If
asked for a moral basis for my duty not to leave this café without paying, you would not for a moment think a physical account of the masses
and forces at play would be an answer, even though the facts about the

129

masses and forces do guarantee that I have the duty. The problem is that they do not give any moral basis for the duty. So it is no objection to my account to say that the facts that would-be consenters look to already guarantee the authority facts.

A more formidable objection is that the duty to consent already depends on prior *moral* facts, which might as well be taken as the moral basis for the authority itself, as well as for the duty to consent. The direct authority objection claims that the consent-requiring facts are already authority-establishing facts. This objection (if it is to be interesting) claims that the facts are already a sufficient *moral basis* for authority. However, whether consent to new authority is morally required is not the same question as whether it is present. Normative consent theory explicates the presence of authority in terms of the separate—admittedly still moral—question of when a person would be required to consent to new authority if offered the chance.

This is only part of an adequate reply to the direct authority objection, of course. It might be a good reply to those who think normative consent depends on previously existing authority. I have tried to show how there could be authority resulting from normative consent even if there were not already authority on independent grounds. However, this might be granted by a proponent of the direct authority objection, who might wish to add that, nevertheless, there always is already authority on independent grounds, in addition to whatever ground for authority normative consent provides. I do not want to argue that there is no other basis for authority than normative consent. At the very least, actual consent can be such a basis, and perhaps there are other bases. It is hard to know how to decide whether whenever normative consent grounds authority there would always already be authority on other grounds, too, even though normative consent does not depend on such existing authority. Since it is not clear how this coincidence could be explained by the objector, I believe he bears the burden of proof.

Normative consent rejects the voluntarist idea that you are not under authority unless you have voluntarily accepted it. Still, it retains the idiom of consent rather than simply embracing utterly will-independent requirements of authority. It retains the idiom of consent, of course, by grounding authority in the fact that if you didn't consent, at least you should have. It is natural to wonder whether we are being fickle— granting something to voluntarism, but then not really honoring it.

Normative consent retains, to put it in a way that is usefully vague now, *some* connection to the will. It is intuitively compelling to maintain that there is, putting it vaguely again, *some* moral independence of each person from the wills of others, having something to do with the fact that they, too, have a will that is just as morally important as anyone else's. This is a quasi-voluntarist constraint on authority.[9] This is one sense we might try giving to the idea of natural freedom: no one's will is more authoritative, because of who they are, than anyone else's, and so each of us is free of other wills and subject only to our own. Unfortunately, this exaggerates the situation. My freedom from the wills of other people does not, of course, mean that I am free from true moral requirements. Our respect for the freedom of others finds a limit when their will is exercised immorally, and normative consent tries to capture this fine line. You are not under another person's supposed authority so long as you freely *and morally* decline to accept it. But if your rejection of it is not (or would not be) morally permissible, it is that moral fact that grounds the authority.

As a further concession to freedom, we can add that permissible coercion is not yet warranted by the fact that your refusal of consent was wrong. Some morally wrong choices are choices you nevertheless have the right to make without interference. In any case, authority is not coercive interference with your choices. It is only the imposition of duties, and this is not something you can avoid by immorally refusing to consent to it.

NORMATIVE CONSENT AS UMBRELLA

Direct authority theories, of course, owe us some account of the direct basis of authority, and this has proven difficult.[10] In this section I want to propose a way of thinking about the relation between normative consent theory and several considerations that might seem to support authority directly.

I want to consider several competing approaches to authority that also do not rely on actual consent. My aim is to suggest that they might be conceived so as to be compatible with normative consent theory. What these approaches have identified, if this idea is right, is not any general moral basis of authority, but several contexts in which a person would, if asked, be morally required to consent to authority. The alternative approaches I will consider are (a) urgent task theory, and (b) fair contribution theory. I briefly explain each one and propose reconceiving each as falling under the umbrella of normative consent theory. Space only allows a sketch of how this might be done.

We can distinguish between relatively modest or ambitious uses of normative consent theory. The ambitious approach would be to hold that some authority is based on normative consent and some based on actual consent, and that there is no authority that is not based on one or the other. The more modest claim would be similar, except that it would leave open whether there are some direct bases of authority. I do not choose between these here, but I do want to argue that some cases of supposed direct authority, derived from several different alleged direct grounds of authority, are better conceived as based on normative consent. Whether all alleged direct bases can be brought under the normative consent umbrella (when they are not simply mistaken) is a further question I must leave aside.

First, urgent task theory holds that some tasks are morally so important that there is a natural moral duty to obey the commands of a putative authority who is well positioned to achieve the task if only people will obey. This is somewhat rough, and there are many possible variants, but it will serve the present purpose.[11]

One difficulty for such a view is in the idea of urgency. We cannot get plausible results if we just let this stand for a measure of the great value of something being done. The reason is that some things that would be very great achievements nevertheless make no plausible moral claim on everyone we might try to enlist by commanding them to help. For example, if my religion is the true religion, then it might be the case that a temple to my god would be of great objective value.[12] That would not yet establish that you have any duty to obey my commands to help me build it. Other tasks, such as saving the person drowning at sea, do seem to have a claim on the assistance of whomever I enlist to help me save the person (assuming I am well positioned to organize a rescue, I do not invidiously discriminate with my commands, etc.). The basis of authority, then, is evidently not simply the fact that the task is important. Normative consent theory proposes that in the case of some urgent tasks, but not others, those who are commanded would, if asked, be wrong not to consent to the commander's authority for these purposes. The wrongness of refusing consent, rather than urgency itself, would be the explanation for why some urgent tasks ground authority and others do not.

A second alternative approach to authority is often called the "fair play argument," but might be better called "fair contribution argument." It says, roughly, that it is wrong to take advantage of the cooperation of others in an arrangement from which one benefits without contributing one's fair share. Nozick and others have presented examples that seem to meet this criterion but intuitively do not generate obligations, such as cases where the benefits are either unavoidable or at least not actively taken.[13] Some writers have tried to limit the criterion to especially important benefits, but these adjustments face problems of their own.[14]

Consider fair contribution theory under the umbrella of normative consent theory. The question now would not just be whether one is benefiting without contributing, nor would it necessarily focus on the importance or nature of the benefits. Rather, there could be a variety of reasons why it would be wrong not to consent to authority in certain contexts of fair cooperation. The importance of the benefits and costs might certainly be relevant. But there is no obvious warrant for inferring a duty to comply from facts about costs and benefits. Normative consent theory asks which cases of this kind are such that it would be wrong not to consent to authority if one's consent were solicited. The advantage of this step is that it is often easier to see that such a refusal to consent would be wrong than it is to grant that, lacking consent, it would be wrong to disobey commands.

Consider the honest effort of a putative authority to distribute benefits and burdens fairly in order to accomplish a task that requires widespread contribution and has morally important effects. For example, consider a state collecting taxes in order to provide for national defense. Suppose, though, that the state is fallible and does not always distribute burdens quite fairly. The obligation to contribute *fairly*, then, would not generate a duty to comply. If offered the chance to consent to being under this state's authority, however, the fallibility of the commands might not be an adequate reason for declining. The commander's aiming at fairness, and maybe some reasonable tendency to approximate fairness, has something to do with the moral story here, but it is not simply a duty to do one's fair share. It is the requirement to consent to this fallible person's authority so long as there is a proper and competent effort at fairness (or something along these lines). Since refusing to consent would be wrong, you cannot escape the authority by pointing out that you would not have consented to it. The result is a duty to comply with the commands even when they are mistaken. I have not tried to specify which precise features of the case have ensured that it would be wrong not to consent to the authority. Still, this is enough to suggest that fair contribution theory might best explain authority when it is understood as falling under the larger umbrella of normative consent theory.

This at least suggests that the difficulties faced by direct theories cannot be assumed to infect the normative consent umbrella in the same way. The moral considerations for or against a duty to consent will often be different enough from the moral considerations for or against a duty to obey in the absence of any normative or actual consent.

It will be useful to bring together my conclusions about political legitimacy and authority in a summary way. Recall that legitimacy is the permissibility of coercively enforcing commands. As discussed in chapter 3, no justification for coercion can succeed if it relies on doctrines that qualified views could reject. If the justification avoids relying on such doctrines, then maybe the coercion is justified, but I do not take a stand on what else might be necessary or what collection of conditions might be sufficient. For example, I leave open whether my actual consent to coercive enforcement is necessary for its permissibility. It is, however, not sufficient, since even if I actually consent, the coercion (even over me) is not permissible if the justification relies on any doctrines that could be rejected from a qualified point of view (whether or not I happen to accept the doctrine myself).

Authority, by which I mean the moral power to require action—can, in principle, be established even without a generally acceptable justification if normative consent (the moral duty to consent to authority if offered the chance) is present. Actual consent is not required for authority, though it might be sufficient if it were present. So, on the view defended here, there can be authority without legitimacy.

Can there be legitimacy without authority—permissible coercion without an obligation to obey? I am not sure. Even if the justification were generally acceptable, it might still be wrong to coerce me unless I actually (and without disqualification) consent to the coercive enforcement regime. Still, it is possible that all of this could obtain without normative consent. That is, in such a case there need not be a moral obligation to consent to authority if one had been offered the chance. So, if a person actually accepts a coercive enforcement arrangement, and there is no qualified basis for rejecting it, then the coercion would be permitted even if there were neither actual acceptance of authority—the moral power to require action—nor any obligation to accept the commander's authority (normative consent). As for the authority and legitimacy of political structures that meet the criteria of epistemic proceduralism, I argue that owing to normative consent they are authoritative, and also that they at least meet the general acceptability condition for legitimacy, whatever other conditions on legitimacy might be appropriate.

In the next chapter I will propose an account of why, under the right conditions, people would be required to consent to the new authority of democratic legal arrangements that meet the demands of epistemic proceduralism. Normative consent is the umbrella, but we need a more particular account for this particular context.

Original Authority and the Democracy/Jury Analogy

WE HAVE SEEN THE STRUCTURE OF EPISTEMIC PROCEDURALISM in chapter 6, and a general nonvoluntaristic approach to political authority, the normative consent approach, has been laid out in chapter 7. In this chapter I will argue that an epistemic proceduralist account of democratic authority can be grounded in normative consent. I try to bring together several promising considerations from the excellent literature on political obligation and then link them up with the theory of normative consent. I believe the resulting account avoids many of the most important difficulties for previous attempts to account for political authority.

It will be helpful to begin by briefly describing the strategy of argument. Much of what epistemic proceduralism has to say about democratic lawmaking generally can be observed in a familiar setting, that of a criminal justice system of trial by jury. I begin by arguing that a jury trial system has the authority to require punishment or exoneration, and that this depends neither on anyone's consenting to it nor on the system's being authorized by any prior political procedure. It has what I shall call *original authority* in that sense. The argument in the jury context states and responds to the general objection that there cannot be authority without consent or some other voluntary act of acceptance. The general response is to use the idea of normative consent, but more is required to show that normative consent applies there. That is, I argue that the conditions that support the authority of juries do so by making it morally required for individuals to consent to that new authority arrangement. If our earlier discussion of normative consent is sound, this would establish authority even if no consent was given or solicited.

By reflecting on the original authority of a jury system, I hope to identify several considerations that morally explain it. These would not only shore up our confidence in it, but they are then available to apply in other contexts. In particular, of course, I will then argue that these conditions apply in a very similar way to the question of the authority of democratic lawmaking institutions. The reasoning for democratic authority is meant to stand on its own two feet, more or less. The suggestion is that we can see how such an argument would go by trying something closely parallel to the argument that supplies the moral basis for the original authority of jury systems. To anticipate, both systems serve urgent collective tasks with institutions that can publicly be seen to have some decent tendency (better than or at least nearly as good as any other and also better than random) to produce good or correct decisions. There is no pretense of justifying particular institutional details in either context. If the arguments succeed as far as they go, then that would become an important further topic.

There is a methodological point that might preempt certain misunderstandings and objections. I divide my arguments into two kinds here. One kind is aimed at giving the reader sufficient reasons to believe in the original authority of a jury system. Only the other kind tries to provide an account of the moral basis or justification for it. So, first, I hope to make the authority claim intuitively plausible, giving reasons of an intuitive kind to believe it. But these will probably strike many of us as highly provisional, vulnerable to being overridden without support of other kinds. This is where it is important to consider what might be the moral basis for this authority. If no good account of the moral basis could be found, we should wonder if there is one, and believe in the authority less confidently or even not at all. But I do offer an account of its moral basis, which I then apply to the case of democratic politics. First, though, I consider the jury context in some detail.

PREJURIA

Imagine Prejuria:

> The men and women of Prejuria have held their community together tenuously for some years even without any commonly accepted criminal justice system. There is widespread agreement, even among the troublemakers, that certain things are unjust: theft, assault, fraud, slander, and so on. There are even well-known social rules that specify which of the unjust things are, as it were, the community's business. Some people call these laws, but they are not enforced in any public way. The rules do specify the punishments for each "crime," but there is no institution devoted to accusing, trying, or punishing anyone. People form their own judgments and treat each other accordingly. This causes some serious

problems for the people of Prejuria, as the case of Prudence Powers illustrates. Ms. Powers, who owned one of the community's general stores, was seen by at least a dozen people (so they say) sneaking out the back of Faith Friendship's general store, with which Ms. Powers's store competes for customers, just before Mrs. Friendship's store burned to the ground. This struck many people as less than surprising, Ms. Powers being a ruthless businesswoman when she isn't busy entertaining one man or another. This was a year ago, and Ms. Powers has since found it impossible to live a decent life in Prejuria, since no one will talk to her, do business with her, or intervene when she is verbally or even physically accosted, which often happens if she goes out in public. She reasonably fears leaving her house now and lives on the meager provisions she makes herself. It so happens that this roughly corresponds to the punishment—extended imprisonment—that is known, in the public rules, to be associated with the crime of which she is accused. Everyone realizes, though, that she is also in danger of being killed by some of the community's rougher elements.

Let us call this the story of *Anarchic Prejuria*. We should also consider a variant: *Epistocratic Prejuria*, in which there is an institution for accusing, trying, and punishing, if you can call it an institution.

The church fathers meet on Friday nights, and they let it be known on Saturday mornings what needs to be done to whom. They have said that Prudence Powers ought to be confined to her home for nineteen years.

In a third and final rendition of Prejuria,

A group of citizens has invented a system whereby a panel of six citizens is randomly chosen and asked to hear the case against any accused person and the case in that person's defense, and to make a decision as to whether the named punishment shall be imposed or not.

Call this *Juristic Prejuria*, a transitional phase, if it should hold up, to a successor community, *Juria*. There is nothing like a legal basis for these proposed jury trials, which are the brainchild of a private group, Citizens for Public Justice.

Suppose that these three scenarios are all available to citizens of Prejuria. If enough people accept and comply with any of them, then that will be the way things are done for the foreseeable future: anarchic, epistocratic, or jury-based administration of criminal justice. Obviously, so long as the details are filled in right, the jury-based system is the one we should hope they choose. Unfortunately, our question is a more difficult one: supposing the jury system gets going, do the citizens of Prejuria have an obligation to abide by its decisions? We do not always have an obligation to obey the commands of a system simply because we think it is a good thing. On the other hand, its being a good thing can, along with other features of a case, contribute to the case for an obligation to obey, and in this case I think it does.

Here is the shape of the argument before turning in more detail to several points that it depends on. First, in Prejuria, there is no qualified disagreement with the proposition that the jury system will be more likely to promote substantive justice than the anarchic arrangement, and also better than a random procedure for choosing decisions. This depends on some features of the jury system to be discussed later. (Now here, of course, we commit ourselves to a small part of the content of our acceptability requirement, the principle saying which points of view are qualified and which not.)[1]

Second, whether or not the epistocratic arrangement, in the hands of the church fathers, would do even better than the jury system, there is indeed qualified disagreement about that proposition. Roughly, this is because they are so demographically narrow (all adult male coreligionists). My argument here is the same as my general argument against invidious comparisons in political justification (see chapter 2, "Truth and Despotism"), and I say no more about it here. The importance of this reasonable objection to the epistemic value of the system of the church fathers emerges when we ask whether the system would receive normative consent: would citizens be morally wrong not to consent to its new authority if they were given the chance? I contend that they would not be wrong—such consent would not be morally required of any citizen who (within a qualified point of view, not just any point of view) doubted that the church fathers would be substantively any more accurate than anarchy.

By contrast, however, no qualified person could doubt that the jury system (suitably constituted) would perform better than anarchy, and so there isn't the same basis for refusing to consent to its authority if given the choice. This is not yet a positive argument for an obligation to consent to the jury system's authority. Prejuria meets several further conditions, which we will look at shortly.

Finally, those considerations will persuade some readers that there is an obligation to obey the jury in Prejuria. Some others, however, will wonder how such a duty can simply befall us—how we can be obligated to this arrangement even without consenting to obey it, or without even voluntarily doing anything to join ourselves with it. Here is where normative consent emerges as the deepest level of justification of authority: it is no objection to the authority of the jury to say that you have not consented to it if, as I argue, refusal of consent would have been morally wrong and null, resulting in authority in any case. That gives the shape of an argument. Let us turn to considering the points in more detail.

The Antivigilante Principle

So far, all I have argued is that one particular excuse for not consenting—qualified doubts about the epistemic value of the arrangement—is not available in the case of the jury (though it is available as a reason for not consenting to the authority of the church fathers or any other epistocratic proposal). The invalidity of one particular rationale for withholding consent hardly establishes an obligation to consent. So we need something more, some positive support for the original authority of the jury system. As I have said, there are two kinds of support to distinguish: reasons to believe it, and a moral basis for it. I begin in this section with reasons to believe it, before venturing an account of its moral basis. Should we believe that the spontaneously created juries in Prejuria have the authority—the moral power—to require of certain individuals that they punish or exonerate defendants as the jury system decides? I believe that there is an antivigilante principle that strongly suggests just that.

Locke argues persuasively that a condition in which anyone may take it upon themselves to punish those who deserve punishment will be a chaotic condition that is bad for everyone. We would all be better off if there were an organized justice system in which certain parties judged and punished, and the rest were obligated to refrain from punishing even where it was deserved. This is one particular line of argument for the principle that,

> when there is a system that serves the purposes of judgment and punishment without private punishment, then private punishment is morally wrong.

Let us call this the *antivigilante principle*. It could be argued for in different ways. I will simply assume that the principle is true. It is likely to be accepted even by many who would doubt or deny that there is ever a distinctively political obligation to obey the law, and so by assuming it, we will not be begging the question against them.

We are assuming that crimes and punishments in Prejuria are not set by any laws. Intuitively, though, the application of the antivigilante principle does not seem to be limited to a system that enforces man-made laws, and indeed Locke's argument emphasized the enforcement of moral laws of nature forbidding such things as murder, assault, and theft.[2] There are at least some moral rules that, when enforced by the right kind of system, trigger the antivigilante principle, empowering the enforcers to forbid private punishment when someone has been exonerated by the central enforcement system.

Under the right conditions, according to the antivigilante principle, public exoneration is final. That is, even if the defendant is guilty and does deserve punishment, if the public justice system exonerates him, then individuals are forbidden from correcting the error on their own initiative by carrying out the deserved punishment. Most of us are viscerally more resistant, in general, to punishment than we are to exoneration, even if we do not doubt that justice does sometimes call for punishment. It seems more important to exonerate the innocent person than to punish the guilty. So reverse vigilantism—privately exonerating the erroneously convicted person (say, by freeing the person from jail, etc.)—is less unattractive than vigilantism, or punishing the erroneously exonerated. On this way of looking at things, the primary purpose of a public justice system is not punishment but exoneration. The most urgent thing is to prevent private punishment, and the best way to do this is to have a visibly adequate system of punishment. We must publicly punish not because punishment is so important, but to forestall private punishment. By punishing in a way that is publicly seen to be adequate, it becomes morally indefensible to punish privately. Public exoneration is final.

I do not know whether this asymmetrical view of the relative importance of due punishment and due exoneration is correct, but I do not want to delve into it here, and so I will only assume the antivigilante principle, that when there is an adequate public justice system, then even when it erroneously exonerates someone, that is final, and private punishment is morally forbidden. This is an instance of political authority. It is, or so I will argue, a moral power to forbid the action of private punishment. I will leave open whether or not there is also an anti-reverse-vigilante principle, which would be a moral power to require (of jailers and so on) punishment.[3]

Notice that there is nothing to the antivigilante principle unless private punishment might otherwise have been permitted. Is there, as Locke claims, a natural permission to punish? We can take it for granted that private punishment is inaccurate and destabilizing. Locke obviously knew this when he, nevertheless, held that if the only alternative is the unchecked reign of thugs and thieves, private punishment is permissible. We do not have to assume that the permission extends as far as retaliatory killings. For our purposes what matters is whether there would be any significant private punishments that would be permitted in such a condition. If so, then this gives some substance to an antivigilante principle that would then forbid these private punishments when there is a public system in place.

We should think first about the milder kinds of punishment, although we will not get much from the analogy unless it is punishment of a coercive kind, something more than, say, a refusal to associate with a person known to have stolen from you. Upping the ante just a little, consider a village thief. In the absence of a public system of judgment and punishment, would it be permitted for the members of his community to forcibly exclude him from social and communal venues and events such as taverns, shops, gatherings, meetings, and so on? I think the answer is rather obviously yes. There is, then, a natural "right" (more accurately, a permission or moral liberty), of some scope, to punish certain moral wrongs when there is no public system of judgment and punishment. Perhaps even more would be permitted, but this is enough for our purposes. The antivigilante principle says that once there is an adequate public system of judgment and punishment in place, such forcible exclusion would no longer be permitted (although people would remain free to choose whom to associate with and so on). If he is publicly exonerated this is final, and private punishment would be wrong.

It might be objected that this antivigilante principle is not a form of authority at all. It simply states some conditions under which it would be wrong to engage in private punishment, but it is not a case of a moral power of one agent to require action of another agent. It would be easier to show that the anti-reverse-vigilante principle was a kind of authority. There, at least, there is pretty clearly a command to the jailer to punish, and to not privately exonerate, the convicted person. Things are less obvious in the case of the antivigilante principle. The public judgment and punishment system in a condition such as Prejuria does not explicitly or obviously issue commands to everyone to refrain from vigilantism.

Authority is the moral power to require or forbid actions, not merely the moral power to do things that happen to result in requirements or prohibitions, something that we all do all the time (when I walk into the street, the driver gains an obligation to slow down, etc.). Does an adequate public system of judgment and punishment forbid private punishment, or does it merely result in that prohibition? Only in the first case would it be a case of authority.

Let us give a name to the sort of case that we are hoping to avoid here. A *side-effect case* is one where a requirement or prohibition is the result of certain acts of mine but where they are no part of the point of the act. These are moral powers to bring about requirements or prohibitions, but not moral powers to require or prohibit, and so not authority in the sense we are after.[4] We want to know that the moral power that the juries would have to prohibit private punishment is not just a side-effect power. Consider a case in another context where something is forbidden without an actual command against it, and yet the resulting prohibition is not merely a side effect either. If I post a flyer on a public bulletin board, say an ad for a car I am selling, it becomes morally wrong for others to post a flyer in that very place, covering mine. This is not commanded by me or anyone in any obvious way. And yet it is not merely an extraneous side effect. The resulting prohibition is especially important to the whole point of posting the ad in the first place. A second example: you can forbid me to ask you on a date by wearing a wedding ring. Neither you nor anyone commands me not to ask you on a date. The prohibition is not the result of a command. On the other hand, the creation of that prohibition is such an integral part of the point of wearing a wedding ring that we should regard it as a moral power exercised by wearing the ring. The wearer of the ring has the moral power to forbid people from asking her out, and it is not just a side effect.

I do not know how to give precise conditions for side-effect versus non-side-effect cases, but I contend that the prohibition on vigilantism brought about by an adequate justice system credibly declaring the intention to serve the purposes of judgment and punishment in a centralized public way is not a side-effect case. It is not just that the agents who invent and run the public justice system can choose whether to produce the obligation or not; that would be compatible with its being a side effect. It is that the resulting prohibition on private punishment is especially important to the whole point of developing the public justice system in the first place. The justice system has the moral power to forbid

143

private punishment, not merely the power to bring it about that private punishment is forbidden. It is, then, a case of political authority.

Spontaneous juries are highly plausible cases of political authority, ones it will be hard for the philosophical anarchist to deal with. This claim of mine would be on sounder footing if we had an account of the moral basis of this authority, and I propose a deeper basis later. But if you grant it, you must reject both philosophical anarchism and voluntarism. The spontaneous juries in Prejuria would be cases of political authority even without any consent or voluntary act that incurs the obligation. I hope to have provided good reasons to believe this, but in order to solidify that belief, and to use what we have learned to support epistemic proceduralism's claim to the authority of democratically made law, we need a deeper general account of the moral basis of the authority in the jury case.

Before turning to that, we should pause to look at the map for this chapter. The destination is the conclusion that (at least certain possible) democratic arrangements would be authoritative because it would be wrong not to consent to their authority. Having just argued that there is authority in a different context—new juries in Prejuria—we will next consider a moral basis for that authority. Finally, I will argue that the democratic context parallels the jury context in the right ways, so there is the same kind of moral basis for the authority of democratic arrangements with the features specified by epistemic proceduralism. I turn now to an account of the moral basis for the authority of juries in Prejuria.

An Approach to Authority

Over the years, it has proven difficult to find a satisfactory account of political authority. The account I propose here brings together elements from several familiar accounts in a new way. The long list of challenges to accounts of political authority cannot be engaged here, but I will take up a few of the main challenges I think the view must face and argue that it succeeds in overcoming them.[5]

We should begin outside of questions about authority, by considering what sort of duty we have to contribute to the solution of big problems such as poverty around the world. It is common sense that we should support institutions that address the problem, or we should contribute to some extent in other ways on our own, or both. There is disagreement about how stringent these obligations are, but few people think they place no obligations on us at all. Certainly, it is debatable, but it would be progress to show that political authority is no more problematic than humanitarian duties. Let us define as,

Humanitarian duties: duties to contribute to the solution of great humanitarian problems either by making a positive difference or at least by acting in such a way that if people generally acted that way the problem would be significantly lessened or solved.

Humanitarian duties are not necessarily duties to obey anyone, and so in assuming that they exist we will not be begging the question in favor of political authority. Obedience to supposed authorities might sometimes be an effective way to help solve humanitarian problems, other times not. So far, this is not enough to support authority of the kind we are after, the kind where a command creates an obligation even apart from whether obeying it (alone or together) actually does help solve the problem it aims to solve. Even philosophical anarchists, people who deny that there is political authority, accept that we often have reason to do as authorities command. For example, what is commanded might be independently morally required (refrain from murder), or we might be morally required to coordinate our actions with others (drive on the right), and so on. What they doubt, and what I want eventually to claim, is that we sometimes have a duty to do as the state says because it has said so, even apart from whether doing so best serves any of the purposes that are in view. That is the kind of authority that is often claimed by, or at least on behalf of, states, and once it is formulated in this way it is easy to see why political philosophers often meet it with skepticism. I want to argue that political authority can be supported as one kind of humanitarian duty, a category of duty that it is very difficult even for opponents of political authority to deny.

What is the humanitarian problem to which political obligation might, in some sense, be a solution? We don't want to get ahead of ourselves. We want to begin with an account of the authority of juries in Prejuria—their moral power to forbid private punishment. Only then will I try to show that a similar approach will account for the political authority of laws made by a suitable democratic system. So we begin with this set of questions: What is the humanitarian problem to which the juries are part of a solution? In what way does this morally ground the authority of juries? How does the account of these things avoid certain well-known challenges to theories of the moral basis of authority?

If poverty, when it exists, is a humanitarian problem, then so is anarchy. "Anarchy" is a vague term, but here I will mean specifically the absence of a public system of judgment and enforcement such as we see in Prejuria. I assume, with Locke, Kant, and many others, that this is a disastrous condition, and I assume that people have a humanitarian duty to contribute to its remediation. I do not assume that they have extremely stringent duties to do all they can in this direction, but at least a duty to do their fair share. I will define a fair share as a contribution such that if everyone made a similar contribution the humanitarian problem would be solved or greatly improved. This is too vague to tell us just what would count as such a contribution, but that will not matter for present purposes, which involve sketching an approach to authority that solves some familiar problems and which could be extended to the case of democratic authority.

So, assume there is an obligation to fairly contribute toward remediation of the humanitarian problem of what I will call *juridical anarchy*—the absence of a common system of judgment and punishment. There are contributions of different kinds, but one kind will be obedience. The problem will not be solved until there is a justice system that is generally complied with. Even though my own compliance will make no significant difference, since others will either comply or not largely regardless of what I do, it would be unfair of me not to comply for this reason even as others do comply. And what is needed is for people to comply even when, at least in some cases, they do not themselves believe that the jury's verdict is correct or they believe that the punishment is unjust (leaving aside here what the limits to this might be). The result is authority. The spontaneous jury system obtains the moral power to require or forbid certain actions.

This is too fast, of course, for several reasons. Perhaps the most important is that, as bad as judicial anarchy is, it is not plausible that we have a duty to obey a judicial system administered by the Hell's Angels, or even the church fathers. So the duty to contribute by obeying is not based simply on the fact that judicial anarchy is bad. It rests on certain features of the jury system. In particular, the duty to obey the jury system in Prejuria stems partly from its having, in a way that all qualified points of view can accept, a decent tendency to make accurate judgments of guilt or innocence, and to assign appropriate punishments. This is the element of the account that will be most important when we eventually apply the approach to the authority of democratically produced laws—the publicly recognizable epistemic value of the procedure. But, first, there are several important questions that we need to take up about the general approach.

The approach so far resembles an account of political authority that has been much discussed in recent years, based on an idea of fair contribution to important tasks. This "fair play" approach faces some important problems, and so it is important to distinguish the approach I am taking from that one, at least briefly. The standard versions rest on the fact that the agent benefits from the scheme, and so she is a "free rider"—taking advantage of others—if she does not contribute. My approach rests instead on the moral importance of the humanitarian problem. I am not free riding in the standard sense if I let the problem of grave poverty be addressed by others without helping. The system that results might not benefit me in any way, and so I am not "riding" at all. This is an advantage for my approach, I believe. The idea of free riding does not seem to cover cases where the advantages are not actively sought or taken. Arguably, I am not taking advantage of others unless I am somehow *taking* something, but it is difficult to establish that most citizens are taking benefits (as distinct from merely benefiting) in the relevant sense.[6] On the approach I have sketched, no use is made of the idea of taking advantage of others. The claim is simply that humanitarian problems cast duties over us all, and that it is not fair for any person to leave the solution of the problem to others.[7]

A second challenge that has often been pressed against the standard fairness accounts is that it is easy to devise counterexamples, cases that meet the proposed conditions but that intuitively do not result in an obligation to obey. For example, I cannot be obligated to help run a radio station just because I sometimes turn it on and enjoy listening.[8] My approach avoids these counterexamples by concentrating on the need for solutions to humanitarian problems, not all kinds of beneficial projects.[9]

There is another common approach that mine resembles in some ways, what we might call the *urgent task* approach. Very roughly, these are approaches that say that some task is so important that people are obligated to obey if someone sets themselves up as an authority in a way that would solve or significantly reduce the problem at hand. The central problem for this as an approach to political authority is that it has trouble explaining why I have an obligation to obey the laws of my own particular state, and not (at least not to the same extent) the laws of other states—what Simmons calls the *particularity problem*.[10] If the French are obligated to send their money to the French government because of the great importance of the problems the government will use the money to solve, then why wouldn't all people around the world have the same responsibility for helping the French government solve those problems? Since humanitarian tasks seem to broadcast their obligating force to all moral agents equally, they can seem like an unlikely basis for differential obligations to obey one's own particular government.

Simmons makes a useful distinction between two kinds of pressing tasks and argues that there are problems with using either of them in this kind of theory of authority.[11] The first kind of pressing task is familiar from duties of rescue. However, even if duties of rescue, such as the duty to save the proverbial drowning baby in the nearby fountain, have the potential to supply some particularity, they do not seem to have another feature that my view requires, namely, a fair division of responsibility. Even if few people are helping, I am not permitted to stop at the level of aid that would, if exerted by everyone present, save the baby, but that will not, by itself, do any good at all. I must do more than a fair sharing of burdens would require. Applied to the context of political authority, this rescue model would implausibly suggest that, for example, I must not only pay the taxes required by law, I must send considerably more if others are shirking. Likewise, I need not send any if enough is being sent by others. This is not how political authority works.

The second kind of pressing task yields duties of charity (as Simmons calls them), such as the duty to contribute to alleviating hunger in the poorest parts of the world.[12] Simmons seems to grant that these duties exist and that they are characterized by something like a fair division of responsibility.[13] I am not obligated to give and give to the distant poor simply because others are not giving enough. Charity matches political authority better than rescue in this respect. The problem, he argues, is that duties of charity cannot explain the particularity feature in the idea of political obligation.

Simmons thinks that the wide-ranging duty of charity cannot explain any duty to obey the laws of one's own particular country, whereas a more local duty to remedy an emergency does not have the fair-share feature of the duty of charity: one can be simply excused if the problem is distant, letting the burdens fall on those nearby. Simmons's distinction between duties of charity and duties to rescue (183) is not as clear as it looks at first. There are, of course, local and temporary emergencies, such as a child lodged in a well, or a disastrous hurricane. But what is the contrast class? Simmons speaks of the chronic global problem of hunger and poverty, but this is nothing but a constant (and perhaps systematic) set of local and temporary emergencies—individuals whose health and lives are in danger. We could hold that the burden falls exclusively on people who are nearby, but for some purposes we think of these local emergencies as part of a chronic problem that places duties on all humans everywhere. The question seems to be how a task could have both the fair-share feature of charity tasks and the particularity of rescue tasks.

These can be combined if the way to address the charity task is by organizing in certain local ways. Suppose we see the problem of political organization as a global problem: people need health, security, and justice everywhere, and we are all called upon to help provide it. Accepting the authority (within limits) of our local states is one way to do our part. States have not magically arranged borders along just the antecedently correct lines, or any such thing. Their significance stems from their availability and effectiveness, such as it is.

If this is right, then we should be able to imagine a similar framework for addressing global poverty in a way that generates obligations to one's own particular local agency. Suppose that an agency such as Oxfam were to set up offices around the world, where each office promulgated amounts and forms of aid that local individuals are expected to contribute. Different locales will have different abilities to pay, different trade-offs between time and money, different resources or skills to contribute, and so on, and so different districts would produce different requirements. It is plausible to think that one's duty of charity in this case (we are assuming there is some such duty) would require complying with the requirements of the local Oxfam office rather than striking out on one's own and helping as one sees fit. It certainly does not seem as though each of us would be required to attend equally to all the local offices and their requirements. The large or global problem would have generated duties of a local or "particular" kind. Of course, this would depend on further conditions such as that Oxfam is reasonably effective, that it is the only one, or it is the salient organization to focus one's efforts with, and so on. But it looks like duties that Simmons calls *duties of charity* (contrasted with *duties of rescue*) can indeed generate requirements of a suitably "particular" form, requirements to abide by the commands put forward by the agency in one's own district.

The spontaneous juries that arise in Prejuria have a similar structure. The need for judgment and enforcement of the relevant moral rules is a pressing one everywhere, and it might well be that one good way to address it is to divide the world into districts. The overall system is promoting a perfectly agent-neutral value, a species of justice. And, as Waldron points out, there is plausibly a moral requirement on everyone everywhere to promote and sustain, or at the very least not interfere with, just institutions. This requirement might very possibly have the sort of obligation-limiting feature of the idea of a fair contribution that Simmons grants in the case of duties of charity. In any case, this duty to uphold just institutions is separate both from the duty to contribute to solving the humanitarian problem and also from the local requirements (Waldron calls them *range-limited* principles) applying to people in a particular (e.g., districted) way.[14] The duty to uphold just institutions does not generate a duty for Prejurians to obey all the rules of other jurisdictions. Their duty to obey the rules in Prejuria stems from the districted solution to the urgent task, which is global in scope, of putting people under the auspices of just institutions. Crucially, these localized duties are not to be thought of on the model of duties of rescue. They are part of a system devised to address the nonlocal urgent task of bringing people under adequate procedures of criminal justice. As the slogan goes, "Think globally, act locally." The particularity problem, then, does not appear to be an insuperable difficulty for approaches that ground authority in an important moral task that the system of authority credibly claims to address.

It might seem as though the reference to the global problem is superfluous and the duties of Prejurians simply stem from the need for criminal justice in Prejuria. The problem with putting it that way is that it does not explain why these needs in Prejuria put duties only on Prejurians rather than on everyone in the world. That problem is solved if the duties of Prejurians are seen as implications of their, and everyone's, duties to contribute to the global need for criminal justice, with the particularity of each person's duties stemming from the fact that the best solution is a districted one.

Bringing these points together: great needs can generate obligations to help solve them. In some cases the appropriate solution will direct individuals' obligations not to the problem itself, but to some particular part of a system that addresses the problem. Duties of charity (in Simmons's term) can both call out to everyone and also yield duties of a particular or local kind in this way. This sketches the general kind of approach I will be taking to the question of political authority. For convenience, call it the *think globally, act locally* model of political authority or, for short, the *global/local model*. I will not belabor the way in which

I believe it would account for the duty to obey the juries that arise in Prejuria. Briefly, there is a great need for people to be under a justice system of judgment and punishment, and the appropriate system for solving this problem divides people into local districts. I now fill this approach in further by responding to several natural challenges.

Enter Normative Consent

Even if the global/local model explains a duty to contribute to the solution of a global problem,[15] more needs to be said to explain how it gives rise to authority. The reason is that authority has a special and somewhat surprising structure, as we have seen. Even where authority is, in a certain way, based on its addressing some great need, the obligations it generates are not conditional on whether the command is the best or right command, nor on whether obedience is the most effective way for me to help address the underlying great need. So, the challenge is this: even if the global/local model explained how I might get an obligation to direct my efforts to some local portion of the system that is addressing the need, something more would be needed to explain why I would be obligated to *follow orders*, to do what I am told because I am told.

One way of pressing that challenge would be to insist that while some obligations, such as obligations to help with systems aimed at alleviating famine, might just befall us, obligations to do as we are told are not like that. Moral agents possess a special kind of freedom from each other's authority. It cannot simply befall us, but can only arise subject, in some way, to our own will. I have been carefully vague in phrasing the claim. It does not say that there is no authority without consent, but only no authority that is not, in some way, connected to our will. This is the *quasi-voluntarist constraint* that we granted for the sake of argument in chapter 7.[16] This constraint implies that we cannot fall under another's authority simply on the basis of the moral urgency of some task. This constraint would be met, of course, if actual consent to authority were present. The problem is that there simply isn't actual consent to political authority by all those whom the law purports to obligate.[17] The question is whether some weaker connection to the will is more widespread and also sufficient to supply what is appropriately demanded by a quasi-voluntarist constraint.

In chapter 7, I argued that political obligation could be grounded without consent, but on normative consent—the fact that consent would have been morally required (even prior to any assumption of authority) if it had been solicited.

Normative consent names a moral obligation, when there is one, to consent to proposed new authority. It is, I believe, morally equivalent to a promise to obey. In the context of Prejuria it would be a moral obligation to consent to the proposed new authority of the juries. We have looked at a model of obligation to obey that emphasizes the fact that the obedience is a contribution to a pressing humanitarian task. When we turn to normative consent we are not asking, at first, about a duty to obey, but a duty to consent to the new authority—a duty, not to obey, but to promise to obey. This raises the following problem: even if obedience is a contribution to the task of establishing criminal justice, merely promising to obey is not a contribution to that same task. All the promising in the world will not bring about criminal justice without people actually obeying the juries' commands to punish or exonerate. Obedience to the juries is a contribution to criminal justice in a way that merely promising to obey is not. The question is how to use the local/global account as an account of a duty to *promise* to obey, even though promising is not a contribution by itself in the absence of the actual obedience.

It will help to distinguish between two distinct pressing tasks. The first is the one we have mainly been considering: the task of putting people under an adequate system of criminal justice. Call this the *enforcement task*. The second is the task of getting people to have promised to obey an adequate system of criminal justice. Call this the *general commitment task*. The duty to promise to obey, a duty that would establish normative consent to the authority, stems from its being a contribution to the general commitment task, not from its being (what is far less clear) a contribution to the enforcement task. The structure of the account, then, is still a version of the local/global model. There is a global general commitment task, and it (naturally or under contingent conditions) calls for a districted solution, in which each person ought to commit to obeying (committing is not the same as obeying, of course) those local authorities. This is a contribution to the general commitment task in the sense that if everyone were to act in a similar way, the task would be met. All this is straightforward so long as the general commitment task can be shown to be important in its own right. This is crucial, since the other task, the enforcement task, while of obvious importance, is not promoted by mere commitments or promises or consent. It needs obedience, and yet the quasi-voluntarist constraint prevents our inferring a duty to obey simply from the importance of the task. The importance of the general commitment task in its own right, then, is our next question.

Put aside the context of authority for a moment. If you promise to meet me for dinner, there seem to be two things of value in view: the honoring of the promise (meeting as planned), and the promising itself.

The Dinner Promise

I would like you to come over for dinner Sunday. As it happens we are very likely to have dinner Sunday in any case. I know you like me and so you want to come to dinner, and you usually do come over on Sunday evening. Still, since I plan to make something special, I want you to commit, to promise.

Why do I want you to promise? No doubt, in many cases the promise will increase the chances of the act because many people are inclined to honor their promises. This is often part of why we want the promise. But there are other ways to increase the chances that you will come over for dinner. Instead of asking for a promise I could let you know that the wine I will be opening is one of your favorites. You were already very likely to come over, and this makes it even more likely, and suppose the chances are increased to the very same extent that a promise would have done. Are they nothing but interchangeable strategies? In some cases, they might very well be. In other cases, though, the promise has a value that is not exhausted by the increase (if there is any) in the chances that the act will be performed.

Here is another context in which the value of the promise is not simply its tendency to make the act more likely:

The College Loan

Danielle's parents offer financial help that allows her to attend college. She is already strongly inclined to pay them back, but they could still increase the chances in two ways, and to just the same extent: they could either point out that if she does not pay them back her income tax will be enough higher that it will take half of the original amount, or they could ask her to promise. They might reasonably want the promise instead of the tax incentive.

The reason cannot be any difference in the probability of repayment, since there isn't any such difference. I am deliberately avoiding offering any account of why the promise is valuable beyond its tendency to probabilize the action, because that is deeper than we need to go. It will even serve my purposes if the value does consist in the promise making the act more likely. The important point in the Prejuria example is that the commitment itself is valuable, whether you think it is for instrumental or intrinsic reasons. If so, then what I have called the *general commitment task*—the task of getting people to have promised—will have an importance that is separate from the importance of the enforcement task. In that case, there is an important task to which people can contribute by promising.

I am taking for granted that there is a humanitarian task of the enforcement variety. What the present approach requires is a general commitment task (in the hypothetical pre-authority condition) that is pressing enough to generate obligations to commit to obey. It would be good to see an example in another context in which we see a similar structure at work. Doctors, upon entering the profession, customarily take a modern adaptation of the Hippocratic oath. They promise to help their patients, to respect their privacy, and much else we can summarize as the professional promotion of health. If the task to which doctors are contributing is health, then taking the oath is not a contribution. Or, at any rate, in the manner of the dinner promise, its value seems to outstrip whatever instrumental value it has in getting doctors to act in the valued, health-promoting ways. Increasing the legal consequences of malpractice might have as much effect on performance, but the oath has a value of its own. Moreover, the importance of the task seems to put trained doctors under a moral obligation to take the oath. We can describe it as contributing to a separate task beyond the health-promotion task, namely, the associated commitment task. Whatever the effects of commitment on health, it is important to have our doctors morally committed to its promotion in the ways that the oath accomplishes. A similar story could be told for a variety of oaths of office. What these oaths show is that in the presence of certain sufficiently important tasks there can be a great value to an associated commitment task, and this can rise to a level where individuals are obligated to commit by taking the oath.[18]

We can step back now and note a few things about the resulting overall approach to authority. My view is similar to Wellman's[19] in detaching the duty to obey from benefits received or from any voluntary transaction, and tying it rather to a morally important task to which I have a duty to contribute my fair share. But it is important to see that on my approach, the individual's duty is not meant to be analogous to a duty to aid or rescue. There is a hypothetical duty to accept the authority; this fact yields the authority of the law, and then the duty to comply is simply based on the authority of the law. This duty to obey the law no longer engages with issues about when aid is or is not required, and does not depend on whether one's compliance will actually make any difference. You could find yourself with an obligation to obey a law that asks a great deal of you—military service, for example. A moral duty to provide aid might be too weak to explain this given the high costs and small impact of serving in the military. The explanation is, rather, that you would have been wrong not to accept such authority over you, and so you are under such authority as if you had.

As is well known at least since Rousseau, the expected cost of accepting authority over you is moderated by the relatively small chance of having the greatest costs actually imposed on you.[20] So the obligation to accept the authority, which derives from an obligation to share in providing an important good, is not as likely to run up against the problem of excessive cost. The expected cost of accepting the authority is not high enough to negate the duty to do so. And, of course, the normative consent approach does not try to show, as much social contract theory does, that it is in the agent's best interest to agree to the authority arrangement. Rather, we argue only that the hypothetical agent would be morally wrong not to agree to the authority arrangement. This will often be the case even if this duty conflicts with one's overall best interests. Some costs might be great enough to cancel the duty, but the relevant costs are not those of obedience but those of accepting authority, since that is the act we are, in the first instance, trying to show is obligatory. If it is, then duties to obey follow from this fact. But now considerations of costs will not have the same role. The duty to obey, on my view, is (unlike the duty to *promise* to obey) not a duty derived from its being a contribution to an important collective project. It is, rather, a duty to act as you would have been morally required to promise to act if you had been asked. This, as the normative consent approach suggests, would be a duty just as stringent as if you actually had promised. The duty to aid someone because he is in need is more severely limited by the costs of providing aid than a duty to aid someone because you promised you would.

The normative consent approach avoids another challenge for accounts based on a duty to help provide aid. It can be difficult to show that the only way, or even the best way, to help provide aid is to obey the law. For example, if the aim is to provide security for people, then why must I contribute by obeying the law rather than by directly protecting a

155

few people? Having discharged my modest duty to help, would I then be free to disregard the law? If, on the other hand, I had actually promised to obey the law (or would have been required to à la normative consent), there is no way to keep the promise by making alternative contributions to security.

In order for there to be such a duty to consent in the imaginary condition, it would have to be highly important not only that people obey, but, in any case, that they promise to obey. We have seen that sometimes the state of affairs in which someone has promised is valuable in its own right. Similar considerations suggest that sometimes the condition in which a group of people have each promised is valuable (as in the case of the Hippocratic oath). I contend that in Prejuria this kind of widespread promise to obey the juries would be valuable enough to produce a duty on each person to contribute to this general commitment task by giving their own consent to the juries' authority.

The Democracy/Jury Analogy

This long discussion of the juries in the imaginary land of Prejuria sets up a fruitful analogy. The authority of the juries rests on the duty of the Prejurians to promise to obey them, a duty that in turn rests on certain features of those juries and certain background conditions. In particular, it depends partly on the fact that a (suitably constructed) jury system has an epistemic value that no reasonable or qualified point of view could deny. The institutional details that best promote epistemic value of juries are not for us to dwell on. If the normative framework laid out here is promising, then it would guide a more specific inquiry, but the details of the particular historical and cultural setting of the system would also be important. None of this is within my purview here. I conclude by calling attention to the general structure of the analogy, and a few key features of the juries that would translate into a democratic context.

The value of the jury case, recall, is meant to be that the structure of epistemic proceduralism seems to capture a very natural view of the authority of properly constituted juries. Their verdicts (within certain limits) produce obligations of compliance even when they are mistaken, and this authority rests partly on the fact, acceptable to all qualified points of view, that the jury system has epistemic value—an ability to do better than random at producing substantively just verdicts. If the epistemic proceduralist structure, and the normative consent account of its connection to authority, are thought to be sound in the jury case, then this is strong support for a parallel argument for the original authority of properly constructed democratic procedures on the basis of their generally acceptable epistemic value, in accord with the same epistemic proceduralist structure of the authority. In particular, that authority derives from the procedure's epistemic value but obtains even in the case of substantively erroneous decisions (within certain limits). And the authority is original in the sense that it does not derive from the authority of any prior procedure or source that produced it, avoiding the threat of an infinite regress. The parallels between the jury case and the larger democratic case are very strong, and so the main lines of this phase of the argument can be sketched briefly.

The essential elements of the argument for the authority of the jury system are all present in a democratic system of government. First, there is a very great value, one that no qualified point of view could deny, to having laws and policies that are substantively just. Second, a proper democratic procedure, like a jury, is (or can be) demographically neutral, blocking the qualified objections that would be possible to any invidious comparisons. Third, a democratic procedure involves many citizens thinking together, potentially reaping the epistemic benefits this can bring, and promoting substantively just decisions better than a random procedure. So, fourth, I conjecture there is no nondemocratic arrangement that all qualified points of view could agree would serve substantive justice better. In light of all this, citizens would be morally required to consent to the new authority of such a democratic arrangement if they were offered that choice. Non-consent would be null, and so the fact that no such consent is normally asked or given makes no moral difference, and so any existing democratic arrangement that meets these conditions has authority over each citizen just as if they had established its authority by actual consent.

The democracy/jury analogy is used to support the plausibility of the structure of epistemic proceduralism as an account of authority. The argument for democracy's epistemic value does not rest on the analogy with juries, even though in both cases it surely has much to do with thinking together. Nor is the authority of democratic decisions or of jury decisions based on their having a high degree of reliability. Rather, it is based on their having *some* epistemic value, and their being (at least nearly) the best epistemic instrument available so far as can be determined within public reason. We would naturally doubt the authority and legitimacy of a criminal trial system that did not have very high reliability, but I believe this is simply because we are inclined to think that the best system available for that purpose should be highly reliable. If a trial system were only moderately reliable, but still the best available, I believe its verdicts would still require our compliance. We would still be required to refrain from being vigilantes or antivigilantes. The system would still have the moral power to require or forbid action. The reliability we expect in larger political decisions is probably much less. Since the best methods available are less reliable than the best trial systems, less is required in order to ground authority.

How Would Democracy Know?

IN THIS CHAPTER, I will outline a way of thinking about how democratic political decision making could have the epistemic value that epistemic proceduralism relies on for its theory of authority and legitimacy. I argue that only an extreme skepticism would deny the underlying epistemic capacities and mechanisms that are needed. However, for those minimal epistemic capacities and mechanisms to lead to good democratic decisions, things must be arranged in a certain way. Democratic theory that emphasizes the value of public deliberation is often criticized just at this point. The prescribed arrangements are held to be utopian, or inappropriate, or both. Our discussion of utopophobia and aspirational theory in chapter 14 ("Utopophobia") helps us to navigate those waters. Here, I will introduce the idea of an ideal epistemic deliberation, contrasting this idea and its theoretical role with the Habermasian idea of an ideal speech situation. By explicitly acknowledging that the achievement of this ideal epistemic deliberation is not an appropriate practical goal (and so the question of whether it is utopian is beside the point), we can explain more clearly how, nevertheless, it plays an important role both in theory and in guiding practice. This prepares the way for an explanation of how actual arrangements, which should and do differ dramatically from that ideal, could have the ability to ground legitimacy or authority of actual democratic decisions. Here, it is crucial not to be utopian, even though we should not succumb to an exaggerated utopophobia either. These questions about real democratic practices are more fully answered only after chapter 10, in which I give an account of the centrality and epistemic role of nondiscursive direct action in politics.

Before describing the ideal epistemic deliberation and its theoretical role, I begin with a simplified way of thinking about how we might evaluate epistemic proceduralism's epistemic claims.

Primary Bads as the Epistemic Benchmark

According to epistemic proceduralism, democratic authority rests on democracy's tending to make better decisions than random, and better than alternative arrangements, so far as can be determined within public reason. Some topics for political decision are much more important than others, of course, and so we wouldn't know much just by knowing democracy's rate of accuracy. What if it got most things right, but none of the most important things? A full theory of the weighted importance of different topics would be intractably complex. To combine the idea of weighting with the idea of better than random performance, it is useful to narrow our focus to a few especially important matters, what I will call *primary bads*. It would be absurd to think that democracy's authority could be vindicated merely by performing better than random on these matters. That is not my suggestion. Rather, I hope to support the conjecture that a proper democracy will tend to perform better than random across the wide range of issues it would face by arguing that with respect to the primary bads it would perform *far better than random*. If we show that the primary bads would be *reliably* avoided, and why, then we can argue from there that this supports the supposition that the general run of decisions would be made with better-than-random accuracy: after giving due weight to the more important decisions, and factoring this into the evaluation of performance (a correct answer on a more important issue counts for more), the result would be better than a random procedure. It is the overall weighted score that epistemic proceduralism needs to be better than it would be in a random procedure. I will speak of an overall weighted score, but I am not offering any specific weights beyond carving out a category of primary bads.

A brief remark on which decisions we are evaluating: one question is what counts as a political decision for these purposes. At least all legally valid laws and policies seem to count. We do not need to say more than that for present purposes. When we ask whether democratic institutions make good decisions, there is an initial problem about what is to count as a democratically produced decision. It would be possible to hold that even in a democracy, not every law and policy counts as democratically produced. Decisions by unelected judges, regulations from appointed agencies, the selection of a president by an electoral college—these and many other laws and policies are produced in ways other than being voted on by citizens. A few matters are determined by referendum. Then there is a much larger set of very important decisions that are made directly by citizen voting: the election of senators, congressional representatives, and numerous state and local officials. The decisions that these officials make are another matter. Those are obviously not decided by citizen voting, since they are made by the officials, be they legislators, executives, or whatever. But the decision of who shall hold the office is an instance of direct democracy. When we ask whether democracy makes good decisions, we must recognize that its decisions include any law or policy, whether produced by direct popular vote or not, whose legitimacy or authority is held to derive from its democratic production broadly conceived. The regulatory decisions of an appointed agency are surely included. The commissioners are appointed, but in a democracy (characteristically, if not by definition) any government official is either elected or appointed by someone who is elected, or at least by someone whose appointment is traced in this fashion back to someone who is elected. All the official decisions of all these people must be counted as among the democracy's decisions. I propose, as I have said, to concentrate our attention on a small list of especially important matters, which we can call primary bads. If this list is selected properly, it will have certain features that will support our using it as a rough indicator of democracy's performance overall. I begin by describing four important features for this list, and then propose a particular list.

Weight

The first important feature that these issues should have is that they are among the most important issues that are subject to political decision. Even if we cannot give a complete list of all issues weighted by importance, we can identify some issues that are so important that performance on these would swamp questions of performance on lots of smaller matters. Among the most important things that politics must do is to avoid the worst disasters, such as war, famine, and genocide. Failure to prevent these (insofar as they are politically preventable) would be such a momentous failure that even good performance on lots of smaller issues would seem very likely to be outweighed in our overall evaluation. There is no determinate list of the most important disasters to avoid, since these are matters of degree. The list must be determined partly by great weight of this kind, but with an eye to the other criteria for inclusion.

161

Variety

Second, the list should include issues that exhibit enough variety so that we will have some reason to extrapolate from performance on this set to a great number of issues not on the list. If they were too alike in certain ways, this ability to extrapolate would be missing.

Tractability

The list should be empirically and theoretically tractable. By this I mean that it should avoid unnecessary length, complexity, or empirical inscrutability. Something along these lines is already implied by the qualified acceptability requirement itself, I suppose. But even if it were not for that requirement, and we were free to reason about the whole truth, our capacities are limited. The list will be of little use if it is very thorough but impossible for us to use to draw any conclusions. Suppose, for example, it contained thousands of separate genuine disasters that are important to avoid. It would be impossible to treat them all separately and arrive at any conclusions. I will stop well short of thousands, with exactly six.

Public reason

Third, as required by the qualified acceptability requirement (see chapter 3), the list should be seen to be capable of serving its function from within the wide variety of reasonable or qualified points of view. So the question is not what are really and truly the most important issues. Some of the most important issues might well be left off, and that would not defeat the list's purpose. The list needs to serve its purpose within public reason, and this limits what we may put on it. The primary bads are like Rawls's primary goods in this way. Rawls proposes a list of goods that can be used to specify how well a person or group is faring in society for purposes of evaluating the society's justice. It does not matter if this list does not express the truth about what is good for persons. It need only be agreed by all reasonable comprehensive views that these goods are important enough that they can usefully serve for these heuristic purposes. (Primary bads are not meant to measure individual well-being, of course, but to help estimate a political system's ability to make good decisions.)

One thing that the public reason criterion suggests is that it might do us more harm than good to commit ourselves to any controversial conception of justice. The list I propose does avoid this. And generally, there are many gross injustices that are not on the list despite their importance, and even though they might be within public reason, but that is not a flaw if we can usefully think about performance on those matters by thinking about performance on matters that are on the list. For example, racial apartheid is a gross injustice—a disaster. But it may turn out that our thinking about the avoidance of, say, genocide will tell us enough.

Since there might be more important matters that are controversial and unavailable to public reason, good performance with respect to the primary bads is compatible with terrible performance with respect to the whole real truth about justice. In that case, if the divergence is severe enough, then there might be sufficient moral reason to depart from the norms of public reason. There is much to be said for abiding by a public view shared by all qualified points of view. But in the end, there might be more to be said for, say, saving the human race. It is not clear how great the gap must be between what good can be done within the public conception and what good can be done only by stepping outside of public reason before public reason loses its decisive moral claim on an agent, but I assume that it often retains such a claim even if nonpublic reason points to some alternative that would perform marginally better.

Here, then, is a list of primary bads (in no particular order) that might be used to investigate the claim that democracy tends to make good decisions.[1]

Primary bads: war, famine, economic collapse, political collapse, epidemic, and genocide.

The terms in the list are shorthand for a more complex set of things. For example, famine, epidemic, and genocide are evidently always great disasters. On the other hand, I assume that war, economic collapse, and political collapse might be necessary evils in some extreme cases. Wars of self-defense or humanitarian intervention, for example, are sometimes justified, and they are not then disasters in the relevant sense for our purposes. Economic or political collapse is a disaster only if the continuation of the existing system is not an even worse ongoing disaster. Obviously, then, it is only unfortunate examples of war and collapse that I am counting as primary bads.

Are we to judge a government's decisions solely by its bearing on its own people? Surely not. Each of these is a terrible disaster wherever it occurs, and so it would be perverse to judge a government only by how well its own population is spared these things, leaving all others to fend for themselves. Still, our focus should be disproportionately on the people within the government's own jurisdiction, since this is normally the sphere within which the government's decisions have the greatest causal impact on avoiding the listed evils.

There is another complication about how to factor in primary bads across borders. Even if one country could help prevent famine in another, its responsibility to do so is sometimes less than the responsibility of the country threatened with famine. Even if it should do something, the distant country might not have a duty to endure sacrifices as great as the home country must endure in order to prevent the famine. It is easy to say that all countries should do what they can, but it is probably not strictly true. It may be that an outside country could help more if it risked everything, including the basic health of its own economy. But that might be more than it is required to do to prevent a famine in another country. I do not offer or defend an account of why countries might be especially responsible for their own people. I mean only to point out that this is a common view and one that would support thinking of the primary bads especially in the internal domestic way, as things from which governments must especially protect their own people. Again, this would still be a matter of degree, and countries do have duties, of some degree of stringency, to avoid these evils wherever they are in danger of occurring.

This is a good place to make clear that selecting political arrangements according to how well they perform does not make the overall theory of legitimacy and authority a consequentialist one. The idea of consequentialism is philosophically slippery, since some have argued that the normative content of any moral theory can be put into a consequentialist formulation.[2] That obviously cannot be the view of consequentialism at play if someone accuses my view of being consequentialist. The objection must be that it has the normative content characteristic of consequentialist theories, and so it must be taking a narrower view of consequentialism, possibly meaning agent-neutral consequentialism (utilitarianism is the classic example). If the objection means that on my view a government is permitted to do anything necessary to avoid primary bads and promote good consequences in other ways, then it is false. Government may not promote these aims without moral constraint. It is not as if it is permissible for a government to execute innocent people—say the hungry—if this would help avoid a famine. This is an agent-centered restriction, and does not posit just another consequence to be avoided.

A second way in which the theory is not consequentialist is that it steers clear of asserting much about the true standards of justice and common good by which governments should ultimately be judged. The primary bads are things that all reasonable views of these matters will agree are enormously important to avoid, but each view will have its own list of other things that matter at least as much. Some of these may be consequentialist, others not.

There is a third respect in which the overall view is not consequentialist. The general acceptability condition, which says that political justification must be acceptable to all qualified points of view, entails that if there is a true view of what the best consequences are, but this is not acceptable to all qualified points of view, it is not available in political justification. This is a fundamentally anticonsequentialist requirement.

As for weight, I will assume without argument that the avoidance of each of these six things is highly important on any reasonable view of the ends of politics. Of course, many people will think these are not as important as certain other goods or bads. Even if we left the public reason requirement aside, the list might serve its purpose even if some things that are just as important, or even more important, are missing from the list. Perhaps in that case they should be added, or perhaps they are best left off for reasons of tractability. In any case, the public reason requirement gives us good reasons to leave some truly important things off the list. If Christians are right, damnation of large numbers of souls might be among the most important things to be avoided. Leaving aside the issue of tractability, this Christian view is not held by everyone who ought to count as reasonable or qualified for purposes of delineating public reason.[3]

A final, and possibly disappointing, point about our use of primary bads is that we will not, in the course of this book, attempt to decide with any specificity whether democratic arrangements recommended by epistemic proceduralism would perform well with respect to them. The point of introducing them is to suggest a fruitful way of pursuing the question of how well we should expect certain democratic arrangements to perform. It is part of the framework I am proposing for defending a democratic account of legitimacy and authority, but there is not enough material within this framework alone to allow that question to be seriously addressed. A lot more institutional specificity and empirical inquiry would be required.

In particular, I will not take up the question of which rights should be taken off the normal political agenda. I assume that there must be some of this, but it can take various forms and involves rights of different kinds. For example, there are rights to speak, associate, and participate that are crucial to the good functioning of majoritarian procedures, and it will certainly make sense to treat these specially. Beyond these, it might be necessary to take certain other matters off the majoritarian agenda too, even if they have nothing to do with supporting democratic procedures. I am not confident, for example, that rights of religious freedom, or rights against extravagant punishment could be explained as protecting some crucial ingredient in majoritarian procedures. Furthermore, there are different ways to give certain rights special treatment. Some might still be under democratic control but along with institutional barriers to change, as in the case of the U.S. provision for the amendment of the Constitution. Other rights might be put outside of democratic authority altogether if this provides the most effective overall system for promoting justice in a way that is recognizable by all qualified points of view. For example, if democratic procedures are, as epistemic proceduralism conjectures, among the necessary ingredients in a legitimate and authoritative political arrangement, then rights to democratic participation might, in some form, be outside the discretion of democratic procedures altogether. In that case, no democratic procedure could conjure the authority to morally cancel these rights. And perhaps even some rights wholly extraneous to democracy should be likewise taken out of democratic hands as well. I do not say which if any of these rights should be given special treatment, but even this much raises a natural question. If the most important things were looked after by democracy-limiting rights, couldn't the democratic procedure itself safely be understood as a fair contention among voters' interests? Epistemic proceduralism says that this depends on which overall system would (in a publicly recognizable way) best promote justice. But the misfortune or victimization of minority fractions of the populace cannot, almost certainly, be adequately looked after by antecedently specified rights if voters look out mainly for themselves. As we have seen, famines provide a good example. Usually, only a small fraction of a country's population is affected even by the largest famines. Self-interested voting will not address the danger, and it is hard to see what kind of right might protect people from starvation unless voters collaboratively look out for justice and the common good.

Although I will not discuss these questions in any detail, it is important to emphasize that epistemic proceduralism approaches these questions in a distinctive way. Democracy is not the foundational value. It is not, so to speak, an axiom but rather a theorem. I argue, or conjecture, that it is the solution to the question of how to honor both a certain epistemic imperative that might seem to lead toward epistocracy, and the qualified acceptability condition on political justification. Still, the solution to this problem might well be a democratic arrangement that includes special protection for certain rights quite apart from whether they themselves serve democratic values.

We should admit that just as we are evaluating epistemic proceduralism by its expected performance on certain matters, we could evaluate epistocratic arrangements in a similar way. It might seem, then, that the qualified controversy around any invidious comparisons—about which I have made much—is beside the point, since some epistocratic arrangement either performs well with respect to primary bads or it does not. But while such performance is, in principle, an empirical question, it is a very difficult one to confront with good empirical evidence. So the question is, unavoidably, not how a given regime does perform in our experience, but how we would expect it to perform. My argument has been that any invidious comparison aimed at establishing a form of epistocracy will make claims of differential expertise, and so claims about expected (but not actually observed) performance that are open to qualified disagreement. Perhaps no such qualified disagreement would be possible if the arrangement were put to the real empirical test, but we must proceed without that luxury.

How Much Epistemic Value Is Needed?

Epistemic proceduralism rests political authority and legitimacy partly on whether the political system produces good decisions (though this puts it only very roughly, as we will see). Still, it is natural to object that democratic arrangements, by placing important and difficult decisions in the hands of the masses, are deprived of any substantial epistemic resources. The ignorant may well outvote the enlightened few with regularity. Thus, either democratic politics lacks authority and legitimacy, or I am wrong to claim that these depend on the system's having epistemic value.

It might seem as though epistemic proceduralism must deny that the ignorant masses will often outvote the enlightened few. I propose to grant it. It might seem that I need to argue that democracy is the epistemically best arrangement. Rather, I grant that it is not. It might seem that I must at least argue that democracy usually gets the right answer. I think that is far more than I need to argue. My epistemic case for democracy requires only very modest epistemic claims on its behalf: (a) that some democratic arrangements perform better than a random choice from the alternatives presented, and (b) that they not be too much worse than any nondemocratic arrangement, where (c) these propositions (a) and (b), and the cases for them, are formulable within public reason—doctrines, arguments, principles, and so forth, that are acceptable to all reasonable or, as I prefer to say, qualified points of view. If democratic arrangements are shown to be probably better than random, then my argument against the appeal to invidious comparisons does the rest of the work, showing that the epistemic case for any nondemocratic arrangements is bound to go beyond what can be accepted in public reason.

So the task of this chapter is to argue, in a fairly indirect way, that some democratic arrangements are epistemically better than random, the argument proceeding within the terms of public reason. It is a very modest epistemic claim that is required, then, so modest that I believe opponents are immediately in an awkward position. Indeed, another way of putting this chapter's task is as an effort to defeat a certain kind of skeptic, the one who denies that any (nonutopian) democratic arrangements could tend to perform better than random. So, we need to make an epistemic case for democracy, but the epistemic value does not need to be particularly great. I will refer to this important point as epistemic proceduralism's *epistemic modesty*. It is a crucial part of the case for epistemic proceduralism, giving it an advantage over correctness theories—those that link authority or legitimacy to the actual correctness of democratically produced laws and policies. Those views, if they hope to defend the authority or legitimacy of very many laws, require much more epistemic value of democratic procedure than epistemic proceduralism does. It pays to keep in mind that epistemic proceduralism has no ambition to invent political procedures that will give citizens decisive or overwhelming reasons to believe that the majority is correct. The proceduralism in epistemic proceduralism is the fact that it lets there be legitimacy and authority even when the majority is mistaken (within certain limits, as we have seen).

FORMAL AND SUBSTANTIVE EPISTEMIC VALUE

In some cases, we can know how someone will perform on some task because we know the content of the standard (e.g., the answer key), and know the person's particular skills and abilities on those specific questions. We might know that Bill will perform well on a zoology test that is coming up, because we know that it is about fish, and Bill is an expert on fish. In other cases, we can estimate someone's likely performance even if we do not know the content of the standards of correctness. You do not need to know much at all about what questions will be on a biology test to know that, for example, a group of students cooperating will probably perform better than any of them would perform alone; or that the person who composed the test would probably do very well; or that the students who studied will tend to do better than those who did not.

The right answers to the questions political communities face are often controversial. If we tried to support a political system's epistemic value—its tendency to get the right answers—by starting with controversial assertions about what the right answers are, the whole account would inherit the controversy. It would be an advantage if we could make the epistemic case in less controversial terms. This would require us to supply reasons for thinking a certain system tends to get the right answers, whatever those right answers might be.

Call a *substantive epistemic account* an account that, first, posits some conception of justice or common good and, second, claims that democratic procedures are likely to get things right according to that standard. For example, consider a view that posited Rawls's two principles of justice as the standard, and then argued that certain democratic procedures tended to promote justice according to those principles. By contrast, consider a *formal epistemic account* according to which a democratic process is held to have a tendency to get things right from the standpoint of justice or common good *whatever the best conception of those might be*. The formal epistemic approach makes no appeal to any specific conception of justice or common good and so would be untroubled by the fact that there is reasonable disagreement about which conception is best or correct. Such disagreement would not hamper the epistemic approach if it could be established beyond reasonable disagreement that whatever the best or correct conception of justice or common good is, certain democratic procedures have a certain tendency to produce outcomes conducive to justice or common good.

To some, the formal epistemic approach sounds far-fetched.[4] How could we have any confidence in the ability of a process to get the right answer if we don't even know what would count as a right answer? But notice that this is a common situation in epistemology. We often do not have independent access to the truth by which we can calibrate the epistemic value of some method or process of investigation. Consider the scientific method. When some scientific procedure is held to have epistemic value, the argument must normally proceed in what I have called the formal epistemic manner. Arguments must be offered to show that, whatever the truth is, this process has certain tendencies to ascertain it.[5] If democratic epistemology is treated in a similar way, formally rather than substantively, qualified disagreement over the correct conception of justice or common good is no obstacle to an epistemic conception of democratic authority.

A natural objection here is to say that a particular scientific experiment can often be confirmed by other experiments, or by ordinary perception, or in other ways. The epistemic value of each experiment is, according to this objection, supported in a substantive, not a merely formal, way. This raises the question of why those "confirming" methods should be believed, however. Where do we get our confidence in their epistemic value? Formally or substantively? If substantively, then this question arises again about the source that is supposed to have supplied the substantive test: How do we know it is to be trusted? Moreover, even if we do have independent access to, say, whether certain predictions are verified—perhaps our sensory experience is to be trusted at that point—good predictive performance is often taken as evidence that other claims in the theory are likely to be true. Those further claims are not verified by any independent access to their truth, and so that method is formal.

Our approach to epistemic proceduralism is quite similar. There is, I argue, independent access to some of the content of justice or the common good, namely, the primary bads. That is, it can be treated as part of the best public conception of justice that those things are unjust when avoidable, and the performance of democratic procedures can be evaluated partly be their tendency to get the right answers—to avoid the primary bads. But just as with a scientific theory whose predictions can be independently verified, there are further claims that are taken to be supported by good performance on those matters. In the democracy case, good performance with respect to primary bads is taken as support for thinking the same procedure would tend to perform well on other matters. This extrapolation is a formal epistemic method, as is the inference from successful prediction on some matters to likely truth on other matters. The formal epistemic method, then, is familiar and above reproach.

There is no avoiding the formal epistemic approach entirely. The lesson here is not that it is somehow the only epistemic approach, or the privileged one, but only that it is a legitimate approach. There would be no advantage in using the formal mode of epistemic argument unless the result were a less controversial argument. There are two reasons to avoid controversy: First, there is the banal reason that a writer would like as many readers as possible to be persuaded. But, second, we are operating within a conception of political justification that makes political authority and legitimacy conditional on there being a justifying account that is acceptable to all reasonable or qualified points of view. We do not need to decide whether the controversy we could expect about conceptions of justice and the like is unavoidable even among reasonable views. We can usefully avoid that difficult question if we can give an epistemic argument that does not rely on any substantive conceptions of those matters. Then, even if there is reasonable controversy about justice, we will have avoided it.

Of course, the formal epistemic argument might also be controversial even among reasonable or qualified views, and then the formal mode of argument would lack that advantage. I will argue, however, that there is no reasonable or qualified controversy over the formal epistemic arguments I will employ.

Ideal Epistemic Deliberation

Overall, epistemic proceduralism is aspirational, meaning that it proposes a framework for institutions that could actually work to supply authority and legitimacy even if this is not how things work now, and apart from how much chance we think there is of this occurring. However unlikely it might be, people could behave in ways that would render democratically produced laws authoritative and legitimate owing partly to the epistemic value of such a procedure. The question remains, where does such a democracy's epistemic value come from? We are not just interested in the question of how citizen behavior could improve. We want to know what the mechanism is by which this better behavior would render the overall procedure one with a tendency to make good

171

decisions. Condorcet's jury theorem is one mechanism that has been proposed; the democracy/contractualism analogy is another. Since we will reject those in later chapters, we would like something in their place.

We get a clue from our discussion of the democracy/contractualism analogy. I delay the full details of that argument until later, but it will help to sketch the main points here. It is sometimes held that justice or rightness is a matter of what would be acceptable to all participants in some hypothetical collective choice situation. Rawls's original position, Habermas's ideal speech situation, and Scanlon's initial contractualist situation are all examples. Some democratic theorists have argued that actual democratic procedures might resemble the morally fundamental hypothetical contractual situation (as I will call it) closely enough that it would tend to arrive at the same decisions. Since they count as correct, this would give democratic procedures epistemic value. But contractualist theories of justice or rightness cannot, on pain of circularity, have participants armed with views about justice or rightness. So, instead, they must address some less impartial reasons for their choices. The moral heart of these accounts, then, lies in each having a veto power in order to protect themselves against the pursuit by others of their own personal concerns. The veto power is not a feasible or desirable feature of real democratic arrangements, of course. But without it justice would certainly not be promoted by voters looking out mainly for themselves. They must look out for justice directly. But this destroys the analogy between the hypothetical contractual situation and any plausible or desirable actual democratic arrangements. There is no such analogy to support the epistemic value of democracy.

The democracy/contractualism analogy is unsound, or so I argue. But there is another analogy that offers more promise. It strictly fails, too, but the final account I will propose will make important use of this second kind of analogy. Suppose that good democratic deliberation were modeled on a different hypothetical deliberative situation: not a hypothetical contractual situation, but an ideal epistemic deliberation in which the primary question of justice is directly engaged and debated. Unlike the hypothetical contractual situations employed by some moral and political theories, this ideal epistemic deliberation is not morally fundamental; it is not designed to explicate or constitute the nature of morality or justice. On this view, participants would, unlike contractors, recognize the prior authority of principles of justice (even if they did not know what their content was). They would directly address that question: What does justice, independently constituted, require and allow? One candidate for the more fundamental standard of justice is, of course, contractualism, involving its own different ideal deliberative situation. But nothing about the introduction of the ideal epistemic deliberation depends on contractualism being the best account of justice itself, and we will not assume that it is.

On this model, the claim that democratic decisions tend (to some extent) to be just or right by independent standards (call this the tracking claim) would be supported by a stronger isomorphism than is available to the democracy/contractualism analogy: (a) in this case, unlike that case, the primary question is addressed in both the ideal and real deliberations, and (b) neither this hypothetical deliberative setting nor the real deliberative setting needs a unanimity rule, since neither is meant to capture the deep structure of moral reasoning, with whatever individual inviolability that might involve (represented in contractualism by a veto power). Also, (c) neither the ideal nor the real deliberators would see themselves as free of all prior normative constraints. The prospects for analogy or resemblance between the ideal and the real are greatly improved. By the same token, any resemblance between the ideal epistemic deliberation and the morally fundamental standard should it happen to be contractualist is beside the point.

Now this brief description illustrates a view that I reject in the end. Call it the *epistemic mirroring view*, contrasting with the simpler democracy/contractualism analogy. However, sketching the view is a useful step toward explaining the view that I favor, which I will call the *epistemic departure view*. In the epistemic departure view the aspirational level, describing actual practice that is possible and hoped for, is not meant to mirror or approximate the ideal epistemic level, much less the morally fundamental standard. The reasons for this have to do with what I will be calling *countervailing deviations* from the epistemic ideal, but a fuller explanation of this point will have to wait. The epistemic departure view will need more explanation (especially in chapter 10), but I introduce it here to avoid giving the impression that I am endorsing the epistemic mirroring view. I compare the democracy/contractualism analogy, the mirroring view, and the epistemic departure view in figure 9.1.

Calling the ideal epistemic deliberation an ideal might tempt us to think it should be sought or promoted, but, as should be clear now, that is not the role it is playing here, and I will argue later that there are

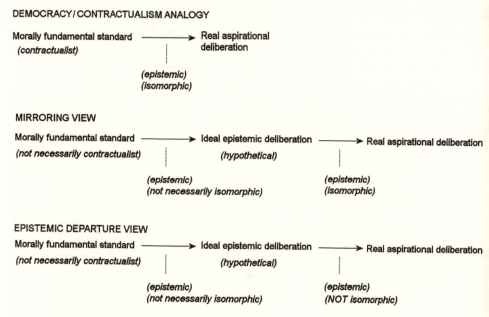

DEMOCRACY/CONTRACTUALISM ANALOGY

Morally fundamental standard ⟶ Real aspirational
  (contractualist)   deliberation

                        (epistemic)
                        (isomorphic)

MIRRORING VIEW

Morally fundamental standard ⟶ Ideal epistemic deliberation ⟶ Real aspirational deliberation
  (not necessarily contractualist)   *(hypothetical)*

              (epistemic)   *(epistemic)*
              (not necessarily isomorphic)   *(isomorphic)*

EPISTEMIC DEPARTURE VIEW

Morally fundamental standard ⟶ Ideal epistemic deliberation ⟶ Real aspirational deliberation
  (not necessarily contractualist)   *(hypothetical)*

              (epistemic)   *(epistemic)*
              (not necessarily isomorphic)   *(NOT isomorphic)*

Figure 9.1

strong reasons *not* to seek or promote it. It is an ideal, but not in the aspirational sense. Its achievement, even if it were possible, is simply not a sensible practical aim at all. Nevertheless, it plays an important role in the theory. And for the time being, for purposes of exploring how democracy might have epistemic value, we can begin by asking how democratic practice would have value if it fully mirrored the ideal epistemic deliberation. If we can answer that, then we can turn to the fact of unavoidable deviations, in practice, from the ideal and consider whether they are too damaging. I will argue that they are not—that realistic (nonutopian) democratic practice can have epistemic value despite profound and unavoidable deviations from the ideal epistemic deliberation. It will help to have a rather different name for the ideal deliberative situation to help us remember that its nature and theoretical role are different from the ideal deliberative situations in many theories influenced by Habermas. I will hereafter call it the *model deliberation.*

The model epistemic deliberation may or may not be the most effective epistemic arrangement conceivable. That is not at issue. The goal is to establish that it would have significant epistemic value, and then to consider whether significant epistemic value is likely to survive the differences between this ideal and actual practice. For the moment, we are leaving actual practice aside. It is important as one considers the elements of such an arrangement to remember that we are not describing a state of affairs that epistemic proceduralism recommends or aspires to. That would indeed be objectionably utopian. The model epistemic deliberation is an imaginary situation with an important role in the theory, but its role is not that of a goal. As we will see shortly, it serves as a kind of template by which to mark and measure deviations and devise epistemically remedial responses. But more on that later. Here, then, is one way of describing an imaginary model epistemic deliberation.

- *Everyone has full and equal access to the forum*: This element of the model deliberative situation would contain a number of provisions meant to structure participation so as to prevent the influence of inequalities other than the rational merits of what is said. For our purposes we do not need to specify these in any detail, and there are bound to be different ways this could be formulated.[6] Among the central provisions, however, there would be at least the following.
- *Everyone has the same chance to speak as everyone else*: We imagine no one facing any more obstacles than anyone else faces to expressing their views, arguments, and objections on the matters at hand. We don't say that everyone actually does participate equally, only because that would seem to be a difficult thing to quantify even in theory (some people say a lot more with fewer words, and so on). We do assume, however, that whatever causes some to participate more than others, none of these causes biases the forum for or against any of the issues in question.
- *People only say things that they believe will help others to appreciate the reasons to hold one view or another among those that are in question*: Besides excluding utter irrelevancies, and pure repetition, we assume that no one speaks in ways that are meant to move opinions other than by inducing an appreciation of genuine reasons for the view they are led toward. It would be wrong to think that so-called emotional appeals are always manipulative in this way. Cold logical discourse is just as open to abuse as communication that is moving or evocative, and yet both can induce appreciation of relevant reasons.
- *Anyone whose interests are at stake in the decision is either present or represented by an effective spokesperson*: By "interests" I don't mean only potential changes in one's well-being. A person might be done an injustice whether or not she is harmed, and I mean to include this kind

of interest as well. Recall, the results of the model deliberation do not define or constitute justice, and so considerations of justice and other moral questions are part of the deliberation.

- *Everyone has as much time to speak as they wish*: No one is stopped from speaking, since there is no limit on time or the patience of the others.
- *Everyone has equal bargaining power*: We assume that no one is in a position to fear retribution from others who know that they take one view or another. We could model this by assuming no one is under anyone's power in that way, or assume that no one would retaliate in such a way, or in other ways. I assume no one has this kind of power over anyone else in the deliberation.
- *Everyone equally credits and attends to the contributions of all others*: This I take to be more or less self-explanatory.
- *Everyone recognizes (or tends to recognize) a good reason when they see one*: This is also self-explanatory, at least so long as it is granted to me that there is such a thing as a good reason for a political decision. I take that for granted here.
- *Participants strive to address the "devil's advocate"*: There is a danger that some significant considerations will not come up at all simply because they aren't taken seriously by any or many of the participants. The group's "center of gravity" on a matter could thereby play a counterepistemic role in determining the decision.[7] I assume that participants present and take seriously views they reject whether or not any participant actually advocates these views.

The list is to be constructed by asking what set of conditions will make it plausible that, on the sorts of issues that political communities will face, a deliberation conducted under these conditions is likely to have a significant tendency to make decisions that are morally right by standards that are independent of the results of this deliberation. Primary bads would be fairly reliably avoided; overall decisions would be better than if they had been made randomly. Many will likely object that this ignores what we know empirically about the epistemically distorting effects of much real-world deliberation. That would be a fair point if the disappointing empirical results were observed in contexts where the preceding conditions are met, but they obviously do not, since no empirical context could meet the conditions. This is hardly a full response to the empirical critics of deliberation, but it does show that their relevance to the claims about the model deliberative situation is uncertain even if their results were (which I do not concede that they are) damning in real deliberative contexts.

If we ask why it is that two heads are better than one, or why thinking together in a communicative way is epistemically better than thinking alone, one element that deserves more discussion is the dispersal of knowledge. The idea of dispersed knowledge is central to Hayek's work on economic markets, and it is worth looking to his work for clues to how to use this idea to support the epistemic value of democracy.[8] This is, however, contrary to the thrust of his own views, and the difference is instructive. In short, Hayek neglects the importance of people addressing the primary question, which for simplicity we might formulate as "What ought we to do?" There is dispute about whether markets in which participants seek only to promote their own interests would promote interests (or otherwise treat people) overall in a just way, or as ought to be done. Part of the reason for doubting this is based on assuming that utilitarianism is not an adequate account of what ought to be done, saying, as it does, that what ought to be done is to maximize aggregate human well-being or desire-satisfaction. Whether or not that standard could be met by markets in which each promoted only her own interests (and others insofar as one happened to care about them), it is not a plausible standard insofar as it allows that some people's interests may be utterly neglected, in ways repellant to our common sense of what is right. This argument resembles the one we used against the democracy/contractualism analogy. Here it is used to suggest that even though there is much dispersed knowledge about human interests, including the special perspective each person has on his or her own interests, neither markets nor majority rule in which participants address only their own interests or reasons will bring these things together in the way they ought to. Both mechanisms allow certain people's interests to be neglected in morally objectionable ways.

A second point, though, is that even if we waived our objections to utilitarian moral principles, so that self-interested markets and self-interested majority rule might do better than we would otherwise think, what epistemic reason would there be for limiting participants to this self-regarding issue and relying on an epistemic invisible hand? It is natural to suppose that there would be even more epistemic value if each, incorporating his or her special self-regarding information into an overall view, were to apply intelligence directly to the question, "What ought we to do?" Not only might each come to a more accurate view on that question, but also now they are in a position to reason with each other about a common topic.

The argument for markets on the basis of dispersed knowledge is an important insight, but it is easily abused. For example, it is sometimes suggested that market rivalry on prices is analogous, in its epistemic contribution, to controversy among scientists about the best theory.[9] In both cases, there is a certain kind of rivalry, and in both cases there is epistemic value in the multiplicity of perspectives that are brought together. But the epistemic mechanisms are very different, and this points to a big advantage in the scientific case. All the scientists are addressing the same question: "What is the true theory?" Entrepreneurs are each addressing a different agent-centered question: "What will maximize my profits?" This advantage involved in addressing a common question is available to my conception of democracy, but not to market arguments, not to (possibly market-inspired) self-regarding conceptions of the proper content of a vote, and not to the democracy/contractualism analogy.

There are arguments meant to cast doubt on a person's ability to form adequate views about matters that do not directly affect his or her own interests. Schumpeter may have originated this line of thought.[10] The central idea is that if I am not the one likely to suffer the consequences, then I am more likely to impose costs on others irresponsibly. While there is certainly something to this point, it would be easy to exaggerate its importance. Perhaps people care more about their own pocketbooks than they do about whether their country or world is just. If so, they might be less diligent in seeking out accurate information about justice. But what matters is not whether they are less concerned, but whether they are sufficiently concerned that they will apply their intelligence productively to the matter. People's concerns range beyond what affects them personally. It would be absurd to deny that people put substantial effort into forming their views about how adequately justice, rights, freedom, and other values are being realized in the larger world.

People have plenty of moral defects, of course, but also plenty of prudential defects. We know voters lack all kinds of important information about politics and the realization of political values (see my discussion in chapter 14). But, plainly, that does not yet show that their efforts in pursuit of those values are too blind to be of any use. That would be no more persuasive than concluding from the fact that people lack important information about their own interests that individual efforts in the market are too uninformed to be of any use. In both cases, people have intense concerns, and this leads them to apply their intelligence to the questions, even though—again in both cases—they do so in deeply flawed ways. There may be some epistemic disadvantage in addressing issues that are outside one's narrow interest horizon, but there are also epistemic advantages when many people are addressing a common question and thinking together. There is no devastating case here against the epistemic value of deciding political questions politically rather than through markets.

My point is not to dismiss or deny the flaws, blind spots, and pathologies that are well known in studies of deliberation and communication in political and nonpolitical contexts.[11] Nor is it to deny (or to concede) that these are more damaging in political than in prudential contexts. Rather, I am denying that they are bound to be too severe for the purposes of epistemic proceduralism conceived of as an aspirational theory.

I do not mean to suggest that the giving and receiving of reasons addressed to a common topic is the typical mode of political action. Nevertheless, I believe it has a privileged place in the best normative theory. As I will argue in chapter 10, nondiscursive uses of power in politics have their place, and they are not peripheral to democratic practice, but central. Still, normatively, the best account of the justification of direct action treats it as remedial: as seeking to remedy a power imbalance that is otherwise ineluctable, and so to neutralize that imbalance's distorting epistemic effect. As I will argue, this kind of behavior is normal and central to good democratic practice because in the real world there will always be various ineluctable and epistemically distorting power imbalances. Still, in the normative theory, the purer reason-exchanging mode is primary, since it dictates proper uses and limits of the direct action mode; but more on this in chapter 10.

DOES CONSISTENCY MATTER?

Epistemic proceduralism looks for whatever procedure will most reliably produce a just decision, so long as this case can be made in a way that is acceptable to all qualified points of view. I argue (simplifying here) that this is best accomplished through a democratic arrangement in which, after public discussion, individual votes are aggregated, and the decision is made by some form of majority rule. It is natural to think of this as the formation of a group judgment out of the aggregated individual judgments, but it turns out that this would raise further questions. A process of judgment is reasonably held to certain standards, such as logical consistency. Some have argued that a plausible list of these standards cannot be met by any rule for aggregating individual judgments.[12] The proof of this is complicated, as are the interesting questions about whether the conditions could be adjusted to avoid the result. Rather than delve deeply into these matters, I hope briefly to indicate why epistemic proceduralism need not be concerned about how these matters might turn out.

It will help to have one simple example of the challenge to judgment aggregation.

THE TENURE EXAMPLE

A university committee has to decide whether to give tenure to a junior academic (the *outcome* or *conclusion*). The requirement for tenure is excellence in both teaching and research (the two *reasons* or *premises*). The first among three committee members thinks the candidate is excellent in teaching but not in research; the second thinks she is excellent in research but not in teaching; the third thinks she is excellent in both. So a majority considers the candidate excellent in teaching, a majority considers her excellent in research, but only a minority—the third committee member—thinks the candidate should be given tenure.[13]

If epistemic proceduralism needed the results of majority rule to count as judgments, this would be a serious difficulty. The judging agent would be profoundly lacking basic capacities of reason. However, it is not clear that epistemic proceduralism has any need for the idea of a group judgment in the first place. If we speak of what a majority thinks about one thing or another, no individual or group is shown to hold inconsistent judgments. The committee apparently has the authority to decide by majority rule whether to grant tenure, and when it does so it makes a decision, but unless we are forced to say it also makes a judgment (which then might be held up to its other judgments to check for consistency), there is no inconsistency afoot.[14]

To see how this helps avoid the challenge, suppose there is a panel of medical experts I want to consult in order to determine the best course of treatment for a serious condition I have. Suppose that majority rule after discussion is epistemically the best way of identifying the most beneficial treatment options for me. Now it is true that a majority might say to do x, another majority might say that if x is done then do y, and yet another majority might say not to do y. But this should not trouble us if we have independent reason for thinking that this majority method for determining whether to do y is epistemically the best. What I want is the best treatment, and I do not care much whether the group of experts can be conceived as making collective judgments at all, much less judgments that are logically consistent. If this is right, then the problems about aggregating individual judgments into collective judgments pose no trouble for epistemic proceduralism, which has no need for the idea of a collective judgment at all.

Why Not Regency?

Supposing we understand the epistemic value of multiple people thinking together, it would not yet be clear why we should need more than a few. Why not have rule by a small group of decision makers—a *regency*—that is randomly chosen so as to avoid invidious comparisons?

The epistemic argument for democracy rests heavily on the unavailability of invidious comparisons. As we saw, that, by itself, would not explain why a coin flip is not good enough, since it avoids any invidious comparisons. So we add that if intelligence could be applied to the problem at hand, without making invidious comparisons, that would be desirable. A first step might be to say that the random choice of a single ruler is likely to be better than a blind random procedure. Then we add that multiple rulers are likely to be better than one (not, as we will see in chapter 12, for jury theorem reasons, but based on the epistemic value of thinking together). The question becomes whether and why there is any epistemic basis for extending the vote to all adults (as I assume democracy does, at least on some matters) rather than a smaller, randomly selected group.

I assume for simplicity that all and only voters are discussants, a point I return to later. The value of multiple discussants lies in the infinite variety of possible important reasons. A few people, within limited time, can only notice and explore so many considerations. When it comes to political questions, the variety of potentially relevant considerations, and the relevant points that arise for each consideration in turn, is always vast. More minds will tend to bring more relevant reasons into play, and this (other things equal) has epistemic value. Assuming for simplicity that all and only voters are discussants, this is some support for universal suffrage, at least among adults. But it is wildly infeasible to have all adults vote on all political matters, and so there must be representatives for this purpose. If we ask whether representatives should be elected or, say, randomly selected, there is one important reason for having them be elected: it is not infeasible to have all adults free to vote in periodic elections, and so this is a way to partially harness the epistemic benefits of the whole large group.

If we ask why assemblies should be as large as they typically are, rather than much smaller, we again balance the epistemic benefits of larger numbers against feasibility. This explains why everything is not a referendum, and also why there is a representative assembly rather than a small regency, but it leaves a range of sizes for the assembly, and I have nothing more to offer on that front. Constraints of feasibility do not obviously preclude a legislative assembly of 5,000 members, so more would be needed to explain why this is or is not a good idea.

Universal voting rights are not required in order to get the benefits of discussion among all adults. That only requires universal discussion rights. In principle, it would be possible to let all discuss and have only a small randomly selected set of voters. Is there anything wrong with this? I make only two points: First, most decisions in modern democracies are, by necessity, made by representatives, not by all adults, and they do indeed benefit from the rights of all members to discuss the matters at hand in public. Second, it is true that all adults are free to vote in electoral contests, so we might ask whether there would be anything wrong with having even elections decided by only a small randomly chosen set of voters, after plenty of discussion by all. Once the epistemic benefits of wide discussion are obtained, why also have everyone vote? I leave the question here, except to say that I do not see in this arrangement anything that is particularly offensive or contrary to the moral spirit of democracy if it turned out to have pragmatic advantages.

THE ROLE OF THE IDEAL

I have tried to establish that in the imaginary situation I call the model epistemic deliberation we have excluded the main sources of bias and error in interpersonal deliberation, and taken advantage of the epistemic benefits of thinking together, resulting in a tendency to make good decisions. But this situation is entirely hypothetical, as I have repeatedly emphasized. It is not a goal to strive for, and it is not even, as we will see in chapter 10, something to be approximated as closely as possible. Its theoretical role is different. Real democratic deliberation will be, and should be, very different from this, but we want some reason to think that it could, under nonutopian assumptions (maybe they are likely to be met, maybe not) tend to produce roughly the same conclusions as the ideal epistemic deliberation despite the great differences in the two contexts. A fuller explanation of this idea is the topic of the next chapter.

The Real Speech Situation

The Ideal Deliberative Situation

Public political deliberation lies at the center of many recent normative theories of democracy, as we've seen. Everyone knows, however, that politics is not, and probably could never be, mainly a matter of the impartial exchanging of reasons. How are these two things compatible? How can deliberation belong at the center of normative democratic theory even though it is by no means the predominant form of political activity even in favorable conditions? We have seen how the idea of a model deliberative situation might, in principle, be central to the theory even without being central to practice—how our epistemic goals might not be best promoted by maximizing resemblance to the model deliberation. In this chapter we look more closely at how the hypothetical model deliberation informs practice in this somewhat indirect way.

Jürgen Habermas spawned a new way of thinking about the moral dimensions of democracy with the innovative concept of an "ideal speech situation." That, at any rate, is the famous phrase, deriving from Habermas's general account of descriptive truth as whatever could survive a certain idealized structure of interpersonal communication. Actually, the idea of Habermas's that is more relevant to politics is his conception of an ideal practical deliberation, and the two are not just the same.[1] Nevertheless, the "ideal speech situation" is an evocative phrase that has caught on, and we can safely treat it as the overarching idea that unifies Habermas's approaches to descriptive and normative validity. The Habermasian idea is that democratic legitimacy and authority might be explained if actual democratic practice could be shown to produce laws and policies that would have met with unanimous agreement in a certain ideal deliberative situation. One natural basis for thinking some actual democratic practice had this feature would be if it resembled ideal deliberative practice very closely. Some have been led to call for a democratic politics that seeks to resemble ideal deliberations,[2] though I will give reason to doubt that this is Habermas's view. More important, I will argue that it is an implausible view. The Habermasian approach is central to my topic, but my aim is not at all exegetical. Rather, I want to describe and defend a model of civility in political participation that gives a principled place for sharp, disruptive, and even suppressive participation under the right circumstances, without jettisoning the whole idea of an ideal deliberative situation. I will suggest that this view, which I call *wide civility*, should be more congenial to Habermasians than they might think, but that is secondary.

Some, including Habermas himself, hope that the ideal speech situation could supply a philosophical explication of truth itself, or at least of objective validity of normative statements, without appealing to anything outside of our own rational and communicative capacities exercised in real life. The merits of that ambition are outside of my concern here. My own interest in the model deliberation is as a plausible epistemic device—a way of collectively coming to correct answers and decisions—whether the standards or facts of the matter are somehow independent of us or not. Nothing here depends on whether we think of the truth as discovered or made by ideal collective deliberation.

In the model deliberative situation all affected people (or proxies for them) are given an equal say, untainted by prejudice or by differences in wealth, power, or dishonesty. This puts it roughly, of course, but it is enough for my purposes. This sort of ideal deliberative situation has important epistemic virtues in contexts of collective political decision making. It brings together diverse perspectives, places a wide variety of reasons and arguments before the public, and prevents inequalities of power or status from skewing the results, which will then tend to reflect the weight of the reasons that apply. In short, such a deliberation is likely to produce good decisions.

Should norms of citizen participation aim at making real deliberative institutions and practices as much like the model deliberative situation as possible? Should actual institutions be designed to mirror the ideal deliberative situation so far as possible? I will argue that citizens should not generally act to promote the resemblance between actual deliberation and model deliberation, since this would often mean letting deviations by others skew the results of the process. The conclusions here are significant both for theory and for practice. I hope to account for the important role played in democratic politics by sharp and disruptive political activity, including activity that interferes with communication. Theories that locate the core of democratic legitimacy or authority in public processes of deliberation about political issues can seem to treat sharp or disruptive political activity as marginal, as unfortunate last resorts. This is unsatisfying, since much of democracy's promise derives from our historical experience with brilliant and original forms of direct action. This idea that the paradigm of responsible democratic activity is the calm giving and receiving of reasons stems from failing to put the ideal deliberative situation in its proper theoretical place. It is not something to be emulated in practice, but a tool of thought and analysis by which appropriate sites for political engagement can be identified. Political behavior does not and should not take place in anything resembling the ideal deliberative situation, and so the deliberative mode of behavior is not privileged in practice.

MAKING IT REAL: THE TOWN MEETING

Alexander Meiklejohn famously discussed the traditional New England town meeting in order to illustrate how certain restrictions on expression are compatible with—indeed necessary for—a meaningful freedom of speech.[3] He argued that without rules forbidding such things as talking out of turn, disobeying the moderator, speaking far off the appointed topic, and so forth, the quality of the deliberation at the meeting on the topics at hand would be harmed. He pointed out that even under such restrictions on speech, participants would be free to express their views of the matters at hand, whatever their view might be. There remains, in short, freedom of speech. Even though we know it is bound to fall short, the town meeting is a real deliberative forum in which the model deliberative situation is realized about as well as we could expect to find anywhere. As in the model deliberation, there are severe restrictions, and yet there is also freedom. These are, respectively, the *restrictive* and the *liberating* aspects of the model deliberative situation, and, to a lesser extent, of deliberative contexts that approximate it. The restrictions might be justified on grounds of fairness or individual rights. They also might be justified by the aim of insulating the exchange of reasons from the distorting influence of power of various kinds. This is an epistemic advantage of the restrictive rules. I want to start here, in the town meeting, and then ask whether it is a reasonable aspiration to extend even this imperfect version of model deliberation to communication in society at large. I will argue that it is not. It is not only the pure ideal but also more realistic approximations such as this one that I argue are inappropriate models for political deliberation generally.

The town meeting is a useful starting point for several reasons. In a town meeting the rules tend to be exceptionally clear. I do not mean only the rules of procedure, or the rules that will be enforced, but also the rules of good behavior. The official rules of a town meeting are distinct from the standards of civility or good meeting behavior. For example, the official rules may, by their silence on the matter, permit a recognized speaker to ridicule opponents in a way calculated to disturb the meeting, but that would not settle whether this was within the speaker's duties of civility. This distinction in a meeting context mimics the structure in a broader political context where there are laws permitting and regulating expression, but also a separate set of standards of civility with no force except that of a citizen's duty. The structure of a deliberative forum is made up of both parts, which I will refer to as *institutional* and *moral norms*, respectively. They are restrictions in two different senses, but for my purposes it will not be necessary always to note that difference.

Given the epistemic advantages of these restrictions on communication in the town meeting (as well as whatever non-epistemic moral value they might have), should communication in society generally be similarly structured, so that political decisions can arise from a process with the same moral and epistemic virtues? I will answer "no."

How Society Is Unlike a Meeting

Public communication is a vast category of human behavior. If there is any temptation to extend the norms and restrictions of model deliberation to public communication generally, it is because there is no sharp line defining which public communication is politically relevant. American jurisprudence around the First Amendment's guarantee of freedom of expression is often troubled by this point. Even if it is desirable to have very robust protection for political expression, it is difficult to say for sure which categories of expression could not be political and therefore fall outside the strongest protection. Our question is not the First Amendment question about when speech may be interfered with by legal regulation. We are considering institutional rules and moral norms for the conduct of expression. Still, if the aim is to shape institutions of political deliberation, the same difficulty arises. It is difficult to say what is political expression and what is not. That difficulty could be avoided if the whole domain of public communication were put under the discipline of institutions and norms that are meant to resemble ideal political deliberation. Call this proposal the *wide mirroring doctrine*. It says that public communication, conceived as one large forum, ought to mirror the ideal deliberative forum so far as possible.

To see why the wide mirroring doctrine is unattractive, it is useful to focus on the restrictive aspect of the model deliberation. Recall, all have equal access to the forum, and all address the question of justice or the common good (even if people have differing conceptions of it). Even apart from any sanctions or enforcement mechanisms, these are restrictive. This is not yet to say that the restrictions are not worth it, but first we should appreciate that they are indeed restrictive. Consider a few examples of possible public communication that would seem to be precluded by the norms and rules of the model deliberation:

> Kurt has the money and experience to purchase and run a small publishing house. He publishes books of poetry by himself and his friends. Most poets do not have this sort of access to publication, and so the access enjoyed by Kurt and his friends is unequal, violating the equal access feature of model deliberation.

> Emma, after much study, has come to believe that political states are illegitimate. She makes a point of avoiding the statist assumptions of the political discourse of her time. Emma never addresses political issues in terms of what is just or best for the people of her own nation, preferring to imagine alternative modes of social organization. She and her fellow citizens only rarely find themselves addressing a common question about justice or the common good. This violates the common question feature of model deliberation.

> Francis is a filmmaker, whose work subtly but definitely influences the perspectives and views of millions of people. This is not owing to any rational arguments, which are entirely absent from his films. It is owing to his skill in leading his audience to certain conclusions by working on their emotions and impulses, violating the restriction that limits communication to explicit reason-giving.

These are just a few examples. What I hope they show, in case it needed showing, is that many valuable kinds of public communication would be incompatible with the restrictions in the ideal deliberative situation. This does not settle whether there should be such restrictions, since there are also disadvantages to contexts of communication in which these various restrictions are not adhered to. Each of the restrictions is meant to guard against something that is, other things equal, worth guarding against. Even outside the more directly political forms of expression, it is not desirable to have an idea's influence increase because of the power or rhetorical skill of the idea's proponent, much less because it plays to prejudices on the basis of race, gender, or class. Since external sanctions are not at issue, it might seem as though it would be preferable if these norms were in place throughout society, in that people enforced them on themselves. The examples of Kurt, Emma, and Francis strongly suggest, I believe, that even the self-imposed norms of model deliberation would, on balance, not be a good thing in society generally. There are too many valuable products of the human mind that would be suppressed if the egalitarian and public-spirited norms of the model deliberation were to characterize all areas of public communication.

Ordinary Politics

We have looked at the narrow formal political context of a New England town meeting, and at the very broad domain of public communication generally. We turn now to what I will call the *informal political public sphere*, a forum with a scope that is intermediate between the other two. This is the domain of political speeches, candidate or citizen debates, opinion journalism, letters to the editor, political advertising, political demonstrations, political art and expression, and so on. Roughly, it is the political activity of nonofficials, or officials outside their formal institutions such as the legislature. Even though the boundaries are not definite or clear between political and nonpolitical areas of the informal, nonofficial public sphere, there is a rough distinction that is hard to deny. The norms that should govern the political part are, I will argue, different and more restrictive than those that should govern the nonpolitical part, and yet not as restrictive as the norms appropriate to the most formal parts of the political public sphere such as official decision-making meetings of legislators. This intermediate domain is the world of ordinary politics, and so the norms that apply here are absolutely central to the conception of a citizen's role and duties in the political process. Since this domain is informal, there are no rules of the kind that characterize official meetings, except, that is, for any laws that might regulate informal political expression. If we ask what form we want communication in this sphere to take, and we assume broad legal protection of freedom of expression, the emphasis falls on moral norms. I will speak mainly, then, of the shape of citizens' duties of civility (leaving it as an open question how far civility requires politeness).

The informal political sphere is intermediate between formal politics, and non-(or hardly-) politics, and the norms appropriate to it reflect its intermediate position. On one hand, the informal political sphere exists alongside the relatively nonpolitical areas of public communication, and so it is relieved of the burden of ensuring, within its own scope, outlets for brilliance, passion, creativity, provocation, and so on. These are provided for to some extent by the light restrictions in the nonpolitical public sphere. On the other hand, the absence of the deliberative norms has its costs. It would be epistemically costly to let power, position, and passion determine the course of political decision making. This might seem to suggest that the informal political sphere should be governed by the deliberative norms. Two questions arise: Would this be desirable if it were possible? Even if it were desirable, how should deviations be dealt with?

First, would it be desirable, if it were possible, for nonofficial public conduct of political deliberations to hew to the norms of the ideal deliberative situation? With one important caveat, I believe the answer is yes. The caveat is that since the boundaries between the political and the nonpolitical areas of public communication are so unclear, imposing the deliberative norms on the political sphere would be bound to impose them to some extent on the gray areas between political and nonpolitical communication, risking a chilling effect on expression that really ought to be free of these restrictions. Nevertheless, this does not mean that the restrictions are not desirable in the definite cases of political expression. They are desirable here for the same reasons they are desirable in the New England town meeting.

Still, there are differences between the formal contexts of the town meeting and the informal political sphere that suggest they must be treated differently. Even if it would be desirable for the deliberative norms to be respected by all in the informal political sphere, nothing even approximating this is likely. This presents a profound version of the problem of second best. The problem of second best, in general terms, is the fact (when it is one) that when one of a number of desiderata is not satisfied, the other desiderata are no longer appropriate. That is, a situation that departs even further from the original list of desiderata may be better than one that more closely conforms to them.[4] In the informal political sphere, since serious deviations are sure to occur, it is important to see that the best response might be certain further deviations. This is the crux of my rejection of the mirroring doctrine, the suggestion that real deliberations should mirror, so far as possible, ideal ones.

The mirroring doctrine suggests shaping the duty of civility by positing a duty to behave in the ways that participants would behave in the model deliberation, at least as far as each person can. The wide version would apply this to all public communication. Narrower versions would apply it only to all political communication, or even only to formal political deliberation (I will support that narrowest version). On the mirroring view, the ideal sets each person's duties irrespective of how other participants are actually, in the real deliberative situation, behaving. Some of our duties are indeed fixed irrespective of the behavior of others, such as the duty not to torture innocent people for the thrill of it. Other duties set one standard of behavior when others are complying with a similar standard, and a different standard otherwise. Consider the duty to drive on the right-hand side of the road in the United States, as the law requires. This is certainly a duty so long as most others are complying with the law, but the duty lapses if most people are driving on the left. Or consider the duty not to interrupt in discussion. It is a duty that probably applies only to the case in which most people are refraining from interrupting. If interruption is already rampant, then noninterruption may no longer be required.

Call duties of this kind, ones that apply only so long as others are, for the most part, also complying, *collective action duties*. They raise a number of interesting questions, but my interest is in exploring what comes of the duty when the collective action breaks down. The original duty lapses, but what, if anything, arises in its place? The duties of civility are best seen as collective action duties, ones that have one content when people are generally complying with the highest standard, but then a new substitute content when that is not so—when general compliance breaks down. Notice that I do not say that anything goes when compliance breaks down. Rather, one's duties change, adjusting to that circumstance. So the question becomes, what is the new content of the duty of civility when there is not general compliance with the initial high standards? What we need is what we might refer to as a *breakdown theory*, a principled account of this new substitute duty of civility. It will vary, no doubt, according to the sort of breakdown that is in question.

We might respond to a breakdown of high standards of civility by supposing that civility no longer has a place at all. No holds barred, we may now do as we please. But that would seem to depend on showing that no new standard of civility can serve, even partly, the same purposes and values as the one that has broken down. If a new standard can serve these purposes, this is a reason for thinking of it as coming into force. The account offered here is based on the idea that when the features of ideal democratic deliberation are not generally met, there are often new standards that will serve, though not necessarily as effectively, the same purposes and values that gave the initial high standards their point.

We can apply this idea, in a quick preliminary way, to the mirroring doctrine. It says that actual political behavior should resemble, so far as possible, behavior in the ideal deliberative situation. Suppose this is plausible so long as compliance is widespread. There is still the question of what to do when compliance is not widespread. It is not obvious that the duty to comply with power-free deliberative norms remains intact. In particular, when power enters the fray on one side in a dispute, the norm that tells us to refrain from using power in that way neither remains intact nor means no holds are barred. This rejection of the wide mirroring doctrine, as I will go on to argue, is the best way to account for the role of political action that is disruptive of reasoning and communication, including many familiar sharp political tactics.

MARCUSE AS A PRECURSOR

Herbert Marcuse offers perhaps the best-known defense of sharp and disruptive interventions in political expression, and I believe his theory is usefully interpreted as a "breakdown theory" of this kind.[5]

Marcuse agrees a great deal with Mill's view in *On Liberty*.[6] He agrees with Mill that there are objectively correct answers to many normative political questions.[7] He also evidently agrees with Mill that under favorable conditions the truth will tend to prevail in the course of full open public deliberation.[8] He agrees with Mill that among the set of conditions that are most favorable to the social discovery of truth is a widespread tolerance. By "tolerance" Marcuse means restraining oneself from interfering with the expression by others of views with which one strongly disagrees. Tolerance is not only one among the social conditions favorable to the social discovery of truth; that epistemic function is what gives tolerance its point. As Marcuse succinctly says, "The *telos* of tolerance is truth."[9]

Tolerance does not, by itself, promote truth, however. It does so only in conjunction with certain other conditions. This gives rise to questions that Mill said little about: What are the other conditions that join with tolerance to promote truth? What is the effect of tolerance when those other conditions are violated in various ways? What implications does this have for the practical question facing a citizen: "Ought I to be tolerant of this highly disagreeable view?" Marcuse offers a rough account of the circumstances of tolerance and an argument that they are pervasively violated at least in modern America.

On Marcuse's view wider standards of civility (as I call them) come into their own when there is a failure or breakdown in the conditions in which tolerance serves its purpose. Applied to the matter of civility in political expression, the breakdown approach asks what is the point of narrow civility? If we follow Mill's and Marcuse's approaches to tolerance of expression, we will answer that an important part of narrow civility's point is as part of an arrangement in which the exchange of ideas will tend to promote true or at least objectively better views and social decisions. The *telos* of civility is, in part, truth. Plainly this is not its only point, but it is worth seeing what follows from its having this point.

Assuming with Marcuse and Mill that the value of orderly deliberation is that it promotes the truth, or wisdom, or quality of the resulting social decisions, narrow civility no longer promotes the truth once the other components of an orderly but free deliberation are missing and if standards allowing deviations from narrow civility could serve to remedy the epistemic situation. In general, the defective background conditions permit transgression of narrow civility for remedial purposes, but only within the constraints of a wider civility. For convenience I will refer to this normative structure as one of *constrained transgression*.

How do wider standards of civility serve the epistemic goal in these defective conditions? Marcuse argued that in this era there is a systematic cluster of interests (especially those associated with owners of productive capital) that have disproportionate control over the course of public, especially political, discussion. As a result, certain favored points of view can be made to attract more support on grounds other than their merits—the actual reasons that exist in their favor. Behavior outside of the narrow bounds that would make sense under more ideal conditions is permitted in order to partially restore the truth-promoting value of public discussion.

From an epistemic viewpoint, the relevant breakdown might be said to consist of *power's interference with reason*.[10] The justification for wider standards of civility in these conditions is, roughly, that they partially remedy the power imbalance. More precisely, they use countervailing

193

power to remedy epistemic distortion wrought by the initial insertion of power. The remedy might sometimes be conscientious suppression of an overrepresented message, or in other cases it might be the introduction, through sharp transgressive methods, of an underrepresented message.

The circumstances of narrow civility in political expression, then, include the condition of power's noninterference with reason. It would be absurd to think that this condition could be fully met in any real context of public political expression, but that does not deprive the idea of normative significance. Habermas, Marcuse's leading successor in what is known as the Frankfurt school of critical social theory, adopts the idea of power's noninterference with truth as the core of his moral and political theory without supposing that it is a condition that could ever really be met. Habermas holds that a legitimate political arrangement is whatever would, hypothetically, be unanimously accepted in a practical discourse situation involving all affected in which, roughly, power does not interfere with reason.[11] It might seem that since power always is actually interfering with reason, this account will leave it entirely to the philosopher, rather than to any public process, to ascertain the conditions of justice or legitimate government. Habermas, however, insists that the philosopher cannot credibly claim to know what such an ideal discourse would produce absent actual discourse.[12] But actual discourse always falls short of the ideal discourse, and normative conclusions must be drawn by concentrating on these discrepancies. The greater the shortfall, the less the moral legitimacy of the normative conclusion, since this enlarges the biasing role of the philosopher's own particular perspective. Marcuse's view is often criticized as arrogantly bypassing public discussion and presuming to know its proper conclusions. On the contrary, Marcuse's view is most charitably read as advocating remedial interventions in the discursive system so as to restore some presumptive normative significance to its conclusions. One strategy that is suggested by this approach is not to try to generate the conclusions by a solitary application of reason, but, as far as possible, to approximate real social conditions in which either power does not interfere with reason *or, failing that, find some remedial feature that would support our ability to infer from the imperfect real discourse to conclusions about what would have been accepted if it had been ideal.* Such a view admits from the beginning that real discourses are not ideal, but still gives the idea of ideal discourse—the idea of power not interfering with reason—a central critical role.

If we stick to the epistemic point of standards of civil political expression, we will be led to a new, more permissive set of standards in which advocates of the view that is disadvantaged by the appearance of power may permissibly press their own viewpoint with an added degree of power. The more permissive standard is defended on the grounds that this might countervail the antirational effect of the initial pollution of the discourse by systemic power that irrationally favors one side.

When power distributions trigger wider standards of civility, this dispensation is not given to all speakers whatever their message. It is only remedial if wider standards are given selectively to those whose viewpoints are being denied their due hearing by an imbalance of power. The limits of a wider idea of civility are naturally suggested on this account. Even on a Marcusean analysis there would be no apparent justification for such extreme suppression of a message that it disappears from public awareness altogether. The power imbalance argument provides only a basis for leveling the playing field in order to partly recover the epistemic virtues of freedom of expression that Mill emphasized.

AGAINST LEVELING POLITICAL EQUALITY DOWNWARD

I want briefly to mention an important but distinct way in which departures from the equality of the model deliberation might be called for in practice.[13] Here we see a distinctive institutional implication of epistemic proceduralism as compared especially with fair-proceduralist views, and non-epistemic versions of deliberative democracy.

Here the structure is not one in which some people depart from the ideal in order to countervail the epistemic effects of certain other people departing. Still, it is another example of the problem of second best. Owing to one unavoidable deviation from the ideal deliberative conditions—namely, the violation of the assumption that there is unlimited opportunity for everyone to have as much input as they like—an additional deviation becomes appropriate. Unequal opportunity for input should be allowed, to some extent, if by doing so the overall amount of input is increased and as a result the expected epistemic value of the overall arrangement is improved.

Epistemic proceduralism holds that the epistemic value of the process, according to public reason, is one of the primary driving factors in designing democratic institutions. So, even though there are probably epistemic gains from equalizing everyone's opportunity for input, there can also be epistemic losses if this equal input is at too low a level.

Inequality of opportunities for political input may be called for on epistemic grounds so long as it provides more input opportunity for everyone and it is not too unequal. This is more than a mere logical possibility. I want to sketch a simple voucher scheme that represents one way such improvements may actually be induced. My goal here is not to solve the many logistical problems involved in implementing such a scheme, but to present a basic mechanism that appears to have this potential. It is important to keep in mind that the inequalities introduced may be so great as to cancel the epistemic advantage of the increased quantity. However, we can see that the inequalities might sometimes be very modest, and that this general strategy admits of many variations, some of which might be able to do even better than my examples. The proposal is just one way of illustrating how there can be sound epistemic reasons for rejecting the standard (popular among democratic theorists) of equal availability of political input.

If a person's share of the total quantity of influence exerted is expressed as a fraction of that total, then influence would, of course, be a zero sum—a gain somewhere would mean an equivalent loss somewhere else. But, of course, if one's share of wealth were expressed as a fraction, then wealth too would be a zero sum. We know wealth can be increased for some without decreasing the wealth of others, and so a person's share can be understood in absolute as well as comparative terms. The same is apparently true of political influence, or if the word *influence* suggests otherwise, it is true of political *input*. Let *input* stand for an individual's absolute quantity of political participation (measured, for simplicity, in money), and let *influence* stand for a person's fraction of the total political input. If everyone wrote more letters to their congressional representative annually than they now do, the total quantity of input would increase, and no person's absolute quantity of input would decrease. Even if influence is (defined as) a constant sum, the quantity of input is not.

Assume that everyone is supplied with resources for political use at the highest level compatible with everyone having an equal amount. Now allow additional expenditures through and only through government-supplied vouchers. These have a cash value when contributed to certain political endeavors such as election campaigns, and no value otherwise. Each next or marginal voucher a person buys costs more than the previous, but has only the same value as the last. The cash value of the voucher is then paid, by the administering agency, to the campaign that receives the voucher from a citizen. But the purchase price was more than this, and the extra amount retained by the agency goes into a fund that is used to subsidize the price of vouchers, making them more affordable. This subsidy can be structured in countless ways, and I will sketch only one, which I will call the singular voucher version of progressive vouchers: suppose the money in the fund is distributed among all those who are happy to receive only their one government-supplied voucher (call this the singular voucher). These are available for free, or if "earnest money" seems like a good idea, to avoid frivolous uses, then they are cheap. Their value is determined by the size of the fund and the number of people who want the singular voucher. Anyone who wants to contribute more than the singular voucher will have to purchase progressive vouchers and may not receive a singular voucher. This will become clearer with later examples. But first some general points.

If we assume that some citizens would pay more than the cash value for progressive vouchers[14] if this were the only way to have additional political input, then this will raise money to pay for singular vouchers that are free or very cheap for anyone who wants one. The result would be a distribution of political input in which more is available to everyone.

Consider a community of 200,000 voters, the size of a small city such as Providence, Rhode Island. Suppose that the maximum equal level of contribution without vouchers would be $5 per voter per election cycle, yielding a total expenditure of $1 million. Now suppose we allow vouchers in addition. Let each progressive voucher have a value (redeemable by campaigns) of $50, but they cost more than this. To buy one costs $50, to buy a second costs $88, next is $153, then $268, and the fifth and final permissible voucher costs $469. (The marginal rate of increase is 75 percent, but this can easily be varied for other scenarios.) Each voucher is still worth only $50, but people who can afford it and want to have more political input may well pay more than the cash value; indeed, that cash value has nothing to do with what a voucher will be worth to a citizen. Nevertheless, I will assume in this example that not many citizens will buy many of these increasingly expensive vouchers. (This grants something congenial to opponents of my thesis. If more bought vouchers, my conclusion would follow only more easily.) Suppose that only 5 percent of voters buy any progressive vouchers: 5 percent buy at least one, 4 percent go on to buy two, 3 percent buy three, 2 percent buy four, and 1 percent buy all five. Buying all five costs

$1,028, but a person's input is valued only at $50 times the number of progressive vouchers she buys and uses, in this case $250, plus the amount that was already being spent under the maximal equal scenario, or $5. The total input for the maximum spender under these assumptions is $255. These purchases build up a fund of $2,628,516. Dividing this into a free or cheap singular voucher for every voter who chose not to purchase progressive vouchers (95 percent of all voters) yields a singular voucher worth $14. I assume for simplicity that all remaining voters receive and use a singular voucher (though, if not, they can be worth more). What is the result of this arrangement?

First, whereas previously no voter contributed more that $5 to political campaigns, now no one contributes less than $19, since no one is without the $14 voucher. Everyone contributes more than they did before, including those who contribute the least. Second, we have introduced inequality of input. The vast majority are contributing at a value of $19, and a few at a value of $255, and some in between. The highest is about thirteen times the lowest; on the other hand, a campaign can get as much by winning over a small coffee meeting of thirteen of the poorest voters as it can by wooing any single fat cat. Third, since the distribution is Pareto superior, the total contribution is also greater. It has gone from $1 million to $5,128,516—more than quintupled. This greater quantity, we are assuming, has positive consequences for the epistemic value of the process, at least under favorable conditions, and so long as it is not too unequally distributed among participants.

The degree of inequality is certainly minuscule by the standard of actually existing politics in the United States,[15] and the increase in the total is enormous by any standard. We have no basis for saying there is, or is not, a net epistemic gain, but this should be enough to suggest that the general strategy of progressive vouchers may offer a way of combining the epistemic values of the quantity and of equal distribution in a way that political egalitarianism—the principle insisting on equal opportunity for input—cannot. Political egalitarianism would have mandated the maximal equal level of $5 per person for a total of $1 million, forgoing the additional $4.1 million of input that could be induced if a certain (modest?) amount of inequality (with no invidious comparisons) were acceptable. Political egalitarianism is a crude and implausible principle, even though there are good reasons for keeping inequality within certain limits.

THE IDEAL SPEECH SITUATION IN ITS PLACE

Contrary to a common interpretation of him, Habermas does not believe that actual institutions should resemble an ideal deliberative situation as much as possible. It is not just that this is unrealistic or utopian; he argues that it is not even desirable. It is preferable to have a "wild," "anarchic," and "unrestricted" public sphere on which formal political institutions can draw, even though this does open the informal public sphere to morally undesirable biases and inequalities. Habermas is not explicit about the value of a less disciplined informal public sphere. Also, it is not quite clear what the importance is of the idea of an ideal deliberative situation if it is not to be emulated in society at large. There are a few possible answers suggested by Habermas's discussion.[16]

First, why is it desirable to have an unruly informal political sphere, one in which equal access, time, and power are not guaranteed? One obvious reason is that the informal public sphere will be the source of ideas whose value lies outside the political, and so whose origins in egalitarian conditions will tend to matter less. Second, even politics benefits from a rich and productive background culture. Even if not every product of public deliberation has the potential to enrich political thinking, an environment that includes boldness, surprise, and offense is one that will have a wider variety of original ideas, gestures, and confrontations from which to draw in political thinking. Much of this raw material would never exist in a setting structured so as to prevent any influence other than the 'forceless force' of the better argument.

If the model deliberation is not to be emulated in society at large, what is the importance or value of the idea? One part of an answer is that the model deliberation is apparently to be emulated in more formal political institutions, a point to which I will return. A second part of the answer is that the ideal deliberative situation, even existing only in thought, serves as a template against which to judge reality in order to identify and deal with deviations.[17] This naturally raises the question of what is to be done when such deviations are identified, since we know that approximating the ideal is not the goal. That is the question to which my suggestions about breakdown theory in general, and countervailing deviations more specifically, are meant to provide part of an answer.

The goal of making deliberative heaven on earth, of seeking to make real political institutions resemble as closely as possible the structure of the ideal deliberative situation, leads to an implausibly narrow conception of the public sphere and of the duties of civility. An alternative way of using both the idea of an ideal deliberative situation and actual deliberative processes is a breakdown theory of the kind sketched in this chapter. The ideal serves as a template for identifying breakdowns, which are common and inevitable. Actual practice can be adjusted in light of those deviations, not always to reestablish resemblance to the ideal, but to bring forces to bear, rational or not, that countervail the effect of the initial deviations so far as possible. The result is not any static structure at all, but a dynamic process of deviation and response, aimed at grounding the supposition that the results could have been agreed in an ideal deliberative situation. This approach, for which there is support in Habermas's own writing, seems to be the best way of avoiding the narrow, overly polite conception of duties of civility that might seem to be implied by the central role given to the ideal deliberative situation, while still giving that idea a central theoretical role.

The interest of this approach is not mainly in its endorsement of protest, emotional political appeals, and judicious use of power politics. That is a fairly conventional and time-honored view. It is, perhaps, more interesting to locate this view in a conception of political deliberation that gives a central theoretical role to the ideal in which only the forceless force of the better argument prevails. A second feature of this approach that goes beyond the endorsement of sharp politics is its ability to scale the wider conception of civility in a graduated way, without letting the duty of civility collapse whenever its higher standards are not being generally met.

It is important to ask, as many asked of Marcuse's view, whether a policy of countervailing deviation from narrow norms of civility risks escalating the conflict in dangerous ways. The fact that there is often some risk of this kind is certainly not a fatal problem for the view. Civil disobedience is also a way of escalating a dispute, and often risks further retaliation and escalation, but this is not decisive against it in general terms. The risks of escalation would have to be weighed and judgment exercised in the use of countervailing power as they must be in the choice whether to resort to civil disobedience.

If one instance of power is countervailed by another, it might seem as though it has been neutralized and the power-free ideal has been reinstated. Sometimes, of course, power can actually be neutralized, as when a weapon is brandished but then destroyed or removed from the scene. But countervailing uses of power as I have used that idea here will not normally neutralize the original insertion of power. If you put a gun to my head, and I put my gun to your head in reply, your use of power has been (at least to some extent) countervailed, in the sense that its ability to skew the deliberations has been scaled back by my response. Still, the power-free ideal of the ideal speech situation or the ideal epistemic deliberation has not been restored. Mutual assured destruction might be the best way to countervail the first destructive threat, but it is not the ideal speech situation restored. It is a profound deviation from that situation in an effort to achieve something else: a tendency to get the same results as the (very different) ideal speech situation would have gotten.

Should Formal Politics Be Narrowly Civil?
(Why Not Fight Fire with Fire There Too?)

As we saw, the narrow norms of model deliberation would be epistemically too restrictive and costly if they were to characterize public communication generally. Even the informal political sphere should not be overly disciplined by those narrow norms, but there the strict deliberative ideal should be used as a yardstick to measure deviations. The deviations need to be addressed creatively, however, and not always by simply holding one's own behavior to the standards that others have breached. This leaves the formal political sphere, deliberative settings in which selected participants have formalized roles and responsibilities, and in which legally binding decisions are made. Should these formal political settings operate by the more restrictive approach, trying to resemble the structure of the ideal deliberative situation as closely as possible?

If the informal public sphere is sufficiently unrestricted, then perhaps there is a place for the more restricted discursive forms of interaction specifically in legal forums such as courts and legislatures.[18] But what is to be gained? The reasons given for a wider, more permissive regime in the informal sphere might seem to apply to the formal sphere, too. The breakdown model developed here would seem to imply that even in the legislature there will be deviations from ideal discursive interaction, and that countervailing responses, pulling the structure only further from the ideal, will often be the best way of grounding the presumption that the outcome could have been agreed upon in a deliberation. Why posit the narrow rules of civility that would be appropriate in

201

the counterfactual situation of an ideal deliberative situation even here, in formal politics? Why not fight fire, if it should break out, with fire even in the formal political domain?

The answer, I think, is that formal politics can come closer to the ideal than other settings. This, combined with the availability of the other more permissive contexts for communication, means that there are likely to be more epistemic benefits than costs from applying the narrower norms of civility in formal political settings. We should accept a narrow mirroring doctrine at least with respect to standards of civility: standards of civility in formal political deliberation ought to resemble as far as possible the standards of behavior assumed in ideal practical deliberation.

Even discussion on the floor of the representative assembly (the context in which the term *deliberative democracy* was first devised)[19] will never mirror model deliberation very closely. Representatives are unlikely always to speak sincerely, to refrain from using power or position in lieu of argument, to put forward only their views on the common good, and so on. In spite of all this, we structure deliberations in those formal settings by elaborate rules of order and norms of civility. The restrictions that are typical in those forums are far more severe than we could hope to justify in informal political settings, much less for public communication generally. If they do not really approximate the ideal deliberative situation, is there any real justification for those narrow norms? Perhaps they are nothing but a charade, a bit of theater to encourage the public to feel that this is a genuinely deliberative forum, even though it is no more deliberative than social life generally (which is to say, not very).

We need to look for some difference, some reason why formal politics should be governed by narrow civility while the rest of public communication is not. One of the differences between the formal and the informal political spheres is that the formal political sphere exists in a system of public communication that includes wider, more permissive standards everywhere outside of formal politics. The deliberative norms in one context are not as restrictive overall if one is free to take his or her ideas to a different context that is more permissive. If informal politics employs wider standards than formal politics, then the epistemic cost of imposing the narrow standards in the formal realm is lessened. For example, consider a debate in the assembly about farm subsidies, and suppose that farm interest groups are richer than the opponents of subsidies. This leads to a larger number of representatives lining up to support subsidies in order to attract the campaign funding from the farm lobby. This rationally distorting role of money (if necessary, the reader should fix up the example to make it so) violates ideal deliberative norms. Under narrow standards of civility within the assembly, it would be impermissible to respond by, say, playing recorded sounds of ringing cash registers and mooing cattle every time a representative spoke in favor of subsidies. This politeness has an epistemic cost, insofar as it might let the initial deviation skew the results without any effective response. But the creative use of loudspeakers, or other nondiscursive direct actions, is available (not just legally, but according to the wider norms of civility I have advocated) outside the assembly in the domain of informal ordinary politics. That reduces the epistemic cost of the stricter standards in the formal realm. That is a consideration that is not available to justify strict standards of civility in the informal sphere, since there is nowhere else to go other than reverting to relatively nonpolitical expression in order to fall under more permissive standards, thereby diluting and weakening the intended message.

This suggests that there is some reason for a division of labor between the informal and formal political spheres. The formal sphere aims for some of the reason-tracking virtues of the model deliberation, by imposing restrictive norms governing the proceedings. The informal political sphere operates without those confining norms in order to allow the inevitable deviations to be balanced out by carefully devised counterdeviations. So far, though, this is just an argument for a division of labor between the formal and informal political spheres. We don't yet have any clear reason to assign the more restrictive norms to the formal political sphere rather than to the informal political sphere. I want to conclude by very briefly pointing to some reasons for thinking the formal sphere is especially well suited to the more restrictive deliberative norms, at least so long as the informal sphere and the general public sphere are less rigid.

The formal political sphere is different in some important ways. First, it is relatively clear what counts as internal to the context of the assembly and what does not. For this reason, it is relatively clear when rules would apply and when not. The boundaries between the informal political sphere and the nonpolitical public sphere are less clear. Second, the formal political sphere consumes only a small fraction of life. Restrictions in this forum are not, in a certain sense, as restrictive, since much of life takes place in the less restrictive informal political sphere or in the general public sphere. This is not just the point that there is a division of labor between the formal and informal spheres. The formal sphere is a smaller part of life, by any measure, than the informal. Third, the behavior of participants in the formal political sphere is more easily monitored. The number of people involved is small, and they are publicly visible. This works together with the final point, namely, that reputation pays. In the formal political sphere, participants are punished by the public for untoward behavior as the public sees it.

What these features suggest is that restrictive norms meant to encourage discursive reasoning on equal terms might be less vulnerable to noncompliance, and so more effective, in formal political contexts than in the informal political sphere or in society generally. Moreover, the epistemic costs of these restrictions would be smaller there, partly because the other more permissive settings exist, and partly because the formal settings are a relatively small part of communicative life. Narrow civility might, after all, have a place in real institutions, namely, in the conduct of formal political deliberations, at least when things have not gone too badly wrong.

Conclusion

My aim has been to argue that the idea of an ideal situation of political deliberation is indeed a potent tool in normative democratic theory, but that its role is not as something to be emulated or mirrored in public discourse or even in political discourse. Its role is mainly as a template to lay over actual deliberations in order to identify (not always to mourn) deviations. Once they are identified, the question is what should be done about them. The mirroring doctrine argues that resemblance to the ideal should be maximized. The view I have described, wide civility, rejects the mirroring view, since promoting that kind of resemblance to the ideal would often require acquiescence in the face of serious distortions of the process of deliberation, skewing not only the process but also the decisions that are likely to result. Wide civility calls for countervailing deviations where a countervailing measure can be devised. It is still an account of civility, since even these measures morally constrain people not to merely pursue selfish or sectarian interests as far as one can. Fire may be fought with fire, but a spark may not be fought with a flamethrower. Wide civility folds a lot of sharp, disruptive, and even informally suppressive political activity into a broadly deliberative approach to democratic politics, recovering a crucial part of democracy's moral promise as we know it from historical experience. The specific content and limits of wide civility under various conditions are a further question;[20] the important thing to keep in mind is that it does have limits, and that this can be accounted for by the remedial role that it plays in the account I have described.

Having said all that, however, there is, after all, some reason for formal political deliberation—a narrow context surrounded by other outlets for discourse—to be governed by a narrow conception of civility. Political discourse generally is not like a New England town meeting. On the other hand, New England town meetings, and to a lesser extent other formal political deliberative settings, are.

Why Not an Epistocracy of the Educated?

IT IS NATURAL TO THINK THAT THE WISE OUGHT TO RULE, and yet it is now universally denied. One reason for this is that many people think that ruling arrangements ought to be justifiable in a generally accept-able way. I have adopted that viewpoint in one specific form, the quali-fied acceptability requirement. Given so much reasonable (qualified) dispute about who counts as wise in the right way and other matters, it might seem doubtful that rule of the wise could meet this standard. On the other hand, a decent education, including, say, some knowledge of politics, history, economics, and so forth, as well as close experience with others from diverse backgrounds must be admitted to improve the ability to rule wisely, other things equal, at least assuming a certain measure of good will (otherwise these neutral means might only make a bad person more dangerous). But then why shouldn't there be general agreement among all qualified points of view that citizens with such an education should have more votes than others? Is the only reason for this the assumption that goodwill is lacking? Should we all accept rule of the wise if that condition were overcome?

We have considered and criticized intrinsic procedural approaches to politics and found them wanting. I think that there is no denying the epistemic dimension of political authority, and this conviction lies behind my concern to resist the Platonic idea that the wiser among us ought, on that basis, to have a greater share of authority.[1] In Plato's favor, as I have said, if there are substantive standards of the quality of outcomes, then surely some citizens would be better (less bad) than others with regard to their wisdom and good faith in promoting the better outcomes. If so, this looks like an important reason to leave the decisions up to them.

It is possible to know what is best and yet not choose to do it, and this point might be deployed against epistocracy. Here, though, I will sim-plify matters by supposing (with, for example, Socrates)[2] that the knowers would do what they think is best. Alternatively, if this is too much for you to swallow, just build this extra public-spirited motiva-tional assumption into the characters who will be considered as poten-tial epistocrats. So, I assume for purposes of argument that some are wiser than others in this way, and that they would do what they thought best for the polity. The big question behind the more specific one I will concentrate on is why these wiser folks should not rule: why not epistocracy? The more specific proposal I will consider and criticize is that, in particular, the better educated would rule more wisely, and should accordingly have more political authority.

In *Considerations on Representative Government*, John Stuart Mill notoriously proposed to give more votes to the better educated (among others).[3] In political philosophy it is natural to think of the authoritarian Plato and the liberal antipaternalist John Stuart Mill as having little to do with each other.[4] In fact Mill was profoundly influenced by Plato. The explicitly Socratic spirit of rational examination of our lives and convictions is among Mill's deepest convictions, and gives his influential view of liberty much of its characteristic shape. Mill was also sympathetic to the distinctively Platonic idea that political authority ought to be in the hands of those most capable of exercising it wisely and justly. We find this view in Socrates (or Plato's Socrates) too,[5] but it is developed most fully by Plato in *The Republic*. Like Plato, Mill argued that the superior wisdom of an identifiable minority justified their having greater political influence, in a way. In particular, Mill thought, citizens with a high degree of education ought to have more votes than others, even if all ought to have the right to vote. Mill was mainly concerned not to put the wise in charge, but to counteract the fact that they were likely to be outnumbered. For my purposes it will not matter if we treat that approach together with the rather different goal of seeing that the wise actually rule the rest. In both cases, the wise are supposedly identified and given more voting power per person than others. I will call this general idea an *epistocracy of the educated*, noting that Mill's is a moderate version in which suffrage is universal (one person, at least one vote) and that he is not trying to guarantee in advance that the wise, as a group, are in control.[6]

Mill's version of the rule of the wise, while wildly unpopular with commentators, is actually fairly formidable.[7] It avoids important objections that can be brought against Plato's version of epistocracy, and gains support from certain very plausible and decidedly more popular convictions: many people would accept that there is some kind of education, call it *good political education*, such that the citizenry of a large polity would tend to rule more wisely if they were educated in this way than if they were not. From here it seems only a short but treacherous step to the conclusion that in a society in which only some have this education and others do not, the group of those who do will tend to rule more wisely than the group as a whole. On this basis, we can understand Mill's notorious call for two measures: (1) literacy tests as a qualification for voting,[8] and (2) extra votes for individuals with higher education.[9] I hope to show how Mill tried to support these measures in a liberal framework, and also how the argument fails.

First, I will show what is formidable about Mill's proposal of "plural" or weighted voting that privileges the highly educated. I consider first a point that Aristotle makes against Platonic rule by a small, wise elite. Mill, in effect, takes Aristotle's anti-elitist point onboard, but then improves the case for a moderate epistocracy in response. Then I consider two ways of resisting Mill's proposal. The first, the deference objection, fails, but instructively. The second, the demographic objection, fares better.

Aristotle versus Platonic Epistocracy

In Plato's pure form of epistocracy, the knowers ought to have all political authority, in virtue of their wisdom.[10] Just as reason deserves authority over the other parts of the soul, the knowers in the political community deserve authority over the other parts of the city. Not only should people and classes be placed in the roles to which they are best suited; one role, the rational or knowing role, ought to be in charge of the rest.

Suppose, then, that there are a small number of citizens who have, to an especially high degree, a morally informed practical wisdom and accompanying public-spirited motivation that is pertinent to the conduct of political affairs. In the first instance, I mean by this, say, that each of these people knows better than anyone outside of this group what ought, politically, to be done. Suppose we were convinced, moreover, that the state ought to act in the way most likely to be correct or just, with no other constraints on proper procedure. Assume, for simplicity, that this entails obligations on citizens to comply when the state is so acting. It might seem, then, that the state ought to be ruled by this wise group, and all citizens have a duty to do as this group directs.

Even with this unusually intense emphasis on the tendency toward correct decisions, the conclusion does not obviously follow, as some remarks of Aristotle's suggest.[11] The main idea can be seen most easily if we suppose that the wise group consisted of a single person. Even granting that following her directions would lead to correct political decisions more often than following anyone else's directions, that is an absurd way to frame the alternatives, because there is no reason to think the decisions need to be made by a single person. It is very plausible that decisions would tend to be better if she were to deliberate and decide along with several others, such as the next wisest in the society. The point is obvious in the case of a simple nonmoral test, say of the "standardized" variety used to qualify applicants for college. The single best performer in a group would certainly not do as well as a cooperative effort by the top several performers, even though enlarging the group reduces average competence. The same point is extremely plausible when the task is what to do politically.

Aristotle argued, persuasively, that this consideration counts against the simple argument that the few wisest ought to rule, since they know best what ought to be done. So the question about the wise elite is not whether its members are wiser than others, nor whether as a group it is wiser than any group of others, but whether it is wiser than any group at all, including larger groups that include all members of this wise elite. Aristotle's point is that some larger group, even if the average individual wisdom is lower, might perform better.

Despite this extra epistemic value of larger numbers of decision makers, Aristotle sees that this is too abstract a point to rule out the possibility of a person so much wiser than others that there is nothing to gain and much to lose by his consulting with them. If someone is that much wiser, then that person ought to rule over the others,[12] and if others presume to rule over this person, their supposed authority is null and "ridiculous."[13] So the epistemic value of many rulers is not a general enough phenomenon to block the legitimacy of epistocracy even on Aristotle's view, though it significantly restricts its application.[14]

The basic idea behind Aristotle's point is the suggestion that rule by the few wisest could be improved upon by expanding the size of the group and having its members deliberate with each other before making their group decision.[15] This point leads away from epistocracy, even while granting that some few might be wiser than the rest.

Mill's Epistocracy of the Educated

We will not consider why Mill thinks everyone should have at least one vote. Letting him have this premise favors him by making his proposal less objectionable to democrats. Grant it for the sake of argument.

Mill's proposal of plural voting has two motives. One is to prevent one group or class of people from being able to control the political process even without having to give reasons in order to gain sufficient support. He calls this the problem of class legislation. Since the most numerous class is also at a lower level of education and social rank, this could be partly remedied by giving those at the higher ranks plural votes. A second, and equally prominent, motive for plural voting is to avoid giving equal influence to each person without regard to his merit, intelligence, and so forth. He thinks that it is fundamentally important that political institutions embody, in their spirit, the recognition that some opinions are worth more than others. He does not say that this is a route to producing better political decisions, but it is hard to understand his argument, based on this second motive, in any other way.[16]

So, if Aristotle is right that the deliberation is best if participants are numerous (and assuming for simplicity that the voters are the deliberators), then this is a reason for giving all or many citizens a vote. However, this does not yet show that the wiser subset should not have, say, two or three. In that way something would be given both to the value of the diverse perspectives and to the value of the greater wisdom of the few. This combination of the Platonic and Aristotelian points is part of what I think is so formidable about Mill's proposal of plural voting. It is also an advantage of his view that he proposes to privilege not the wise, but the educated. Even if we agreed that the wise should rule, there is a serious problem about how to identify them, as we have seen in my earlier criticisms of epistocracy. This becomes especially important if a successful political justification must be acceptable to the wide variety of qualified points of view among the ruled. In that case, privileging the wise would require not only their being so wise as to be better rulers, but also, and more demandingly, that their wisdom be something that can be agreed to by all qualified points of view.

Now, of course, there could be as much ground for disagreement about who should count as truly educated as about who is wise. But Mill's proposal is to use some more specific criterion of education, such as the possession of a university degree. That particular criterion, of course, is highly contestable, since higher education has long been disproportionately available to certain groups divided along lines of gender, race, class, religion, and so forth. I return to this issue below. Mill's position has great plausibility: good education promotes the ability of citizens to rule more wisely. So, how can we deny that the educated subset would rule more wisely than others? But then why shouldn't they have more votes?

The Dilemma

It might be held that against most proposed epistocrats there are grounds of objection that ought to be counted as qualified. That is, there is much reasonable disagreement about what qualifies a person as the kind of moral knower that is in question. Rejecting the idea that the pope or the Dalai Lama is a knower in our present sense, even if this should happen to be true, is not crazy or vicious or beyond the pale in any obvious way. There is no adequate reason here to disqualify the objection and override their right to be ruled on grounds that are acceptable even to those who reject the special claims about the proposed epistocrats. This is a premise in my argument, not something I am offering any argument for. Nor is there any pretense, as I have said, of specifying the exact boundaries of qualified objections. Supposing we accept this principle against such invidious comparisons, it has some power against episto-cratic proposals, as we have seen. On the other hand, the rule against invidious comparisons might appear to be in tension with another proposition that many of us will find extremely plausible, and even beyond reasonable disagreement:

> *The political value of education*: A well-educated population will, other things equal, tend to rule more wisely.

I do not intend this to give the name "well-educated" to whatever will lead a population to rule more wisely, making the proposition tautolog-ical. Rather, what I take to be very plausible is, really, two things: First, that there is some way of giving content to "well-educated" so that, as a conceptually contingent matter, a population of people with such an education will tend to rule more wisely. I believe it would distract from my main points to consider here what such an education might be. I ask the reader to insert whatever education makes this most plausible. The second thing that I take to be very plausible is that there is some educa-tion such that it is unreasonable or otherwise disqualified in our sense to deny that a population with that education will tend to rule more wisely. Here are some very generally described candidates that some will find plausible in this role, alone or in some combination: basic literacy, basic

211

knowledge of how one's government works, some historical knowledge, knowledge of some variety of extant ways of life in one's society, some knowledge of economics, some knowledge of the legal rights and responsibilities of oneself and others, basic knowledge of the constitution of one's political community, and so forth.[17]

Again, I will not argue for the assumption that some account of "well-educated" will put political value of education beyond qualified denial. If it is so, it favors my polemical opponent, the advocate of extra votes for the educated, so we may simply grant it for the sake of argument. I will consider two strategies for arguing that even if, for some meaning of "well-educated," the political value of education is beyond qualified denial, nevertheless, it can yet be denied without disqualification that,

> *The epistocracy of the educated thesis*: Where some are well educated and others are not, the polity would (other things equal) be better ruled by giving the well educated more votes.

I think the seemingly small move from the Political Value of Education to the Epistocracy of the Educated Thesis can reasonably be resisted, and so the rule disallowing invidious comparisons in favor of the well-educated portion of the citizenry would remain intact. I think the Millean idea is the most challenging test case for a principle forbidding invidious comparisons; if we successfully defeat it, this will be strong support for the idea that invidious comparisons will never be beyond qualified disagreement.

THE DEFERENCE OBJECTION

If the educated would rule more wisely, then must the consequences of their rule be admitted to be better? For our purposes, the more complicated formulation of this question would be, "If it is beyond qualified denial that the educated would rule more wisely, then must it be beyond qualified denial that the consequences of their extra ruling power are better?" The question poses a challenge to the idea that the educated must be admitted (beyond reasonable denial) to be wiser rulers. The reason is that it is widely assumed that we are not bound to turn our moral judgment over to any other agency, to "surrender our judgment," as the phrase often goes.[18] Put in our terms, it is implausible to suppose that if certain changes are the result of extra voting power by the well educated, then it cannot reasonably be denied that those changes must be for the best. It is not unreasonable or disqualified to refrain from drawing a substantive moral conclusion merely on the grounds that it is the outcome or opinion of a purportedly expert procedure or agency. Suppose we make this a part of our conception of qualified and disqualified considerations: deference to some other agency on substantial moral matters is open to qualified denial.

If deference can reasonably be refused, then the following argument may seem to be available against Mill: whatever the overall long-run effect turns out to be of giving more votes to the well educated, it will not be disqualified to deny that it is for the best. But if they were wiser, then the overall long-run effect would be for the best. Therefore, it is not disqualified to deny that the well educated are wiser. So, Mill's defense of the plural voting scheme is not generally acceptable in the requisite sense—not "such as can be understood and accepted by the general conscience and understanding," as Mill puts the requirement.[19]

This would be useful in turning back the plural voting scheme, but if it could do that, it could also turn back a large chunk of epistemic political argumentation. Notice that the same kind of argument could be used to show that it is open to qualified denial that even universally good education promotes wise rule in a democracy. Again, once the long-term effect is clear, must we take that as a basis for the substantive moral conclusion that those changes are for the best? If nondeference is reasonable—not disqualified—then must we say the epistemic political value of education can also reasonably be denied? Moreover, the epistemic value of any arrangement at all would fit into the same template, not just arrangements involving education. If Mill's plural voting loses on these grounds, perhaps the whole epistemic dimension of political argumentation loses, too.

I think the epistemic approach, including Mill's, can be saved from this objection. The question would then arise whether Mill's proposal can be defeated in a way that leaves other epistemic lines of argument available. For present purposes, this might mean especially leaving intact the proposition that it is beyond qualified denial that some certain good education promotes wise rule. I will turn to a strategy that attempts to do that in the next section. First, why does this more general indictment of the epistemic approach fail?

It is easy to see that a single short-run outcome of a ruling arrangement (e.g., extra votes for the well educated) can resist deference, since the arrangement can be assumed to be fallible, even if it is better than others. So, any particular outcome might reasonably be held to be an error. Things look more difficult when we turn to the long-run overall effect of the arrangement. If it is not, on balance, better, the arrangement must not tend to better rule after all. Accordingly, if the long-run effect of privileging, say, the literate can reasonably be denied to be better, then the tendency of the arrangement to rule better can also reasonably be denied.

But the long run never comes. At any point in time it could be held that the effects so far are only temporary, and so not necessarily for the best. It is true that any adequate argument for the supposedly superior arrangement must employ a time horizon in which the benefits have a realistic chance of being reaped. But the point remains that at the end of any such finite period, it could always be denied that the arrangement's long-run tendencies have played out. It could yet be held that with more time it would perform for the best, but so far it has not. When one arrangement is held to perform better than another, this need not mean that it is *certain* to do so over any finite period of time, but only that it is (to some degree) likely to do so. So at any time after the arrangement is instituted, a person who thinks that so far the effects (compared with the alternative arrangement) are not for the better is not thereby committed to denying that the arrangement is superior to the alternative, in tending to produce better outcomes. So at no time will anyone be faced with the choice of deferring or denying the arrangement's superiority.

This does not fully dispose of the worry about deference, I suppose. If an arrangement is held to be very much better, and very much time has passed, is it *then* unreasonable to refuse to defer? My intuitions still rebel at the idea, but it is deeply puzzling why this should be.[20] Here I only hope to have shown that in the context of epistemic arguments for political arrangements, deference could usually be reasonably avoided even while accepting the superior tendencies of the arrangement.

Recall the complex polemical situation. This saves Mill's plural voting scheme, so far, whereas I hope to defeat it. On the other hand, it does so in a way that also saves the whole prospect of justifying any political arrangement on grounds of its politically epistemic value, such as, for example, generally improved education, or other institutional arrangements such as advocates of deliberative democracy might recommend. The question, now, is whether the case for plural voting can be defeated on other grounds, without defeating the epistemic approach wholesale.

THE DEMOGRAPHIC OBJECTION

In a society in which some have that education and others do not, those who do might yet, on balance, be no better able to rule wisely than others owing to the other epistemically detrimental features of the group. To see the general possibility, suppose that, for some reason, the people who sought education were, statistically, more racist than others even after education. Then, even though the education improves their ability to rule wisely, it would not follow that the educated are better able to rule than others, since their racism might plausibly be held to nullify the epistemic advantage their education might have given them.

Here, then, is a general form of objection to giving the educated more votes, which is compatible with accepting that a good education makes its recipients better able to rule wisely:

> The demographic objection: The educated portion of the populace may disproportionately have epistemically damaging features that countervail the admitted epistemic benefits of education.

A common reaction to Mill's plural voting scheme for those with university degrees has this general form. In our society, it is pointed out, having such a degree is disproportionately the privilege of members of certain races, classes, and (formerly) genders. Even if we grant, for the sake of argument, that everyone acts with goodwill rather than with neglect for the interests of others, people are inevitably biased by their race, class, and gender. Giving extra votes to certain of these groups only compounds the effect of these biases, damaging the expected quality of collective decisions. Exactly what is meant by bias here, and how it leads to increased collective error, would need more careful explanation, but I accept this as a powerful objection.

The demographic objection is also among the best reasons for repudiating literacy tests of the kind that were once employed in the American South, and banned by the Voting Rights Act of 1965. Many people apparently objected to such tests on less epistemic grounds, especially grounds of procedural fairness, but the epistemic objection is also available and powerful: indirectly disenfranchising poor southern blacks by formally disenfranchising citizens who failed certain literacy tests could reasonably be held to deprive the process of an epistemically important perspective on a leading form of injustice. It seems an important consideration even if (as Mill must think) no appropriate standard of procedural fairness would be violated and even if we had reason to assume that those entitled to vote gave full and fair weight to the interests of everyone, to the best of their ability, limited only by their knowledge and experience of what those interests are.

The objection to plural votes for the educated does not require all qualified (e.g., reasonable) citizens to accept the epistemic claims in this demographic argument. It is enough if it is not disqualified (unreasonable) to hold them. In that case, it can reasonably be denied that the educated, as things are, are better able to rule wisely than others. This blocks the availability of the epistocratic rationale, even if it is also qualified to disagree and think that the educated are, even under these conditions, likely to rule more wisely than others. The reasonableness of *denying* this is decisive according to the requirement we have set ourselves: to have a justification for ruling arrangements that is, in this sense, generally acceptable.

As I have stated it, the demographic objection to giving more votes to the educated could be avoided by demographically correcting the group given extra votes. If the problem is an underrepresentation of certain races, classes, and genders, it might yet be possible to select from the educated a subset in which those groups are properly represented (say, in proportion to their presence in the general population). This only works if there are enough members of these groups among the educated, but suppose there are. We select a sample of those who have the benefits of education, and then exclude some of them selectively in order to avoid overrepresentation of any race, class, or gender. Then we give the resulting group extra votes. This deprives the skeptics of their stated reasons for doubting the epistemic superiority of the group that is given more votes. Is this the end of the demographic objection?

Consider a doubter, who points out that even though race, class, and gender have been demographically corrected in the privileged group, we could still ask about religion. Well, we could empirically check to see if there is a significant distortion of the representation of certain religious groups. Then, if there is, we could correct for it in our selection from among the educated. Problem solved. But, the doubter continues, what about sexual orientation? OK, let us check and then fix it if necessary.

But now consider a doubter who alleges that among the privileged group there are not too many whites or men, but there are disproportionately many racists, or sexists. This might not be empirically testable, at least in realistic practice, even if it is true. Call these *empirically latent* features. The claim that by disenfranchising poor southern blacks we would do serious epistemic damage to the democratic process might also be claiming such an empirically latent feature of the arrangement, its truth being impossible to convincingly confirm or disconfirm empirically. And yet, that empirical inscrutability is not clearly enough to disqualify the objection either. The question is not whether it is true that such damage would be done, but whether that view is beyond the pale. We are not carrying a conception of the boundaries of the reasonable or the qualified that we can apply to cases, and so we cannot evaluate the question in that mechanical way. It is worth asking, instead, what we would be committed to if we made the circle of qualification large enough to let this epistemic claim on behalf of poor blacks count as qualified, whether or not we think it is true.

It is hard to disqualify claims that assert empirically latent features of certain arrangements because they cannot be empirically refuted. On the other hand, surely a view should not be counted as qualified merely because it cannot be empirically refuted. Lots of crazy views about ghosts, or conspiracies, or motives, cannot realistically be empirically checked, but they are no less crazy for that. But the view, disputable though it may be, that the otherwise demographically corrected sample of the educated might still contain disproportionately many racists or sexists or people with certain other untestable biases is not like these. It is no less reasonable, perhaps, than someone suspecting that the educated are disproportionately liberal or conservative (and that this has untoward epistemic effects) even before there was any way to check it empirically. At least one might have decent, if disputable, reasons for thinking so.

Taking it a step further: suppose someone objects not on the ground of any particular suspected demographic distortion, but simply on the ground that there might well be one. He does not suspect racism or sexism specifically, but only that the demographically adjusted group of the educated still disproportionately have some epistemically distorting feature or other, some feature that travels with education and so gets indirectly and unintentionally selected for in this scheme. Call these appeals to *conjectural features*.

Consider the case of literacy. How could anyone object, Mill asked, to requiring of voters that they at least be literate?[21] Certainly, it is absurd to deny that a populace would tend to rule more wisely if more of its members were literate. So how can we deny that those who are literate will tend to rule more wisely than random (or than those who are not)? The feature of literacy travels with other features such as race and class in such a way that the overall epistemic effect can reasonably be held to be negative, despite the undeniable epistemic benefits of literacy considered alone. These epistemically significant correlates of literacy can be easily empirically confirmed. So now consider a revised literacy criterion: from the set of the literate, pull a demographically representative sample, removing the sample error with respect to race and class. Now give double voting power to everyone in the repaired sample, and so half as much to all illiterate citizens (and also to others who were excluded as a consequence of repairing the sample with respect to race and class). In this case, the cognized and demonstrable sample biases are removed, and the beneficial trait of literacy remains. My contention is that objections to this scheme on the conjectural grounds that there may remain important sample errors of which we are unaware are not so unreasonable that they should be disqualified. If this seems plausible in the case of a literacy criterion, why not also for any educational criterion?

On what grounds would we put this beyond the pale? It is not automatically qualified just because it cannot be empirically refuted, as I have said. Rather, given the actual history of ruling arrangements that privilege some citizens over others, it also need not be crazy, or based on ill will. I suppose we would want to hear more from someone who would object in this way, but I simply leave the question here.

I do not mean to propose that all objections should be qualified unless they are crazy or vicious; I doubt that would be an adequate approach. Rather, I mean only to raise the question: If objections based on latent or conjectural features of the group that is given more votes are to be disqualified, but they are not crazy or vicious, then on what grounds are they to be disqualified? Probably there are other ways to disqualify objections. I wonder if any of them apply to these objections.

The upshot is this: if objections based on latent and/or conjectural features of the privileged group are not disqualified (and if they are, on what grounds?), then the epistemic argument for privileging an adjusted set of the educated would not be available to justify such a policy, even if all agree that the kind of education in question does enable those who receive it to rule more wisely. I believe that any educational criterion for extra voting power would be open to qualified objections of this kind, and I take this to defeat the idea of an epistocracy of the educated.

Recall the worry we confronted in chapter 2, "Truth and Despotism,"[22] when arguing that the qualified rejectability of all invidious comparisons led to universal suffrage as a default position. The worry was that universal suffrage's merits might also be subject to qualified disagreement. As I argued there, departures from universal suffrage introduce an extra element of rule of some by others, and that element is subject to the qualified acceptability requirement, whereas its absence is not. Thus, universal suffrage is entitled to that default status. In this chapter, the question is not the denial of universal suffrage, but the unequal distribution of suffrage that is plural voting. Still, the argument applies pretty directly. Unequal suffrage introduces an element of rule of some by others that is not present under equal suffrage, and so equal suffrage has a kind of default status as departures are tested against the qualified acceptability requirement.

It is logically possible, of course, that even the improved education of the whole citizenry could have bad epistemic effects that cancel out the epistemically good effects. For example, suppose that by removing illiteracy we not only gain the improved judgment of a literate voting population, but also lose the perspective of illiterate people, something that might be of value in various contexts. This point helps to expose the structure of my argument.[23] The demographic objection, made more precise now, says that it is not disqualified to object to any educational criterion for extra votes on the ground that there might be epistemic value in the perspective of the (relatively) disenfranchised people. That is, the value is plausibly in the fact that they can inject into the process the perspective of some actual citizens or subjects. The loss of the illiterate perspective when there are no longer any illiterate citizens is epistemically more dubious, though I do not mean to deny it altogether. The question is whether it would be reasonable or qualified to deny that the gain from literacy outweighs the loss of the illiterate perspective. Without deriving it from any general theory of qualification or reasonableness, I proceed on the supposition that at this point the epistemic gain cannot be reasonably denied.

Is the Epistemic Value of Equal Voting Reasonably Rejectable?

I have argued that differential voting power on the basis of invidious epistemic comparisons is open to qualified objection. But, then, it looks as if the epistemic value of equal voting might also be rejectable for similar reasons. I am not offering any substantial theory of reasonable or qualified rejection from which this follows, but my argument about latent and conjectural features may be committed to it, and here is why. Suppose there is some argument for formally unequal voting power across certain groups. Suppose the argument is not based on invidious epistemic comparisons and so does not run afoul of the arguments presented here blocking such comparisons. The extra voting power that members of one group have is defended on some ground other than their greater wisdom. But now the question arises whether the lesser voting power of the other voters can be criticized on epistemic grounds. For an arbitrary example, suppose it is rural voters who are given fewer votes per person. Can we argue that there is a reasonable chance that by suppressing the power of rural citizens, political outcomes will tend to be skewed in favor of a distinctively urban viewpoint? This would be a criticism of their lesser voting power on epistemic grounds.

This form of argument for equal voting is very tempting, but it is apparently no better than the argument that the educated will rule more wisely. We are imagining that there is a reason for their lesser voting power even without assuming they are less wise. Suppose, for example, that they are authorized to vote only in some subset of the elections that urban citizens may vote in. Perhaps the reason is only to free them to perform other work (farming, etc.) upon which the society depends. So far, then, there is no invidious epistemic comparison. If there is reason to believe a group with less voting power will be taken advantage of by others since all will favor their own interests, then this may be a fine reason to give them equal voting power. I do not need to address this kind of argument, since this would not be an argument that relies on their having any special insight, but appeals more to motives of partiality. We can more clearly turn our view to a different model by supposing, unrealistically of course, that every voter addressed the common good and without any great bias in their own favor. Now ask what would be wrong with the half-time rural voting scheme? And consider, in this light, the tempting idea that the rural perspective is of epistemic value and is being discounted, thus tending to distort the outcomes.

This idea of the epistemically valuable rural perspective, possessed disproportionately by rural voters, is an invidious comparison. It is true that rural voters are not being held to be wiser overall, but only in certain respects. Still, this more limited invidious comparison must be just as vulnerable to the possibility of latent or conjectural features of an epistemically countervailing kind. Even if they do have a special insight other things equal, it is not unreasonable to worry that being rural might travel with certain insensitivities or limitations that countervail this insight's epistemic value all things considered. (Perhaps rural voters tend to be tradition-bound, or irrationally fond of open spaces, etc.)

One form of this appeal to a group's special insight is the argument that the victims of injustice are especially well located to have knowledge of what justice requires. My argument here rejects this move, and in this context it is useful to reflect on the damage of various kinds that might travel with the victim's insight into the nature of injustice.[24]

This case against topping up unequal votes is not, perhaps, as strong an argument as the case against extra votes for the educated. Claims for a group's overall epistemic superiority may resonate more justifiably with the history of bigotry, sexism, and the like than this more limited claim about a group's special insight. I am not sure we are forced, in the end, to block this latter kind of claim. But I want to steer clear of it if I can, and see whether this turns out to be too restrictive. This idea of "too restrictive" is not a judgment highly disciplined by theory. But if, for example, it becomes impossible to account for convictions that we think we ought to keep, we will think the argument went wrong somewhere. So, I am merely marking the present restrictive move—blocking the appeal to a group's special insight—as something open to reconsideration.[25] It is, in effect, granted to my opponent—who doubts that I can generate plausible results if I accept it—for the sake of argument.[26]

Neither equal voting nor departures from it can be defended, then, on the basis of invidious epistemic comparisons. If the task were to defend formally equal voting power for each citizen, we would need to turn to some non-epistemic consideration such as some suitable conception of procedural fairness or equal respect. The role of the epistemic dimension might recede considerably. My aim, though, is neither to defend formally equal voting power nor to criticize it. My limited aim is to rebut a Millean scheme of extra votes for the educated on the grounds of their greater wisdom. (And, of course, I hope the argument has more general application against a variety of epistocratic proposals, though I do not explore that very far.) Still, it may seem as though we would *eventually* have to resort to non-epistemic moral considerations to justify equal voting, and so this might seem like a dodge. But that supposes that we would eventually want to defend equal voting. I doubt this, for the following reasons. Here are two kinds of formally unequal voting arrangements that I am not sure I would wish to reject:

1. the formally greater voting power possessed by elected legislators, appointed officials, judges, et cetera,

2. the formally weightier voting power conferred by districting arrangements of various kinds, such as a Rhode Islander's greater power over the makeup of Congress and the election of the president than a New Yorker's.

So, arguments against unequal voting power that appeal to a group's special insight face the same problem as arguments for giving some especially wise group more votes: the feature by which the group is picked out for special treatment may indeed be undeniably of epistemic value, but reasonable worries can persist that this feature might travel with some latent or conjectural and epistemically countervailing feature. The same argument that I use to block Millean plural voting can be used against efforts to defend equal voting on the grounds of a discounted group's special insight. But equal voting is a questionable ideal, and defending it is no part of my aim.

To conclude this chapter: epistocracy of the educated is probably the most formidable proposal of a form of epistocracy that makes claims of political expertise that cannot be reasonably denied. Still, I think it fails because of the demographic objection. Even though we must all grant that a better education (somehow conceived) improves the ability to rule wisely, it is not unreasonable or disqualified to suspect that there will be other biasing features of the educated group, features that we have not yet identified and may not be able to test empirically, but which do more epistemic harm than education does good. It is not disqualified to disagree with such skepticism, of course. It is a matter on which there will be reasonable disagreement, and that is fatal to the proposal to use either position in justifying political arrangements. I take this to put the prospects for any form of epistocracy in very serious doubt.

The Irrelevance of the Jury Theorem

THERE IS A LONG TRADITION, at least since Aristotle, extolling the wisdom of groups. This, of course, exists alongside the long tradition denigrating the intelligence of common people. Aristotle gives early voice to both ideas when he says that common individuals are not very bright, but that collectively they are at least better, and possibly wise enough to rule politically.[1] In our own time, we have volumes of sophisticated demonstrations both of the ignorance of voters in modern democracies and of the variety of ways in which collectivities can make better decisions than the individuals they comprise.[2] In this chapter, we look at how collectivities can, under certain conditions, make better decisions than individuals, even without benefit of exchanging arguments, or perspectives, or, indeed, any communication at all. Certain mathematical facts establish just that, and democratic theorists have been intrigued. The most influential of these mathematical results is known as Condorcet's jury theorem.[3] After introducing it and showing briefly how it works, I wish to argue that it is too shaky a basis on which to ground the proposition that voters in democratic procedures tend to make good decisions. We will have to look elsewhere in order to support that proposition, a proposition that is crucial if the authority of democratically produced laws and policies is to be grounded partly in the epistemic value of those procedures, as epistemic proceduralism requires.

Suppose there are two options, and suppose each voter is independently 51 percent likely to choose the correct option (and 49 percent likely to choose the incorrect option): then among a group of 1,000 voters, the probability that the majority will vote for the correct option is approximately 69 percent. If the number of voters is increased to 10,000, then that probability rises to virtual certainty: 99.97 percent. The probability that the majority will support the correct option tends toward certainty as the number of voters approaches infinity. Thus, among electorates of even just moderate-sized towns, much less large nations, the majority is almost certain to choose the right option, just so long as each voter is independently just a little better than random in a two-option choice.[4]

The proof of this striking result is fairly simple, and it is worth presenting an informal version here. Begin with the fact that while a fair coin flipped a few times is not likely to produce a very equal head/tail ratio, with more tosses the ratio becomes more even. With just a few tosses, an outcome of, say, 70 percent heads and 30 percent tails would not be shocking. But with many tosses of a fair coin, a 70/30 split is almost out of the question. With enough tosses it becomes certain that the division will be almost exactly 50/50. This "law of large numbers" is the core of the proof of the jury theorem.

Now change the coin from a fair one to one weighted slightly in favor of heads, so in each toss it has a 51 percent chance of being heads. Now with enough tosses the percentage of heads is certain to be almost exactly 51 percent. The reason is just the same as the reason a fair coin tossed many times produced very nearly a 50 percent split. The more tosses, the closer to exactly 51 percent this weighted coin is likely to be. Now obviously the same would be true if instead of one coin flipped repeatedly, we considered many coins, all weighted the same way, each having a 51 percent chance of coming up heads. The more coins we flipped, the closer the frequency of heads would come to exactly 51 percent. Obviously, too, the same would be true if we had individual voters instead of coins, where each will say either "heads" or "tails," but each has a 51 percent chance of saying "heads." The more such voters, the closer the frequency of "heads" answers would come to exactly 51 percent. Here is the payoff: if the frequency of "heads" is bound to be almost exactly 51 percent, then, of course, it is even more certain to be over 50 percent. So the chance that at least a majority will say "heads" is astronomical—approaching 1, or a 100 percent chance—if the group is large. It gets higher with the size of the group. It is also plainly higher if instead of 51 percent, each voter (or coin) has an even higher chance of saying "heads," say 55 percent or 75 percent.

So if each voter has an individual likelihood above 50 percent (call it $(50+n)$ percent) of giving the correct answer (whatever it is) to a dichotomous choice (heads/tails, yes/no, true/false, better/worse, etc.), then in a large group the percentage giving the correct answer is bound to be exceedingly close to ($50+n$ percent). Therefore, the chance that it will be *greater than 50 percent* is even higher, approximating certainty as the group gets larger or the voters are better. In summary, concentrating on our starting example, if voters are each 51 percent likely to be correct, then in a large number of voters it is almost certain that almost exactly 51 percent will be correct, and so even more certain that more than 50 percent will be correct. Under these assumptions, it is very likely that a proposal winning majority support is very likely to be the best or correct proposal.

The results are very much the same if we weaken the assumption that all voters have the same competence, but assume only an average competence above 50 percent, so long as the individual competences that produce this average are distributed normally around the average. Abnormal distributions change the results significantly, sometimes for better, sometimes for worse.

INDEPENDENCE

The mathematical result is beyond dispute, but it applies only under certain conditions. One is that enough of the votes must be statistically independent. This is often misunderstood. On the overly pessimistic side, many have said this cannot be met, since there will always be lots of influence one on another. Few will be independent of each other. What the theorem requires, though, is not causal independence, but statistical independence. Statistical independence means that the probability of one voter, say Joe, getting the right answer is exactly equal to the probability of Joe getting the right answer given that Jane did. Joe's and Jane's chances of being correct are independent of each other if neither of them gets a higher chance of being correct given that the other is correct.

The jury theorem's independence requirement often inspires either too much optimism or too much pessimism. On the overly optimistic side, some have said that all that is required is that enough voters make up their own minds rather than intentionally altering their votes to follow some opinion leader.[5] But that is clearly not enough. It is logically possible for voters each of whom makes up his or her own mind to vote identically time after time. If too many voters did that, it would radically violate the independence requirements of the jury theorem, which mathematically depends only on correlations, not intentions. Suppose, for example, that Joe and Jane each had a competence of .6, a 60 percent chance of getting the right answer. If they always vote the same way, then Jane's getting the right answer would guarantee that Joe got the right answer. The probability of Joe doing so given that Jane did so would be 1. Since this is greater than the simple probability that Joe gets the right answer (which is Joe's competence, or .6), independence would be violated. It is violated whether or not Joe or Jane based their votes on those of each other. Perhaps they are just very much alike. Voters making up their own minds is not what independence means for purposes of the jury theorem.

We have seen that voters making up their own minds does not guarantee statistical independence. It is also true that voters who do not make up their own minds might yet be statistically independent. Statistical independence is compatible with some degree of deference to opinion leaders.[6] That is, even if several voters are more inclined to vote for A if a certain pundit they all like supports A, this does not yet violate their statistical independence. The pundit is a clear common causal influence on these voters, and so in a certain sense their votes are not causally independent. Nevertheless, they can all defer to this pundit to a significant extent and remain statistically independent, so long as each has some competence with respect to knowing when to defer and when not to defer. That is, if two voters each has a competence that is higher than their fidelity to the pundit (fidelity of .6 means a voter agrees with the pundit 60 percent of the time), then the voters remain statistically independent of each other despite their both being influenced by the pundit. Moreover, since the pundit might be smart, the voters' deference can improve their own competence, with beneficial effects on group competence.

Making up one's own mind is not the issue. The simple fact that voters will share common influences is not fatal to the jury theorem's applicability to democracy, and sometimes enhances it. How much influence across voters the theorem can tolerate, and how much is present in any realistic democracy, are questions that are not yet well understood. The lesson, for now, is that if there is a problem about applying the theorem to democracy, we do not yet have enough reason to think that the problem is a failure of voter independence.

Beyond Binary Choice

In its classic form as proven by Condorcet, the jury theorem explicitly applies only to binary choices such as yes/no, true/false, better/worse.[7] This can look very restrictive. Political choices are complicated, and the narrowing of choices down to two is just the last stage in a process that starts with many more. On the other hand, elections and referenda do often present themselves as binary. Should the law be passed or not?

Should this person be president or that one? Should the sales tax be raised or not? Obviously, at some earlier point there were far more than two things that might be done. So the binary choice condition would not apply at those earlier times. But whatever process leads to the choices I just listed, the binary choice precondition is, starting at that point, apparently fully met.

Nevertheless, it is enormously important if the binary choice condition can be relaxed. It turns out that, in a sense, it can. There are several results along these lines, one of which is proven by Goodin and List.[8] The reasoning cannot be presented here, but the main conclusion of their argument is this: when there are three or more choices, if each voter is more likely to vote for the (objectively) best alternative than she is to vote for any of the other alternatives, the chance that the best alternative will win a plurality increases with the size of the group of voters.

One underwhelming result is that the correct answer is more likely to win than any other single alternative. This is not much use when there are several other alternatives, since their probabilities of winning are cumulative. Even if the correct answer has a better chance than any other answer, the chance of it winning might be far less than the chance of some erroneous answer or other winning. Another result of questionable use for our purposes is that the chance of a plurality getting the right answer climbs quickly with the size of the group if voters' individual competences are better than .5. But, of course, .5 is not a very interesting number when the alternatives are three or more in number.[9] It would be a competence substantially better than random, and so it is a substantial assumption that would need some warrant.

The most interesting aspect of the result is the fact that the chance of the correct answer winning increases with the size of the group, approaching a group competence of 1, or infallibility. This fact seems to hold true even for the crucial case where voters are only slightly better than random, being only slightly more likely to vote for the correct answer than for any other single answer. The stunning thing about the classic binary choice theorem is that, for example, the group competence gets above .97 even where the number of voters is only the size of a small town (10,000), so long as voters have a competence of at least .51. What if there are three alternatives rather than just two? In a group of 1,001 voters with three alternatives, and voters just slightly better than random (.34 chance of the right answer, .33 for each of the wrong answers), the chance of the best alternative winning a plurality is .489, not an enormous leap from the .407 achieved by 301 voters (and the correct answer would still lose more often than it would win). So far, there is no clear explanation of how large a group must be before voters who are just barely better than random would be virtually certain, or even more likely than not, to give the correct answer a plurality when there are more than two alternatives.

I do not want to exaggerate these limitations of the nonbinary applications of the jury theorem. First, we do know that group competence approaches infallibility at some size of the electorate even with just barely better than random individual competence, and many democratic contexts involve much larger numbers of voters than those studied so far. So group competence might well turn out to be very high in those cases.[10] Second, some epistemic theories do not require astronomical group competence. Epistemic proceduralism, in fact, requires only that the group be better than random, and the best (or nearly so) so far as can be established in a way that does not contradict any qualified point of view. The extension to three or more alternatives is certainly progress. The irrelevance of the jury theorem, including extended versions, for our purposes, rests on the difficulty of assuming individual competence that is at least better than random. This in turn rests on two considerations, which I turn to next. One is that systematic thinkers often make systematic errors. The other is what I call the *disjunction problem*.

The Illusiveness of Random Individual Competence

A deeper worry, one that applies in both the case of binary choice and for choices between three or more alternatives, concerns the assumption that voters are better than random. Individual voters might indeed be better than random, but this is not obvious. Factual errors, prejudice, and other factors could, for all we know, outweigh the average voter's margin of better-than-random competence, at least on matters that are sufficiently contested that they end up being settled by a vote. Democrats and Republicans in Congress systematically vote against each other on many issues. Which party should we be sure is at least a little better than random? If they oppose each other often enough, they cannot both be better than random. If one party is, the other party's competence is 1 minus the first party's competence, which must be less than random. But if, as I think, either party could easily be worse than random, then it is hardly absurd to think that due to the same kinds of biases or errors, the average congressperson could have been even worse than random.[11]

Systematic individual biases and errors are, of course, very common, and they represent one kind of challenge that needs to be met before individual competence could be assumed to be at least random. There is a second kind of challenge to that assumption, which I will call the *disjunction problem*. Before we avail ourselves of the assumption that voters are at least a little better than random, we would need to know what random competence would be. In the Condorcetian analysis, what random competence means when there are k alternatives is getting the correct answer with a probability of $1/k$. Two alternatives give a random competence of ½, or .5; four alternatives, ¼ or .25; and so on. Consider a choice among three alternatives: A, B, and C. If we suppose, a priori, that voters are a little better than random, we might let them have, say, a .34 chance of getting the right answer and a .33 chance of each of the wrong answers. But suppose we presented the choice differently: alternative A versus the disjunction of B or C. By leaving the choice between B and C for later, the choice is now binary. Since the choice is now a binary one, are we suddenly entitled to suppose voters must be at least a little better than .5? Is it a minimal, modest assumption that they are more likely than .5 to choose A, which is the right answer? Quite a promotion.

To put the point more precisely, for a set of k alternatives, assuming a competence of $1/k$ implies that if any of the alternatives were disaggregated (showing that it was actually disjunctive) to create $k+n$ alternatives, competence would be somewhat greater than $1/(k+n)$, that is, somewhat better than random for that choice set. It is as if the assumption that looked weak has just turned out to be stronger. An assumption of random competence over k alternatives is, in effect, also an assumption of *better* than random competence for the embedded $k+n$ alternatives. Indeed, if the number of disjuncts is significant as compared with k, then a competence of $1/k$ is *much* better than random for the set of $k+n$.

What this shows is that, since some of a set of alternatives are often really disjuncts, there is no principled sense in which it is a weak or obvious assumption to suppose individuals have better than random competence over a given set of alternatives. Consider the proverbial blind men and the elephant. Each can touch a different part, but this is not enough to identify the kind of animal before them. If they are asked whether the animal before them is an elephant, they are given a binary choice: yes/no. But "no" is the answer they should give if they think it is any animal other than an elephant. "No" means "hippo, or rhino, or mule, or horse . . ." To choose "yes" at the "random" rate of .5 they would need some strong suspicion that it is an elephant rather than *any* of the other possibilities. A competence of .5 would be quite high given that there might be dozens of animals it could be given the little each of them knows. Would an assumption of .5 competence be a blind, dumb, random competence because there are two choices, and even a random device would perform at .5? Or would it be a rather high competence in light of all the possible animals they might be faced with? A random device would perform at .5, but a thinking person might well perform well below that, and for good reasons. Odds are (or might be), given what they know, that it is something other than an elephant. Knowing that the men have a binary choice does not automatically allow us to assume that unless something has gone badly wrong they should have a competence of .5.

This problem might seem limited to the special case in which at least one of the alternatives is disjunctive. But the selection of almost any law or policy leaves significantly different possible ways of instantiating it, not just in the means employed, but also the ends. Should we build a bridge over the channel or not? If so, should it be a four-lane, a two-lane, built now, or later? And so on. So many political alternatives, as presented for social choice, are disjunctive, and so the disjuncts could have been presented as separate choices, giving rise to the difficulty I have pointed to. This difficulty about how to count alternatives raises questions about the a priori assumption that voters can be presumed, for Condorcetian purposes, to be at least a little better than random. And without that assumption, or some substantive support for the competence assumption, the jury theorem gets us nothing.

BAYES IN BRIEF

There is another mathematical approach to group competence, relying on Bayes' theorem.[12] The two main problems I have counted against the jury theorem apply there as well. On the Bayesian approach, each voter takes the fact that many others voted for p as evidence in favor of p. As each revises her own estimation of the probability of p upward in accordance with this evidence, voters bootstrap each other up to very high levels of confidence that p is that case. This Bayesian approach requires that participants take each other to have a competence higher than random. But just as before, the idea of random competence depends on there being some privileged way to count alternatives, and this is the first problem. As we saw earlier, political choices are often disjunctive, and that provides many different ways the choice might be presented. For this reason, there is no sense in which a "random" competence over some particular way of presenting the alternatives can be counted as a weak assumption, as I argued earlier. Also, of course, there are many sources of systematic error or bias that allow for the possibility that voters are very often pervasively worse than random. Again, the assumption that voters are better than random is not freely available, but would need some argument. The stance I have argued for here with respect to the jury theorem applies without alteration to the Bayesian approach to democratic group competence.

Communication

The jury theorem makes no use of interpersonal communication. The Bayesian model has a small social element: participants must be able to revise their opinions in light of information about how many people had certain opinions in the last round. Still, knowing the results of a poll or a vote and using it as data—as Bayesian participants do—is still nothing like hearing people explain their opinions. Discussion is still utterly absent from the model. If the blind men can talk with each other, there is some hope that they can figure out that the object is an elephant, though none could do this alone. But neither the jury theorem nor Bayes' theorem actually models the blind men sharing their perspectives. Under majority rule if they were better than random individually, the group (especially if it is large) will have a surprisingly high chance of being correct. But, of course, they will not be individually very competent, since we know they are each inclined to say that, no, it is not an elephant. That is the end of that story from the jury theorem's point of view. Bayes' theorem adds a layer. After the first round of opinions, each should revise his opinion in the direction of the majority. But this is clearly not going to help anything. If anyone had been suspecting it was an elephant, the large majority against them would disabuse them of that notion, on Bayesian reasoning. Bayesian blind men would not figure out that it was an elephant simply by wondering whether it is, looking at the results, and updating their probabilities. They would

231

need to talk to each other, something absent from both the Bayesian and the Condorcetian model.

Aristotle makes several remarks that sound very much like the elephant analogy:

> The many, of whom each individual is but an ordinary person, when they meet together may very likely be better than the few good, if regarded not individually but collectively, just as a feast to which many contribute is better than a dinner provided out of a single purse. For each individual among the many has a share of virtue and prudence, and when they meet together, they become in a manner one man, who has many feet, and hands, and senses.[13]

At a feast the dishes are publicly shared and appreciated in combination. This is an utterly different epistemic model from the jury theorem. The mathematics of the jury theorem is not really driven by the bringing together of different parts of a puzzle, but simply by the statistical fact that the fraction of a large group that will vote yes will come very close to the probability the individuals have of voting yes. It is a mathematical fact that applies to coin flips in exactly the same way it applies to votes. A large number of weighted coins, each of which has, say, a 51 percent chance of turning up heads, will produce very close to 51 percent heads. Should we say that the coins bring their different perspectives together? Is each coin like one of the blind men in the elephant story? This is clearly a mistake. The reason this is important is that it is very natural and plausible to think that if democracy has any epistemic value it is partly to do with the sharing of diverse perspectives. Many have suggested that the jury theorem is a mathematical formalization of that very mechanism. The coin-flip example shows, I hope, that it simply is not. And this, in turn, is important if I am right that the jury theorem is really not available for these democratic uses owing to the disjunction problem and other problems about the assumption of better-than-random voter competence. We should not conclude from this that the idea of sharing perspectives turns out to be unavailable. The jury theorem, which is unavailable, is a different idea altogether.

THE DISJUNCTION PROBLEM AND EPISTEMIC PROCEDURALISM

According to epistemic proceduralism, under the right conditions, democratic decisions have their legitimacy and authority partly because of a publicly recognizable tendency to make good decisions, at least better than a random procedure. The case for epistemic proceduralism escapes the critique I have laid out against the statistical approaches for the following reasons.

The disjunction problem shows that there is no such thing as an obvious or trivial assumption that voters are better than random. Epistemic proceduralism, however, never makes such an assumption. Rather, argument is offered for the quality of group competence directly, and not in a way that first assumes any particular relation between individual competence and random competence. We do still need to use the idea of better-than-random competence in one way, because that is what epistemic proceduralism requires of group competence. After all, if group competence was not even better than random, then why not choose randomly? So, does the disjunction problem apply again at this level?

First, notice that the disjunction problem does not show that there is no way to define random competence, but only that there is no privileged way to count alternatives that would warrant the intuitive thought that individuals must be at least better than random. Now, we could make the same charge against the idea that the group must be at least better than random. If there are four alternatives presented, then "better than random" means better than .25. But it is odd to think that we can freely assume that if three of the four alternatives are grouped into one disjunctive alternative, leaving only two alternatives, the group competence automatically goes up to .5. That is the challenge of the disjunction problem posed at the group level.

Recall, though, that the lesson of the disjunction problem is that no competence assumption is available, so to speak, for free. We can choose one way of defining random competence, such as the performance of a device randomly selecting from the alternatives however they are actually presented. What we cannot do is go on to assume that people or groups must obviously be at least that good. It is necessary to point to actual mechanisms or other reasons to believe that individuals or groups will actually perform that well. The mechanism I appeal to is interpersonal communication and reasoning about the question at hand. So, consider the blind men and the elephant. On the question "Is it an elephant?" they would individually be no better than random (or worse). Neither the jury theorem nor a Bayesian process of updating beliefs in light of the beliefs of others would yield a group competence above random. But if they communicate with each other, it is highly likely that they would figure out that it was an elephant.

Are we sneaking the jury theorem in by the back door? Suppose we accepted this and said that under proper conditions of communication the group competence on the elephant question, after communication, would be better than random. It follows by the jury theorem that under those same conditions, after communication, individual competence would be better than random. If it were not, then the group competence could not be, as the theorem shows. Someone might say that the jury theorem is playing a crucial role here, since the communication pushes the group competence above random only by pushing individual competence above random and aggregating individual judgments. The jury theorem, though, is about amplifying individual competence to a much higher group competence, and that kind of amplification is no part of the story of the communicating blind men. All the jury theorem adds to our story is the fairly uninteresting fact that if the group competence is above random, then individual competence will also be above random, albeit significantly lower than the group competence. The disjunction problem is avoided because at no point do we avail ourselves of the intuition that the group or the individuals must naturally be better than random. The blind men trying to identify the elephant are individually hopeless. Even so, we expect communication (under the right conditions) to tend to make the individuals and the group better than random (the individuals less so than the group). We define one interpretation for random competence: as good as a random device selecting from the alternatives however they are actually presented. But we do not simply assume individuals or groups are this good. We argue for it on the basis of the epistemic value of communication. Since the disjunction problem only counts against the free assumption of competence better than random, it is not a problem for our approach.

Obviously, I have not given any detailed account of how and when reasoning together will improve group competence. In many settings there are dynamics such as "groupthink," and polarization effects that can undo the epistemic potential of thinking together.[14] Letting the blind men communicate is only meant to illustrate how an account of this kind could provide a basis for the epistemic value of group deliberation, without in any way relying on the jury theorem's competence-amplifying effects, and without making the assumption—discredited by the disjunction problem—that competence above random can be taken for granted.

We should remember that epistemic proceduralism would need it to be the case that group competence was better than random in a certain way, though not simply by getting more correct answers than random. Rather, good group competence on the most important issues could outweigh poor performance on less important matters. So what we would need is not better-than-random competence overall, but an above-random score when the value of decisions is given weight proportional to their importance. As I have discussed in chapter 9 ("How Would Democracy Know?"), we can make this model relatively tractable by listing a set of especially important matters, what I call *primary bads* to be avoided, and then by a mixture of argument and conjecture suppose that sufficiently good competence here will translate to better-than-random weighted score overall. The upshot is that even though epistemic proceduralism does not need the same assumption of above-random competence as the jury theorem, it does still need above-random competence, somehow interpreted, when it comes to avoiding primary bads. It is not yet clear, then, how epistemic proceduralism escapes the force of the critique I have mounted of the jury theorem approach.

In order to extrapolate from good group performance on primary bads to an above-random weighted group score generally, either we need to assume that group performance on other less important matters is no worse than random, or we need to suppose that group performance on primary bads is enough better than random that even poor performance elsewhere would not prevent the weighted score from being above random. I think there is nothing trivial or minimal about assuming that competence on other matters is at least random. One reason is the disjunction problem, and I will not repeat it here. But there is also the less technical point that it is easy to be worse than random if one has a systematic bias, or one's information is faulty in a crucial way. A person performing worse than random on some type of cognitive task is not really much more mysterious than a coin persistently getting heads less then half the time. It must not be a fair coin, and the person must be biased or misinformed or some such thing. So, we are left needing to maintain that group performance on important issues (avoiding primary bads) is, under the favorable but possible conditions that epistemic proceduralism needs, and after public deliberation of certain kinds, enough better than random to outweigh, in the weighted score, any especially poor performance by the group in other areas.

It is true, of course, that if group performance on primary bads is held to be not just above random, but some significant amount above random, then the jury theorem would entail that individual competence is not just above random, but significantly above random (though by a smaller margin than group competence is above random). But it is important to see that this does not somehow make the jury theorem available after all. This still does not give the jury theorem any way to start with information about individual competence and get new information about high group competence. Our reasoning has gone in the reverse order.

Conclusion

There is good reason to turn our focus away from aggregating votes and toward the formation of the attitudes that go into voting. This is an old refrain that deliberative democrats use against models that understand voting as expressing preferences, but it turns out to be appropriate where votes are understood as expressing judgments, too. The leading models that take an aggregative approach to judgments, in hopes of showing they produce a collective wisdom—the jury theorem, Bayes' theorem, and so on—are simply not entitled to the assumptions they need about individual competence. The epistemic engine of democracy will have to lie elsewhere, somewhere that explains how individual judgments come to have the requisite quality.

Another influential explanation of how democracy might have epistemic value draws on an analogy between democratic procedures and a contractualist theory of rightness or justice. In the next chapter we will see that this, too, falls short.

Rejecting the Democracy/Contractualism Analogy

IN THE LAST CHAPTER I argued that epistemic claims for democracy cannot be supported by appeal to Condorcet's jury theorem. In this chapter I criticize a second influential way of arguing that democracy could have epistemic value, specifically on questions of right or justice. The approach I have in mind asserts what I shall call a *democracy/contractualism analogy*. Justice is understood along contractualist lines, to be explained later. Then outcomes of proper democratic arrangements are held to track justice (call this the *tracking claim*), and to do so because they have a structural similarity to the hypothetical choice situation posited in contractualism.

Analogy theories, as I will call them, accept that democracy tracks justice partly because citizens are motivated non-egoistically and in a morally significant way. Given the profound disanalogies between the hypothetical contractual situation and even admirable contexts of democratic social choice, there is no such adequate analogy. Whether actual democratic procedures, or any conceivable democratic procedures, might have justice-promoting tendencies (something I do not investigate in this chapter), I argue that there is no support for this supposition in a democracy/contractualism analogy.[1]

THE ANALOGY

Scanlon's influential contractualist view says that "an act is wrong if its performance under the circumstances would be disallowed by any set of principles for the general regulation of behavior that no one could reasonably reject as a basis for informed, unforced general agreement."[2] Conceived more generally, contractualism holds that the content of justice or right is given by what would be agreed upon by participants in a hypothetical collective choice procedure of some specified kind, including elements that reflect certain moral considerations and not only instrumental reasoning. However, different theorists use different versions of the general contractualist idea. I use the term here to cover a cluster of views that resemble Scanlon's in certain ways.

The democracy/contractualism analogy hopes to answer a standard challenge for the claim that democratic procedures might promote good or just outcomes. With so much disagreement about what is just, how could there be a generally acceptable argument that certain arrangements promote justice? Even if we assume contractualism, and even some particular version of it, there might be disagreement, some of it entirely reasonable, about what principles of justice would be supported by contractualism. As we have seen, some philosophers, especially Rawls, argue that political power can only be justified by appeal to considerations that are beyond reasonable objection, and we are adopting such a constraint in the defense of epistemic proceduralism.[3] Since this is a criterion of what counts as a successful justification, it constrains justifications offered by philosophers as well as by ordinary citizens. Yet others require general acceptability of principles on other grounds such as simple stability. A general acceptability requirement of any such kind would imply that no reasonably disputable interpretation of contractualist justice can be appealed to in a justification hoping to show that a certain political arrangement tends to produce just laws and policy. Because there is some reasonable or qualified disagreement about justice itself, there is bound to be similar disagreement about whether certain political procedures will tend to promote just outcomes.

On the other hand, it cannot simply be assumed that no propositions of justice are acceptable beyond qualified disagreement, even if many are not. I will assume, for example, that famine that could be easily avoided without significant burdens to anyone is severely unjust, and that this is unreasonable to deny. On other matters, such as whether property and taxation systems should work to promote the well-being of the least well-off, or whether recreational drugs ought to be legally forbidden, assume for the sake of argument that there are reasonable objections. The objections, then, would block the use of these views in political justification.

Suppose, then, that because of qualified controversy about the substance of justice, the public comparison of political arrangements with respect to justice must proceed, at least partly, without testing performance by particular judgments of substantive justice. It may be initially puzzling how such a view is to proceed. How could a political procedure be thought to track justice unless it were known what is just and what is not? A contractualist account of justice tempts the following answer:

> *Similar procedures have similar outcomes*: An actual choice procedure will tend to track justice if it is sufficiently like the hypothetical choice procedure contractualism employs in order to explicate the content of justice.

If contractualism itself is taken for granted, this seems to be beyond dispute—its truth guaranteed by the word *sufficiently*—but the question is what guidance it provides for the design of actual institutions. Take for granted that one important goal in the design of democratic institutions is that they promote decisions or outcomes that are just or right by contractualist standards.[4] Call that achievement, if and where it exists,

> *Outcome similarity*: Actual democratic procedures tend to produce decisions that would be produced in an ideal hypothetical contractualist situation.

A natural idea to pursue, then, is the thesis that outcome similarity can realistically be achieved by promoting procedural similarity.

> *Democracy/contractualism analogy*: A tendency of actual democratic procedures to produce outcomes that are right by contractualist standards can realistically be pursued by promoting the similarity (in certain respects) of actual procedures to the procedure in the hypothetical contractualist situation.

This strategy has the potential to ground the claim that democratic procedures track justice even without needing to rely on any claims about what is just and what is not; it is formal in that sense, and so can avoid, if necessary, whatever reasonable controversy there might be about the more specific content of justice. However, some less controversial propositions about justice remain available as test cases. We should not accept the democracy/contractualism analogy if things go too far wrong in these central cases—if, for example, democratic procedures modeled on the contractualist procedure have no tendency to produce the decisions necessary to avoid (avoidable) famine. I will argue that the analogy should be rejected for just this reason.

Several philosophers have suggested this analogy.[5] John Rawls writes, in *Political Liberalism*:

> The guarantee of fair value for political liberties is included in the first principle of justice because it is essential in order to establish just legisla-

239

tion and also to make sure that the fair political process specified by the constitution is open to everyone on a basis of rough equality. *The idea is to incorporate into the basic structure of society an effective political procedure which mirrors in that structure the fair representation of persons achieved by the original position.*[6]

Here Rawls supports the claim that certain political liberties, along with what he calls their fair value (not just their formal equality), will tend better to track justice by virtue of the structural similarity between political procedures and the hypothetical choice procedure in the original position.

A brief note on the term "contractualism": As I am using the term,[7] Rawls is the most influential of the contractualists, but his version of the hypothetical choice situation is not normally used among those who employ a democracy/contractualism analogy. The reason is surely that the "veil of ignorance," which prevents the hypothetical participants from knowing any particular information about their identities, interests, genders, or views of the good is utterly unpromising as something to emulate in the structure of real institutions. Since actual democratic participants will not be behind a veil, there is no hope of securing justice unless each participant is motivated to protect the interests of the other participants in certain ways—a motive that is profoundly different from the motives of the hypothetical contractors. The "fair representation of persons" of which Rawls speaks (see earlier quote) has two entirely different points in the original position and in actual political procedures. The parties in the original position pay no attention to each other, whereas an actual oppressed minority cannot prevail without others joining their cause. Rawls, indeed, argues that voters ought to address justice itself, the primary question the contractual situation seeks to explicate.[8] These points throw Rawls's suggestion of an analogy into serious doubt.

Habermas and Scanlon develop versions of contractualism that do not use a veil of ignorance, and they have naturally been more influential on the analogy theories.[9] Nelson's account of the contractualist situation is strikingly like Scanlon's (and anticipates it).[10] Cohen's view shows the clear influence of Rawls, Scanlon, and Habermas, but employs no veil of ignorance. Barry's version of the analogy argument is explicitly based on Scanlon's version of contractualism. All have the features my argument exploits, though I concentrate on Scanlon's version as a focal point. Hereafter, by "contractualism," I will mean a Scanlonian version—with no veil of ignorance and with contractors motivated partly to accommodate others—unless otherwise specified.

The initial plausibility of the analogy is clear: in proper deliberative democratic procedures, participants are expected to press their own interests and convictions, tempered by a due respect for those of others. Just as with the hypothetical contractors, actual participants' motives are a mixture of self-service and reasonable accommodation of others. That similarity is striking, but I will argue that it is not enough to support the tracking claim—a tendency of democratic procedures to produce outcomes that are just by contractualist standards.

The Failure of the Analogy

Suppose, then, that under the proper contractualist standard of justice, easily avoided famine is almost always unjust (and that this is unreasonable to deny), since remedial measures, or more general policies that guaranteed them, could not reasonably be rejected. First, it is easy to see why egoistic voting will not itself avoid famine: a well-fed majority might fail to support the remedy. As Sen says, famines, even when allowed to run their course, rarely affect more than a small percentage of a nation's population.[11] In majoritarian electoral institutions with egoistic voting it is far from clear how these victims could summon any decisive electoral pressure.

Consider, next, a motivation modeled on contractualism. The motivations that democratic participants would have according to a strong democracy/contractualism analogy are not egoistic. On the other hand, as I hope to show, truly analogous participants will not address the question of justice itself, but only their own interests so far as they can be reasonably pressed. This is not egoism, but nor is it a sufficient orientation to the common good to support the tracking claim under circumstances of real and proper democratic choice. After exhibiting a number of important disanalogies between democratic and contractualist choice, I will argue that justice would not directly be addressed by participants who were analogous to the hypothetical contractors.

Here are several central features of the hypothetical contractualist situation I will consider, drawn largely from Scanlon:

a. The task is to choose general rules that shall apply to all members of society.

b. Agreement is not forced or coerced.

c. Everyone affected by the chosen arrangements is a party to the choice.

d. Participants interact on terms of equal opportunity for input and no unequal bargaining power.

e. Agreement is defeated if it is rejected by any of the individual participants.

f. Participants will not reject any proposal unreasonably.

g. Participants are all motivated to come to some agreement rather than live without any rules.

h. The proceedings are not bound by, and the decisions are not subsidiary to, prior tenets of justice or right.

The democracy/contractualism analogy does not hinge on some general assessment of the degree of similarity. If it did, no theorist could ever have been tempted by it. It is easy to see that no actual democratic procedure could even remotely approximate these essential contractualist conditions. Here are a few important deviations:

Missing Constituents *(not-c): not everyone affected participates*
In actual democracies there is no franchise or other political status accorded to members of other states, children, or members of future generations, all of whom might be profoundly affected by the actions of the state in question. Even among those with rights to participate, many do not.

Unequal Political Power *(not-d): those who do participate are not on remotely equal terms in the relevant sense*
Scanlon stipulates that his contractors have no differential bargaining power one over another. This could never be realized or even approximated in actual political procedures. Certainly the effects of bargaining power can be reduced to some extent in some contexts, and ought to be. But here the question is whether bargaining power could ever be equal enough to ground confidence that the resulting decisions would tend to be what they would be in the hypothetical contractual situation. This is too much to believe.

Higher Law *(not-h): democratic choices are constrained by higher constitutional law*
A morally central feature of the contractualist situation, especially as it has been deployed in political contexts, is that there are no constraints on allowable outcomes other than the proper conduct of the procedure

(including reasonable participation; the strictures of reasonableness itself do seem to be prior to the procedure).[12]

These are all significant differences, but the one upon which I want to rest my objection to the tracking claim is,

The Veto Gap (not-e): *nothing remotely like individual veto power is appropriate in large democracies*

In principle, actual democratic procedures could operate under a veto rule, requiring unanimity for the passage of any measure. However, the veto (unanimity) rule is inappropriate in large political systems such as modern states.

THE INAPPROPRIATENESS OF ACTUAL VETO POWER

The problem is not that a veto rule could not be established, but that it would be absurd to do it. Veto power is a very different thing in the temporal context of actual politics than it is in the atemporal context of the hypothetical contractual situation. In the hypothetical context there is no running polity, but in the actual temporal context there is. A veto power in the real world notoriously makes change far more difficult than stasis, and this privileging of the status quo has no adequate justification. If it were only exercised properly it would have no untoward effects. If only reasonable objections were pressed by the veto, the outcomes would approximate those in the hypothetical contractualist situation. This shows that the veto rule can only be objected to by frankly asserting that it is bound to be used inappropriately. This does not yet impugn the motives of any participants, but it does impugn at least their information and rationality, if not also the motives of some. From a contractualist point of view, the problem with using the veto rule in actual practice is simply that it would often block even proposals to which there is no reasonable objection. I think this can be safely assumed, at least in the large pluralistic polities the democracy/contractualism analogy seems intended to address, even if all voters behaved as best they could.

In many actual democratic states, some individual rights are protected against majoritarian legislation by the higher authority of a constitution. This is sometimes thought of as a kind of veto power, the power of aggrieved individuals to block legislation on the basis of its unreasonable burdens on them. Of course, not all constitutional limits on legislation are proxies for the legitimate claims of individuals. The freedom of expression protected by many constitutions is much broader than what any speaker has a legitimate interest in being allowed to say. Much of what is protected is reprehensible.

Other constitutional rights, such as a U.S. citizen's right against cruel and unusual punishment, fit the case better. However, these are still unlike a veto power in a crucial respect: they depend for their efficacy on a court's acknowledging the alleged violation as a real violation. This requires judges to participate in the process with motives entirely different from the reasonable but self-serving motives of hypothetical contractors (more on this later). Such a system may tend to promote outcomes that are just by contractualist standards, but that is not the issue. Even if it does, there is no structural analogy between the actual and hypothetical procedures that explains this fact. The explanation involves the direct pursuit of justice by some participants, a fundamental disanalogy.

Finally, even if the analogy with constitutional rights were sound, the affected set of issues would still be quite small. The vast majority of collective political decisions would still face a wide range of options that are immune to this kind of veto, including many unjust options. For example, consider the variety of forms a system of taxation might take. There are many possible unjust systems of taxation, but it would probably be inappropriate to prohibit them all in a constitution. On this and other remaining issues, where no constitutional quasi-veto was permitted, there would be no reason to think the presence of reasonable objections would effectively block the offending proposals. Even if it more closely resembled the veto power, the constitutional approach would only account for a very slim tendency of reasonably rejectable proposals to fail in the democratic process.

Large democratic procedures, then, should not give individuals the veto power, since many proposals that should not be blocked would be. The failure of the democracy/contractualism analogy hangs crucially on the inappropriateness of the veto power. To defend the analogy it might be said, then, that real democratic procedures with the veto power are the ideal, the form politics should take if participants lived up perfectly to their responsibilities. Analogy theorists might say that all they ever intended was an analogy with good and proper democratic procedures, not actual flawed ones. It is impossible to deny a strong analogy between contractualism and a highly idealized and imaginary democratic process of that kind. But that is not the influential claim that is in question here. Our question is whether any realistically possible political arrangements, ones that we should aspire to, exhibit the analogy in the way needed to support the tracking claim. It is important to appreciate the severity of an individual veto power in a context of millions of voters. Even if individual moral character could improve without limit, some conscientious voters would be bound not to be fully informed, vetoing proposals to which there is not really any reasonable objection. And it only takes one. Large democratic societies, then, have no good reason to aspire to arrangements in which an individual veto power could reliably be used without error. There is no politics worth pursuing that mirrors this crucial feature of the hypothetical contractual situation. As we will see, this fact fundamentally affects the duties of democratic voters.

THE PRIMARY QUESTION PROBLEM

My aim is not merely to display a dissimilarity between democratic and contractualist choice situations. The two are analogous in some ways, not analogous in other ways. Those asserting the democracy/contractualism analogy are not claiming a perfect resemblance is possible, nor are they merely claiming that some similarities are possible. My thesis is that the analogy fails specifically in ways that will prevent appealing to structural similarities between the hypothetical and actual choice situations in order to support the tracking claim. The contractualist choice situation is unlike (even admirable) democratic choice situations in ways that prevent the latter from having any systematic tendency to produce the same outcomes as the former.

I want to focus mainly on the veto gap in light of a further point about contractualism. If participants do not have a veto, then reasonable objections by a small number will not defeat a proposal unless enough others join them. A single reasonable objector or a small group will be outvoted in a democracy unless either (a) there is a veto power, or (b) other voters join reasonable objections that are not their own. In democratic practice this kind of joining is common, but it is no part of the contractual situation. Contractors are, as I will say, *reasonably self-serving*, and so the power of veto is crucial.

There is an ambiguity in Nelson that is instructive on this point. In following Mill he celebrates the tendency of advocates in an open government to *defend* their proposals by showing that they should be thought acceptable to all or most citizens.[13] Nelson takes this tendency to resemble the motivations of the hypothetical contractors. This kind of "moralizing" of public discourse[14] may well be a good thing, and may well improve the expected moral quality of outcomes, but it does not have any analogue in the contractual initial situation even as conceived by Nelson. He conceives of political justification as showing that a proposal would be accepted in a contractual initial situation. He never suggests that this is what hypothetical contractors try to demonstrate to each other, however, and their doing so would apparently be viciously circular. If they have a standard of rightness available to them, then our philosophical account should pass over them and go straight for that standard. Justification is not a mode of discourse that takes place *within* the initial situation on this kind of view.[15] Insofar as real democratic discourse involves justificatory argumentation rather than simple endorsements or rejections of proposals, the analogy between Nelson's contractual situation and democratic procedures is strained. Nelson switches here to a different (and more genuinely Millean) basis for the tracking claim: that by directly addressing justice democratic participants might tend to track it. This claim, too, would require defense; here the point is that it decisively abandons the analogy argument for the tracking claim.

This point can be put in a more general context. To see this, it helps to introduce a piece of terminology. Some contractualist views are proposed in order to ascertain the content of morality, or some part of it, and others aim to discover the content of political justice. In general, call this issue the *primary question* for a given contractualist theory. In Scanlon the primary question is, "What do we owe to each other?" In Rawls the primary question is, "What is a reasonable political conception of justice?" In contractualist theories the participants in the initial situation are not conceived as addressing the primary question. Parties to Rawls's original position do not ask themselves, "What is a reasonable political conception of justice?" They ask what I will call a *subsidiary question*, "Which of the proposals before me will maximize my bundle of primary social goods?"[16] Scanlon's participants do not ask themselves, "What do we owe to each other?" but rather the subsidiary question, "Do I find this proposal acceptable in light of my interests (reasonably weighted) and in light of my aim of coming to agreement with others similarly motivated?" Several critics of Scanlon have argued that the contractors are themselves, in effect, applying some non-contractualist account of wrongness.[17] Scanlon says explicitly that the account would be circular if that were so, and denies that it is so.[18]

Suppose that rather than applying a noncontractualist account of rightness the contractors apply precisely the contractualist standard of rightness. Here the problem is slightly different. Such an account involves a fatal infinite regress. We, the theorists, begin by trying to explicate justice (to take a political version of contractualism), in terms of what would be agreed by reasonable contractors under proper conditions. But to carry out the explication rather than stopping with this formula we need to give content to the stipulation that the contractors are reasonable.[19] This means (or so this view says) that they, the contractors, will themselves ask what proposals are beyond reasonable rejection. This involves *their* appealing to the contractualist formula, and so they now need to fill in the features and motivations of the hypothetical contractors they are imagining. But those contractors will face that same issue again, and so on. We saw above that if the contractors appealed to a noncontractualist account of right, then our attention should go straight to that standard. The same is true if they appeal to a contractualist standard. The problem, then, is that our attention gets repeatedly shifted to the standard posited by the hypothetical contractors at each successive stage ad infinitum.

There is a good reason for having the parties address a subsidiary question rather than the primary question. If they were to address the primary question, then the whole theoretical apparatus would fail to have any heuristic value in explicating the nature of justice or right. The primary question would remain for the contractors themselves to fathom, and their own choices would be philosophically moot. Thus, it is an important feature of contractualism that the parties in the initial situation address a subsidiary question and not the primary question of justice or morality.

The conclusion to draw is that the contractors we posit cannot themselves be applying the standard of right or justice at all, contractualist or noncontractualist. This is not the same as objecting to giving the hypothetical contractors motivations that are in some way moral or morally significant. This would not by itself undermine contractualism. The idea of a reasonable consideration in the contractualist choice situation could be a moral idea without it being the primary idea that is being explicated. That is enough to show the account would not be circular. And so long as contractualism does not seek to explicate all moral ideas including reasonableness itself, it can help itself to an independent but morally significant conception of reasonableness without threat of circularity. But none of that warrants letting the contractors employ a concept of, specifically, right or justice or whichever primary question the contractualist account is addressing. As we will see next, this point is partly captured by Scanlon's view that hypothetical contractors are motivated only by what he calls "personal reasons."

REASONABLE SELF-SERVICE

It is central to contractualism that the reasons for which proposals are rejected in the hypothetical choice situation are, in Scanlon's term, "personal."[20] One thing this means is that for any rejectable proposal there are personal reasons against it from some relevant point of view. But it also means something more important for purposes of evaluating the democracy/contractualism analogy. It means that the hypothetical participants in the contractual situation behave in a highly distinctive way, from a very specific kind of motivation: they reject proposals only if they themselves have personal reasons against them. For convenience, call this the *self-service conception* of participation.

Personal reasons are by no means all selfish, since many of a person's central interests might concern the fates of others she cares about. Still, two kinds of other-oriented motivation are ruled out. First, impersonal reasons, those that do not derive from any person's personal grounds for objection, are not appropriate reasons for rejection in the contractualist situation. As Scanlon emphasizes, impersonal reasons may be important parts of the story about certain personal reasons—as when a person has a reason to seek a life in which the impersonal values of art or nature can be appreciated.[21] What we owe to each other is not concerned with impersonal reasons except insofar as they figure in personal reasons. Political uses of contractualism, in effect, assume that political justice shares this feature with the aspects of morality that Scanlon addresses.

Second, the contractual participants do not reject proposals on the ground that they are reasonably rejectable by someone or other—call this *anonymous rejectability*—but only for their *own* personal reasons. This is not a point that Scanlon discusses directly, and so we will need to consider whether it is a fair interpretation. But before doing that, it will be helpful to see what is at stake for the democracy/contractualism analogy.

If, as I suggest, contractual participants only reject proposals against which they have their own personal reasons, then if only one person has a personal reason against a proposal, then even if it is a perfectly reasonable objection the proposal would not be sure to be defeated unless that person had the power of veto. Since contractualism ensures that even a single reasonable rejection is fatal to a proposal, the contractors operate, in effect, under a veto rule. This is no objection to contractualism, but it is devastating to the democracy/contractualism analogy. Actual democratic choice procedures do not, and should not, operate under a veto rule. But under any other decision rule a reasonable objection by a single person or small group will not be decisive if participants reject only proposals against which they have their own personal objections.

Either democratic participants are motivated only by personal reasons, or in some other way. If they are motivated only by personal reasons, actual democratic procedures will have no tendency to defeat proposals that are subject to reasonable personal objections unless there are enough such objectors to produce a majority or plurality. The results of even proper democratic procedures, then, will have little resemblance to those of the contractual choice procedure in which even a single reasonable objection is decisive. If, on the other hand, democratic participants are motivated by something other than solely personal reasons, then perhaps a small minority of reasonable objectors can attract enough solidaristic support to prevail by majority or plurality. But in this case the morally desirable outcomes are produced by a procedure fundamentally different from the contractual situation. Here, an individual's vote is determined partly by whether *anyone* could reasonably reject—whether *anyone* has a reasonable personal objection—and so by anonymous rejectability. So the analogy between contractualism and democracy fails either way.

This argument against the democracy/contractualism analogy depends on my supposition that the participants in the contractualist choice situation are motivated to reject proposals only by personal reasons of their own. This is not immediately entailed by Scanlon's insistence that rejectability depends on there being some personal reason against a proposal, since that leaves open whether participants are motivated only by their own personal objections, or also by those of others. If they are motivated also by *anyone's* reasonable grounds for rejection (by anonymous rejectability), so that they would join them by adding their own rejection, then any individual's reasonable grounds for rejection will multiply solidaristically, and could be decisive even in the absence of a power of veto. There would be no need for a veto power, since parties would always, in the end, vote the same way. This would be analogous to an actual democratic procedure in which citizens first determine if they have their own surviving personal grounds for rejection, and then any proposal that is rejectable by anyone is rejected by all. Since actual democracies lack the perfect information, communication, and motivation of the hypothetical situation, the match in their conclusions would not be perfect, but under favorable conditions it might be hoped that often enough a majority would join in any individual's reasonable ground for rejection.

This would obviously improve the democracy/contractualism analogy. But the rejection-joining phase appears to have no independent rationale, and so no claim to be a legitimate part of the contractualist account. This way of giving participants the primary question *in addition* to the subsidiary one involving their own personal reasons would not be empty in the way giving them the primary question alone would be (as discussed earlier). The objection here is, rather, that anything beyond that subsidiary question—captured by the idea of reasonable self-service—is theoretically superfluous.

To see this, notice that similar phases could be added to any approach to moral theory arbitrarily, supporting an equally good analogy between them and democracy. Consider an unorthodox presentation of utilitarianism: In the first phase, we might say, participants enter the amount of their own well-being that is at stake in the various proposals. In the second phase, each determines which proposal would maximize aggregate well-being, and rejects all other proposals. As a result, there is unanimity. So if we said that rightness is the property of being agreed to in this hypothetical unanimous way, we could see that the results would be analogous to a procedure in which democratic citizens each reject all proposals that they believe would not maximize well-being. The obvious flaw here is that the joining phase is simply added on to a self-sufficient normative theory. In the joining phase the hypothetical participants find themselves applying the whole criterion of rightness. But if they have it available, then so do we, even before the joining phase is added. The resulting analogy between democracy and this cooked-up presentation of utilitarianism is, then, artificial.

Adding a rejection-joining phase to contractualism is just as artificial. The crux of contractualism is rejectability from the point of view of an agent's own interests and concerns. What makes an act wrong on contractualist grounds is that any system of rules permitting it would be rejectable from some person's point of view. It is true that it is rejectable only if the person's reasons for rejection survive a due accounting of the reasons others have for rejecting alternatives, but what survives is some person's grounds for rejection. Adding a phase in which all others join anyone's surviving rejection adds nothing and distracts from contractualism's distinctiveness.

REASONABLE ACCOMMODATION

The reasonable self-service assumption may seem to miss the fact that contractualism is normally formulated so that the ideal participants are responsive to the reasonable interests of others. Scanlon writes, "the parties whose agreement is in question are assumed not merely to be seeking some kind of advantage but also to be moved by the aim of finding principles that others, similarly motivated, could not reject."[22] Unlike the parties in Rawls's original position, in which, behind the veil of ignorance, the parties ignore the interests of the other contractors, each Scanlonian party accommodates the interests of other contractors in certain ways. This must be construed without giving the participants the primary question, but contractualism does not intend the participants simply to press their own complaints without regard to those of others. The question is how to interpret this kind of accommodation.

This contractualist element of mutual accommodation can easily suggest the sort of public-interested debate in well-functioning democracies, suggesting a democracy/contractualism analogy. But we have seen that this simple view would illegitimately give contractors the primary question. We need an interpretation of the contractors' mutual accommodation that avoids this mistake. Then it remains to be asked if the democracy/contractualism analogy remains supportable.

So the first step is to interpret the idea of reasonable accommodation in the case of the hypothetical contractors. We can only consider one illustrative approach here. Suppose we interpreted the accommodation phase this way: each party is prepared not to press a personal reason he has against a proposal if this would leave only alternatives to which others had objections at least as weighty. A given contractor does not need to determine (what would amount to the primary question) whether any alternative is subject to reasonable objection all things considered, but only whether the alternatives to the option they would veto are subject to objections as weighty as theirs. If they all are, then a veto would be unreasonable and so they would refrain from exercising it. Call this more limited comparison,

# 1	w	x	y	z
A	1	8	4	7
B	3	5	0	2
C	0	3	4	6
D	1	9	2	5

Figure 13.1

Contractor accommodation: Each party to the contractual situation must ask, for each alternative to the one(s) they would veto, whether there is someone who has as weighty an objection. If each alternative is subject to as weighty an objection by some other person, then no veto is imposed.

Vetoes must leave at least one alternative that is not as objectionable to anyone as the vetoed proposal.

I am not defending this account, nor am I attributing it to Scanlon. My aim is only to show that the idea of reasonable accommodation among the contractors could be brought in without giving them the primary question. The reasonable self-service interpretation of the contractors' motives is not missing this element.

It is helpful to look at a simple example (figure 13.1). Consider Case 1, with persons (or factions of any size) w, x, y, z, and alternatives A through D. Say objections range from low weight of 1 to high weight of 10. Begin with person w. She will veto A if and only if it is not the case that each of B through D is subject to a weightier objection by anyone (including w herself). In this case there is a number higher than 1 in each of the other three rows, so w may not veto A. (In the figure vetoes are signified by numbers in boldface.) In this arbitrary example, it turns out that only alternative B is beyond reasonable rejection. So, in the chart, each cell is evaluated in the following way. Look at the three rows other than the row that cell is in. If all three of them have a number higher than the original cell, then that cell does not warrant a veto. Otherwise it does. That is the right test because there must be at least one

# 2	w	x	y	z
A	1	1	2	2
B	0	9	0	0
C	2	1	2	1
D	2	2	1	1

Figure 13.2

row without a higher number, meaning there is at least one alternative to which there is not as great an objection.

This illustrates the idea of a principle of reasonable accommodation by otherwise self-serving contractors, and a principle that is not yet just giving the contractor the primary question itself. Notice that the test does not involve one contractor asking anything about what others could veto. So clearly it is not the primary question, which is, in effect, the question whether an alternative is beyond veto by anyone.

How does this affect the democracy/contractualism analogy? Consider another case (see figure 13.2), in which x has a much weightier objection to alternative B than anyone has to any other alternative:

Under the veto rule in the hypothetical contractual situation, person x would be able to block alternative B even after reasonable accommodation of the others. But in actual democratic contexts without the veto rule there is nothing to stop alternative B from winning if enough people vote for it. Infact, x could be a faction of any size, such as 49 percent in a majority-rule system. So the point is not just that lone individuals could be oppressed. Given the absence of a veto rule in actual democratic contexts, the democracy/contractualism analogy depends on an appropriate account of the accommodation by some voters of the reasonable interests of others.

Is there some form of reasonable accommodation in voting that is analogous to the form we have just sketched for contractors, and that would prevent proposals such as B from being able to win in a vote? The question is what voting norms can meet the following criteria: (a) voter motivations are analogous to those in the contractual situation (and so do not address the primary question), and (b) the result is some systematic tendency for alternatives that are reasonably rejectable in the contractual situation to lose in proper democratic contexts.

Recall, contractors accommodate each other by refraining from vetoing a proposal unless this leaves some alternative that is not subject to as weighty an objection from someone else as their own objection. Devising an analogous form of accommodation for the case of real voters is not a simple matter. How can the idea of rejecting a proposal be translated into some approach to voting *for* proposals? To avoid the primary question, voters should somehow vote against proposals on the basis of burdens to themselves, though qualified by some reasonable accommodation of others, and in a way that supports a strong tendency for reasonably rejectable alternatives to be electorally rejected. I can see no way of making this work.

We have no account of appropriate voters' motives (as distinct from *contractors'* motives) that shows how to incorporate reasonable accommodation while avoiding the primary question. If democratic procedures do (or could) tend to produce just outcomes by contractualist standards, the explanation does not lie in any analogy between the way in which a contractor is reasonable and the way in which a public-interested voter is reasonable.

CONCLUSION

My objection to the democracy/contractualism analogy, then, can be broken down into these steps:

1. The contractors cannot address the primary question, the impersonal question of reasonable rejectability in general or "anonymous rejectability," but only rejectability for their own personal reasons.

2. Without the contractors addressing anonymous rejectability, the veto power is crucial to contractualism.

3. Actual citizens, if they behave analogously to the hypothetical contractors, will not address the question of anonymous rejectability. This follows directly from step 1.

4. Actual veto power would be crucial to the analogy. (from 2 and 3)

5. The unanimity/veto decision rule is not an appropriate decision rule in real and large democratic choice procedures.

6. Under any appropriate rule, then, there would be a veto gap: proposals that are rejectable in the contractual situation might yet win in actual democratic procedures. (from 4 and 5)

7. Conclusion: the democracy/contractualism analogy is too weak to provide any support for the tracking claim. (from 6)

Democratic participation modeled on the contractualist situation would be self-serving within the limits of reasonable accommodation of others. Voters would not directly address issues of justice, nor would they vote against proposals simply because they were reasonably rejectable by others. As a result, many proposals that are severely unjust by contractualist standards would be bound to succeed. The difficulty is not simply that some injustice would be bound to slip through imperfect institutions and motivations. Rather, this conception of a voter's responsibilities formally protects many injustices from defeat. Reasonably self-serving motivation in actual democratic procedures does not find any justification or rationale in the fact that they would be morally sensible motives to posit in the very different context of a hypothetical contractual situation.

Some readers will have the following nagging worry about my argument. Scanlon's contractors are nothing if not reasonable; so then it must be a mistake to see them as self-serving in the way the reasonable self-service conception sees them. That might seem to be objectionably selfish of the contractors in a certain way, just as it would be objectionably selfish of democratic voters to press only their own reasonable objections, and not also those of others. The mistake, however, is to continue to treat the two cases as parallel. The reason it would be objectionably selfish of democratic voters to confine their attention to their own reasonable objections is precisely because others with reasonable objections do not have the veto power that the hypothetical contractors have. If voters had such a veto power and only used it appropriately, there would be no obvious objection to each voter's using her vote only to pursue her own legitimate interests. In the hypothetical contractual situation, then, there is nothing untoward or unreasonable about the reasonably self-serving motivations of the contractors. Each presses her own legitimate interests only, in a context where all legitimate interests can be sufficiently pressed by their owners, due to the veto power.

Who, you might wonder, could possibly object to a person's using her political power to see to it that her own legitimate interests are met?

Nobody, I suppose. But there is a crucial difference between permitting reasonable self-service among the proper motives of voting and permitting voters to pursue reasonable self-service *alone*, without any requirement to join one's vote to the reasonable objections of others.

Once it is clear that the participants in the hypothetical contractualist situation are reasonably self-serving rather than rejection-joining, it is just as clear that the moral quality of the decisions would be hopeless if not for the unanimity rule—the procedural power of any of the participants to veto proposals. But then it is also obvious that Nelson, Cohen, and Barry do not endorse institutions that closely resemble the contractualist situation, since they endorse neither the motivational trait of reasonable self-service nor the rule in which a lone participant can veto proposals.[23] How, then, can they be committed to the democracy/contractualism analogy?

The explanation is partly that they seem to have interpreted contractualism in a way that makes it more similar to the democratic arrangements they endorse than Scanlonian contractualism actually supports. Contractualism's idea of the contractors' reasonable accommodation of the claims of others is easily confused with the idea that each asks herself which proposals are beyond reasonable rejection. This latter idea, public-interested voting with the public interest conceived in contractualist terms, is a prominent part of Nelson's and Cohen's accounts of proper democratic voting (Barry's stays closer to the motives of the Scanlonian contractors).[24] But it would be a misconstrual of the kind of mutual accommodation that contractualism posits, as I have argued.

The other possible explanation of sympathy for the analogy is a failure to distinguish between a tendency of actual procedures to produce decisions similar to those produced by the hypothetical procedure, on one hand (call this *outcome similarity*), and a structural similarity between hypothetical and actual procedures, on the other (call this *procedural similarity*).[25] The thesis we are examining is that outcome similarity can realistically be pursued by promoting procedural similarity. That thesis faces the serious difficulties I have presented earlier. Perhaps the thesis of outcome similarity could be supported in some other way, such as an appeal to some power of free and open political discussion under the right conditions, in which many voters address and debate (among other things) matters of justice. I have some sympathy with that line of inquiry, but it owes nothing to a democracy/contractualism analogy.

The fundamental flaw in the democracy/contractualism analogy is this: without public-interested voting and participation, it is hard to see how justice could be systematically promoted (as if by an invisible hand), since in democracy—both as it is and as it should be—victims have no veto.

Utopophobia: Concession and Aspiration in Democratic Theory

AS WE HAVE SEEN, political theorists often try to avoid epistemic or instrumental accounts of the value of democracy. Sometimes it is in order to avoid the philosophical commitment to external standards, a strategy I have criticized. But even if there are external standards for political decisions, there are other worries about epistemic accounts of democracy, and it is easy to see why. The level of talent, knowledge, virtue, and motivation that the average citizen brings to the task of voting is low. If there are good reasons in favor of democracy, then, it might seem that they must be something other than its ability to produce good decisions. This is not only the main traditional reason for skepticism about democracy. It is also a strong, perhaps dominant, strain in contemporary thinking about democracy, especially in the political science literature. Skepticism about democracy's instrumental or epistemic value flourished in the second half of the last century, and much current democratic theory takes its inspiration from the great debunkers, Schumpeter and Arrow.[1] I have discussed the relevance, or really the lack of relevance, of Arrow's brilliant work to normative democratic theory in chapter 5, "The Flight from Substance." In this chapter I want to illustrate and respond to a more Schumpeterian strand that emphasizes voter ignorance and irrationality, rather than the difficulties with aggregation discussed since Arrow. Schumpeter writes,

> The reduced sense of responsibility and the absence of effective volition in turn explain the ordinary citizen's ignorance and lack of judgment in matters of domestic and foreign policy which are if anything more shocking in the case of educated people and of people who are successfully active in non-political walks of life than it is with uneducated people in humble stations. Information is plentiful and readily available. But this does not seem to make any difference. (262)

I won't directly discuss the large literature on these matters. The approach I sketch in this chapter could be extended, if it is sound, to other voter vices, including selfishness, manipulation of opinion, and so forth. There are many serious charges against voters, and I want to grant many, though not all of them, for the sake of argument. Rather than challenge the literature that explores the deficiencies of voters, I want to concede much of it in order to explain how it is not as devastating to normative political theory as it is usually thought to be. We need more clarity than is usually offered about the meaning and value of being "realistic" in our theories. There are certainly defects a theory can have that render it objectionably "utopian," but again, we need a more discriminating account of that epithet than is usually given. Jumping all the way to a complacent realism in order to avoid utopianism would suggest an irrational utopophobia, or exaggerated fear of utopianism. In between these extremes lies what I will call *aspirational theory*. As we will see, this approach posits standards that are not generally met (as any noncomplacent normative theory seems bound to do), though they are possible to meet.

THE BAD VOTER PROBLEM

Voters can be shown by many different measures to have little knowledge about the issues and institutions that are in democratic hands. An enormous literature has shown the extent of voter ignorance. There is a large literature that considers whether voters are primarily selfish, though this is more controversial than that their knowledge is very imperfect. A third important charge is that voters, whatever their virtue or knowledge, are irrational, unable to pursue their ends coherently.[2] My goal is not to fully consider the merits and meanings of these charges, nor even to give an adequate picture of the state of knowledge about them. Rather, I mention these three kinds of charges generally in order to turn to the more central question: how should these charges, and others like them, bear on normative political theorizing about democracy? Even this I do not pretend to take up in a complete way. My aim is the modest one of explaining and defending one approach to normative political theory that is not seriously damaged by facts such as these. If my discussion has any special interest, it may consist in the apparent tension between the low quality of actual voter behavior and the epistemic character of my normative theory. The qualms about the quality of voter decisions might be easier to allay if we were satisfied with procedural fairness, or even some more minimal procedural virtue. But we saw in chapter 4 that there are serious difficulties with normative democratic theories of that kind. We need an epistemic dimension, and so we must face the facts about poor voter performance. How damning are they? In this chapter I describe an approach to normative political theory generally in which facts like this can be tamed. I illustrate that approach by concentrating on the charge that voters are disastrously uninformed.

How Bad Are the Facts Really?

There is a lot of evidence that voters lack information and understanding that would seem to be important to making intelligent political decisions. Political science has devoted great energy to documenting the traditional worry that ordinary citizens might not be up to the task of political decision making. In our time, of course, the political decisions voters face are overwhelmingly decisions about what representative to vote for, including officeholders at all local and national levels. That is, voters other than officials do not often vote on binding policy decisions directly. Still, a smart decision about whom to vote for would seem to require some information and understanding about the merits of policy proposals, since these will be some of the major reasons to prefer one candidate to another. Those merits depend on lots of facts, many of them publicly contested. Should I vote for the Republican candidate for the Senate? He supports shifting Social Security funds into private financial markets. How well will they perform? What other effects does this have on Social Security's viability over time? And so on.

The merits, of course, also depend on an understanding of moral matters concerning justice, equity, rights, and responsibilities. Even if putting Social Security funds into investment funds yields more money over time, does this put some people unfairly at risk if the market should be low at a time when they need their support? In addition, intelligent votes for officeholders seem to require information of another kind: information about how a candidate is likely to behave. This, in turn, would seem to require information about the formal and pragmatic powers and constraints of the office in question, some understanding of what the future is likely to bring (partly as judged in light of history), and so on. Is my senator really going to support this Social Security plan? What are the political pressures he faces? Is he senior enough to have any influence?

These facts are important. But it is good to keep them in perspective. Consider an analogy: suppose we turn the wisdom checkers loose on parents and their ability to make good decisions about the lives of their children. Here are some things the checkers might want to know: Do parents understand the psychology of child development enough to know what parental strategies are effective?[3] Do parents know which of the available schools perform better? To know that adequately, do they understand the debates about standardized testing versus other methods for evaluating school performance? Do they know the name of the head of the school board? Do they know the name of their child's guidance counselor? Do parents know the publicly available facts about the pediatricians in the community, such as the places of their degrees? Their additional certifications? Their years of experience? Their malpractice records? Do parents understand the importance of preventive medicine? Do they know which of the available doctors emphasizes prevention adequately? Do parents understand the investment options available in order to effectively save for their children's education? Do they know the facts about the value of a college degree in promoting later happiness and success? Do they understand the differences between term and whole life approaches to life insurance? Do they know the dangers of having guns in the home? Do parents understand basic nutrition, such as the facts about fat, fruits and vegetables?[4] Do parents know the difference between a scientifically supported health recommendation and a mere fad or unsupported alternative approach? Do they know how AIDS is and is not transmitted? What do parents know about contraception?[5] Do they know basic first aid? Do parents understand the risks of lead poisoning?[6] Are parents up to the task of raising children?

Beyond the few studies I have cited, we can conjecture that good further research would show a disturbing degree of ignorance and misunderstanding on matters that would seem to be important to intelligent parenting decisions. Should we be convinced that parents cannot make good decisions for their children? The fate of children is presumably as important as the direction of a political system. Do the data support a severe indictment of both democracy and what we might call free parenting (the legal right to make parenting decisions within broad limits free from interference by the state)? In both cases, there is little doubt that there are experts who know more and might be just as virtuously motivated. In the case of parenting, expert controls on parental choices would lead to better decisions, and better lives for children. In the case of democracy, removing the right issues from democratic control and turning them over to the right experts would lead to better political decisions, and more justice and prosperity.

I mean these undemocratic-sounding claims sincerely. The trick is knowing, and publicly justifying, which experts to rely on for which issues. There are certain people to whom the public often turns for expert political advice, such as pundits, politicians, political scientists, and so on. Such people are often consulted by journalists and, by extension, their readers. They publish books, articles, and columns that are treated with some deference by the public. How expert are they? Well, since there is no publicly agreed standard for scoring their political advice as correct or incorrect, we cannot, as a public, tell. It is not likely that they are, as a class, unusually accurate given that they disagree with each other apparently about as much as ordinary citizens do. We would also not expect someone whose predictions about political events are no better than random to be especially wise in their political advice, and yet there is good evidence that predictions made by this class of putative experts is just that bad.[7] These points do not show that no one has better political judgment than anyone else. I am sure some do. It illustrates the difficulty of identifying, in a way acceptable to the broad range of qualified points of view, a set of experts who could be expected to perform better than the best democratic arrangement.

As I have argued in the case of democracy, the public justification problem places severe limits, giving democracy a special status, since there is too much scope for reasonable disagreement about who the experts would be. But democracy still needs to pass epistemic muster. If it were not at least better than random, we might as well choose policies with a roulette wheel. I assume that something similar is true for free parenting. The claims of parents to control their children's lives cannot be utterly insulated from the question whether this is good for the children. I will not pursue the facts about free parenting, but the example is meant to elicit the intuition that free parenting, despite the disturbing ignorance of parents on many important matters, is still pretty good for children.[8] It might not be the best possible arrangement, but good enough to support the kind of justification that is required. This would suggest that similar ignorance among voters is not automatically a severe indictment of the quality of democratic decisions.

Having reassured ourselves to some extent, we must go on to ask the further question whether voters are up to the job that is given them by an adequate normative theory of democracy. In other words, we might be satisfied that democracy is appropriate even though voters are ignorant, but we might not yet have a good normative theory of how this could be so. One strategy is to modify normative theory in order to scale back its demands on voters.[9] My strategy will be different: I want to defend normative theorizing that holds the real world to higher standards than it actually meets. This, of course, raises the question of utopianism.

Utopophobia: Concession and Aspiration in Political Theory

A normative political theory can be as cynical or as utopian as one wishes, but most theories try to steer between these extremes. The most realistic normative theory of all, of course, would recommend or require people and institutions to be just as they actually are already. As Rousseau said in the preface to *Emile*, " 'Propose what can be done,' they never stop repeating to me. It is as if I were told, 'Propose doing what is done.' "[10] Few writers believe that things are already just as they ought to be, and so normative political theory departs from realism in this strict sense. Any theory that implies criticism of actual institutions or behavior is not as realistic as it could be. For example, a normative framework that criticizes existing legal regulations on political advertising for being either too strict or too lax is not entirely realistic. A theory that criticizes actual voters for being too selfish or too uninformed departs from strict realism in exactly the same way. Since virtually no one will insist on this extreme kind of realism in normative theory, we can safely give it a derogatory label: *complacent realism*.

On the other hand, there are ways in which normative political theory can be morally too idealized. "Utopian" is an epithet used to ridicule theories thought to be too unrealistic. A theory can be too unrealistic in various ways. I will not be particularly interested in theories that go wrong by ignoring certain nonmoral facts about the world. For example, a theory that posited human immortality and unlimited natural resources could be accused of being utopian. A different kind of utopianism is involved when a conception of society posits moral standards for people or institutions that it is impossible for them ever to live up to. We can call this error an extreme version of *moral utopianism* to distinguish it from the other, nonmoral, or factual utopianism. The critique of moral utopianism, I take it, is that it *falsely* imposes those standards, since people are not morally failing when they fall short of impossible standards. There are less extreme versions of morally demanding theory, perhaps not all deserving to be labeled with an epithet like "utopian." I reserve the label for this extreme version. In between complacent realism and moral utopianism, there are important questions about whether and why normative political theory should resist building conceptions of society that require people or institutions to be other than they actually are (though not beyond what is possible for them). Rawls speaks of a "realistic utopianism."[11] I prefer to speak, less eloquently, of the noncomplacent nonutopian range of normative political theories, the range in which most theorists would agree normative political theory should toil.

Consider a theory that held individuals and institutions to standards that it is within their ability to meet, but which there is good reason to believe they will never meet. So far, the theory has no apparent defect. It would be false, by hypothesis, if it claimed that the standards would someday be met. The example stipulates that they won't. It would be morally utopian if the standards were impossible to meet, but, again by hypothesis, they are not. Many possible things will never happen. The imagined theory simply constructs a vision of how things should and could be, even while acknowledging that they won't be. So, for example, suppose this theory posits a conception of democracy in which citizens are publicly and privately virtuous, and institutions are designed accordingly, so that, in the imagined world, laws are just, rights are protected, the vulnerable are cared for, minorities are embraced and respected, and so forth. In an obvious sense this is not realistic. But we do not mean only that it is more than people actually do; that complacent realism is a worthless constraint. And we do not mean that it is morally utopian. No standard of virtue used by the theory is impossible for people to live up to, suppose. People could be good, they just aren't. Their failures are avoidable and blameworthy, but they are also entirely to be expected as a matter of fact. So far, there is no discernible defect in the theory, I believe. For all we have said, the standards to which it holds people and institutions might be sound and true. The fact that people will not live up to them even though they could is a defect of people, not of the theory. For lack of a better term, let us call this kind of theory a version of *hopeless realism*. The name signifies that the theory is not morally utopian, since meeting the standards is possible, and yet there is good reason to believe it will never happen.

It is easy to confuse standards that are impossible to meet with standards that will not be met. It is worth dwelling on the distinction in a general way for a moment. If something simply will not happen, if there is no chance of it happening, we are tempted to describe it as impossible. Suppose someone says that "impossible" just means "zero probability." They are subject to the following difficulty. If something is very, very unlikely, then they must admit that on their use of "impossible" it should count as very nearly impossible. The reason is that their view is that nearly impossible is the same thing as nearly a zero probability. But consider this case: what is the chance that I will move my hands and arms in the same way as the person at the next table in the café for the next five minutes? The probability of this is very, very close to zero, obviously. So should we accept that this is nearly impossible? That would be absurd, unless "impossible" becomes a merely technical term divorced from all its connotations in ordinary use. One point is that even if it were nearly impossible to *copy* him exactly, I could easily make those movements spontaneously, without trying to copy him. This is almost certainly not going to happen, but it would not be *difficult*, and so not nearly impossible. Just look at what he's doing; it's easy. Another point is that even if we mean intentionally copying, I could *roughly* intentionally copy him fairly easily. But the chances of my doing even that are very nearly zero—trust me—even though it would not be at all difficult. It would just be silly and embarrassing, so I am not going to do it. Since this would be easy, it is a mistake to say it is nearly impossible. This shows, I think, that it would be misleading to call things with zero probability impossible. The reason is that things that are unlikely or even certain not to happen are not necessarily difficult at all, much less impossible. We should insist on a difficulty/probability distinction. If something is not difficult, then it is not impossible, but it might yet be very unlikely or even certain not to occur. I assume that ought implies can—that if it's impossible then it's not morally required. I do not accept the very different and perverse principle that if it's unlikely, however possible or easy, then it's not required. It is not the case that ought implies reasonably likely.[12]

This distinction matters a lot for political philosophy. We might not want to set standards that are impossible or unreasonably difficult. But these are not yet reasons for wanting to avoid standards that will certainly or very likely not be met. It is an important question, and one that has not often been directly confronted, what reasons there might be to want normative political theories to set standards that are not only possible, not only not too difficult, but also not too unlikely to be met.

A hopeless theory can be dangerous, of course. The soundness of the standards might lead some to take actions, and this might be bad.

265

Actions in pursuit of what will not ever be achieved can be wasteful or even dangerous. On the other hand, some people might be led to improve themselves or their institutions, even though not all the way (full achievement is hopeless, after all, by hypothesis). This might be fine, and even a good thing. But some things that would be good in a context of other good things can be very bad on their own. An important category of example involves institutions that should be a certain way if only people lived up to their duties, but which only make things worse if people do not live up. So, suppose that people should be much more (even if not fully) impartial in their choices than they are. Institutions in which victims of injustice can claim compensation might encourage partial and selfish thinking, a tendency to think like a victim in order to get the benefits a victim would be entitled to. The best institutions for the best possible people might avoid mechanisms of victim compensation of certain kinds. But when people are very far from the impartial ideal, it might be a disaster not to have these compensatory institutions. The world is not brought closer to the ideal by having the institutions called for in the ideal, even though citizens are far from living up to that ideal. Rather, those institutions only make things worse. Ideals of society often have this sort of holistic character,[13] and so hopeless realistic normative theories pose the danger of piecemeal "improvements" that are likely only to do more damage.[14]

It might seem that a theory is not normative unless it counsels action of some kind. A hopeless theory might seem to counsel no action, and so not to be normative. First, however, a theory can be normative by being evaluative, whether or not evaluation itself counsels action. "Society would be better like this," might be true whether or not there is anything it makes sense to do in light of this fact. Still, this would not yet make it "practical," and that is a separate complaint. But, second, the sort of hopeless realistic theory in question does prescribe action in a certain way. It counsels all people, together, to behave differently. It does not tell each person to do it whether or not the others do, but many prescriptions are like that. A moral requirement to help push a friend's car out of a snowdrift does not say to push futilely even when no one else helps. Nevertheless, you and the folks standing around might be required to help, and this is a practical requirement rather than an idle evaluation. The requirement is practical even if, given what each knows about the laziness of the others, no person is required, under these circumstances, to start pushing. A hopeless normative conception of society might be collectively prescriptive in that same way without being individually prescriptive at all. People should be less selfish in politics, let us say, or they ought to build and sustain certain institutions. Nevertheless, given what each knows about the moral weakness of the others, there may be no action that is required, under those conditions, of anyone (maybe persuasion, or maybe that's hopeless too). So, the fact that under the circumstances a theory doesn't recommend any particular actions by any individual doesn't show that it doesn't counsel action. It remains *aspirational*: it sets sound standards that are not met, but could be met, and it tells us to meet them.

This brings us naturally to the idea of a hopeful (by which I mean nonhopeless) realistic normative political theory. This is one that applies appropriate standards which are not only possible for people and institutions to meet, but which there is no strong reason to think they will not meet. It is hard to resist the sense that a nonhopeless theory is a better kind of theory. I think this is an important mistake. There is no defect in a hopeless realistic normative theory, and so none that hopeful theories avoid to their advantage. Things are better in one way, of course, if the best theory turns out to be hopeful (nonhopeless) rather than hopeless. We should be sad if people will not live up to appropriate standards, and so we are spared this sadness if the best theory is not hopeless. But this consideration is not a reason for choosing a less hopeless theory. That would be simply to adopt different, more easily satisfied moral standards simply for the reason that they are more likely to be satisfied. In general (with some later qualifications about "demandingness") this is not moral reasoning at all. The likelihood that a person will not behave in a certain (entirely possible) way simply does not bear on whether they should. It is not a fact that has that kind of moral significance.

A supposed moral standard's difficulty, the strain or sacrifice that would be necessary in order for a person to meet the standard, is sometimes said to bear on whether it is a genuine moral standard at all, or on whether it provides reasons or duties. So one way in which a normative political theory might expect too much is by demanding something that is possible but yet more than can reasonably be demanded. Utilitarianism is often accused of requiring that we sacrifice our own pursuits and wealth almost endlessly, making the promotion of the total amount of well-being our dominant project. Some say this places demands that agents often have no reason to heed.[15] That would be a defect in the theory even if the demands were entirely possible to meet. To have a handy name for them, let us call such theories *unreasonably*

267

harsh. By definition, then, harsh theories are false. They state standards that are not genuine standards because they demand too much of agents. Needless to say, then, we want a normative political theory that is not harsh in this sense. On the other hand, I have so far not said anything about where the line between harsh and nonharsh theories might lie. I introduce the idea here to point out that a theory might be hopeless without being harsh. As we have said, a hopeless normative standard is one that there is reason to think will never be met, but the explanation might be only that people are unlikely to do what they should do, even where the standards are neither harsh nor impossible to meet. A standard might be unlikely without even being harsh, much less impossible.

There is a place for nonhopeless theory, but it is not somehow privileged. Nonhopeless theory is what we want when we want to know what we should do, in practice, given what people and institutions are actually likely to do. This is obviously an important inquiry. We do, after all, have to act one way or another. Acting as if people or institutions will behave in some better way than there is actually reason to expect might sometimes be a way of improving them. But even in that case, action is to be guided by what we actually think the probabilities are. In other words, an action plan that has false premises about how people or institutions are likely to act is unsound and sometimes dangerous. We need to concede the facts in practice, even if not in our moral conclusions. In addition to aspirational theory, then, we also need what we might call *concessive* normative theory in addition to nonconcessive theory. This is different from what I previously called *complacent realism,* which eschews all aspirational theory. Concessive theory aims to supplement aspirational theory and is not inimical to it in any way.

I emphasize that I do not regard my own theory as hopeless, as one that we have good reason to doubt will ever be met. Epistemic proceduralism, in order to have even the modest epistemic value that it requires, would need certain things from institutions and participants. In particular, individuals would have to orient their participation in public deliberation toward the common question, "What ought we to do?" There is no reason to believe that democratic procedures would lead to anything but disaster if voters looked out exclusively for their own interests or those of people they are especially close to. Unjust wars of acquisition would not be avoided, since the costs to most people could often be outweighed by the expected benefits. Often, only a small fraction of the population are likely to find themselves or their loved ones in harm's way. Famines would often not be avoided, since they never threaten the life or health of more than a small minority of a nation's people. And so on. But as those two examples suggest, it may be that democratic voters do already often vote in non-self-interested ways, and so epistemic proceduralism's needs might not be extravagant.

Still, there are many critics of this general kind of approach to democracy on the grounds that it requires things of citizens that are not actual and are not likely ever to be actual.[16] Rather than take up the empirical questions this raises, I want to see what happens if we grant their empirical claims for the sake of argument. What follows if they are right that epistemic proceduralism's needs are unlikely to be met? The answer is that not much follows if the project is aspirational rather than concessive theory, and that both are important. So, aspirational theory of this kind gets breathing space when we notice that even hopeless theory is not, on that account alone, defective in any way. To help open up that breathing space, I reflect just a bit more on the value that even a hopeless theory can have.

What, then, is the role for hopeless normative theory? I believe it has two closely related roles. The first is that there is intrinsic value in philosophical inquiry if it is done well, and in seeking the philosophically most defensible account of what political arrangements should be like. If the best account turns out to be hopeless, because people are simply unlikely to do what they could and should do, the theory should be undaunted. Call this the theory's philosophical role.

A related but distinct role for normative theory, even if it is hopeless, is a causal one. Reflection on how people and institutions should be can direct our attention and energy to determining how far realism can reach. We sometimes expect too little precisely because we have no normative standard that forces the question of whether more can realistically be expected.

Suppose we are hiking, and we spy a beautiful spot some miles off, down the slope, across the valley. It isn't just beautiful, it looks like a great place to stay, or even to live. Alas, it is not yet clear whether we can get there, so we might try to contain our excitement. Be realistic. Things are fine where we are, so we could just conclude that the new spot is not really worth considering. It is unrealistic in one way simply because it is not where we are. This complacent realism has little appeal. If we admit that the new spot is beautiful, we might nevertheless conclude that it is impossible to get there. (As I go on, let the scenery

269

change from a pastoral landscape to the space of political alternatives.) If we cannot get there, then there is no sense in worrying too much about the different routes we could try. Alternatively, we might think that it is possible, or might be for all we know, but, realistically, we will not get there because we are likely to eventually give up, or to make navigational errors. However, if we are not sure that it is impossible, then even if we are unlikely to get there, it could be worth thinking about how we might. This is not yet the same as recommending that we set out for it. That would be a different and later question. Perhaps the low chances of success will give us enough reason to make other plans. But why jump to that conclusion? After all, the place is beautiful, and for all we can tell getting there is not impossible.

INSTITUTIONAL RETICENCE

People who like "realism" in their theories often want not only standards that have a good chance of being met, but also specific (and non-hopeless) prescriptions for institutions. They sometimes want the theory to say what we should do, now, given the way people actually do act. We have just been seeing how the demand to condition the whole theory on what people actually do, or on what they are likely to do, is an inappropriate constraint on political theory. But what about the demand for institutional specifics? Since some good political theory is aspirational rather than concessive, the question is whether even an aspirational normative political theory should have determinate implications about how institutions should be arranged.

A theory is aspirational in virtue of its use of standards or ideals that are unlikely or even certain not to be met, even though they are not impossible and may not even be difficult. Still, if they are unlikely or hopeless, it might be very difficult to know what the world would be like in other ways if they were met. Suppose we know from experience about the operation of several different political arrangements in conditions where the participants have largely selfish and amoral motives. That is, in addition to what we might know a priori, by, say, running models that assume perfect information and rationality, suppose we also know something about the far more complex situations that actually occur when people fall within a certain range of largely selfish, ignorant, and amoral motivations. This knowledge will be invaluable in choosing between alternative institutional arrangements. To say that this knowledge, gained from experience, is invaluable is to say that without that experience it would have been far more difficult to make detailed institutional choices. Aspirational theory, of course, assumes motives that are, at the very least, far less familiar, and perhaps even largely unknown in human experience. If so, the invaluable knowledge that can be gained from actual experience under those motives is missing. This has the important consequence that aspirational theory will justify and even require a principled reticence about institutional recommendations. Aspirational normative theory will tend to have more reason to avoid institutional specifics than its concessive counterpart.

Concessive theory will be important, since the time comes when some desirable goal turns out to be too difficult or too unlikely to be worth taking on as a practical goal. In that case, we should concede certain unfortunate facts, some of them about human failings, some of them about other things, and chart a more feasible, if less inspiring, course. But let us not concede too much to concessive theory. It can be important and appropriate, but it can equally well be dangerous and irresponsible. Return briefly to our hike, and our view of the beautiful far-off location. If getting to that fabulous place is impossible or unreasonably difficult or unlikely, then a concessive approach will be appropriate. But to jump to planning routes to other less desirable locations right from the beginning, simply because they will be easier, or more likely to succeed, would be premature. The easiest destination of all would have been to stay home, but that does not make it an appropriate goal. There is more to goal setting than likelihood or ease of success. In political theorizing, concessions to the realistic but unfortunate facts are sometimes appropriate responses to a wider-ranging normative inquiry, where more desirable goals have been shown to be impossible or too difficult or uncertain. Other times, such concessions are merely symptoms of utopophobia. It would be irresponsible to set small and narrow goals without good reason to think that bigger and better things really cannot or will not be achieved.

Why Vote?

It is often held that citizens are not just unlikely to inform themselves and participate constructively, they are perfectly sensible not to do so.[17] Since a person's single vote is virtually certain never to make a difference, he would be foolish—both prudentially and morally—to sacrifice other projects for the purpose of devoting time to learning about politics or standing in line to vote. The crucial assumption here is that we have no moral reason to vote because (as I grant) it will not make a difference. But difference-making is only one of the ways in which we can have moral reasons to do something. Sometimes we have simply promised to do it, and have a duty to follow through whether or not it will make any (other) difference (though that would not apply to the case of political participation and voting). Sometimes we have a duty not to take something that belongs to another person—say, one of the many dollar bills in your rich neighbor's wallet—even if it would not be missed. A better analogy for our purposes might be this: suppose that if enough of us arrayed ourselves at the edge of town at midnight on the first day of each month, we could deter a dangerous gang from moving in (that is when they would otherwise try). It is virtually certain that my presence will not make or break the effort. There will either be enough people or not, but it will not depend on a single person. Still, I think there is a clear moral reason to join this effort. Of course, some people can be excused if they have more important things to do, but there is a significant moral claim on them that would need to be overridden. In a similar way, there are disasters kept at bay by enough people thoughtfully going to the polls, and there are serious reasons to join that effort, even though they can certainly sometimes be overridden by other weighty matters.

Normative Efficiency

There is yet another way in which a theory can demand too much of the world, namely, if it demands more than is necessary to accomplish the same theoretical purposes. If a theory means to account for authority of democratically produced laws, then it will, among other things, say what conditions must be met, such as certain procedures, including the roles or rights of participants, and so on. Some theories will have stronger conditions than others, conditions that are met, as we might put it, in fewer possible worlds. If a theory with weaker requirements is, in other ways, just as good an account of the authority of laws that meet the conditions, then this looks like some kind of advantage for that theory. It is not easy to say exactly what kind of advantage it is, however. This is not a theory that is more likely to be true, after all. It is a theory whose requirements are more likely to be met, but that does not sound like an advantage. If it were, why not go straight to the least demanding theory of all: whatever is, is right? Or, in the context of authority, whatever laws are made, by whatever methods, are authoritative. However, we should doubt that the maximally weak theory can actually succeed as an account of authority. It can *say* that all laws are authoritative, but can it explain how this is so? So to isolate the supposed advantage in question, we should concentrate only on theories that are equally good as accounts of authority. As between two theories of authority that are equally compelling as accounts of what is authoritative about the laws in question, is the theory that explains this without depending on as many (or as strong) necessary conditions a better theory?

The question is similar to the question whether a scientific theory that, while equally good in other ways, posits fewer entities, is a superior theory. Occam's razor famously asserts that it is. The issue also resembles the slightly different question whether a simpler theory is, other things equal, a better theory. (This is not the same as Occam's issue, since a theory's simplicity might stem from something other than its smaller ontology.) In all these cases, whatever kind of advantage such less committed theories are supposed to have, it does not look like it is the advantage of likely truth. I believe that in all these cases, the advantage is a rhetorical or polemical one, but this is a more important matter than this might make it sound. Arguments are put forward in order to move people from their present commitments to some new ones by way of logic. An argument can be sound and yet fail if its premises are not acceptable to the intended audience. Arguments with weaker premises are more powerful, even if they are no more sound, if their premises are acceptable to more actual or possible target interlocutors. A theory of political authority will imply the form of argument for moving from certain premises to the conclusion that a law is authoritative. If an alternative theory just as successfully proves the conclusion with weaker or less controversial premises, then it is a better and stronger argument in a perfectly familiar sense. There are two sides to the point. One side is that an argument that is just as good on other grounds at establishing a conclusion, but does so with weaker premises, is a stronger argument. Call this an argument's *efficiency*. The other side is that an argument that establishes a stronger conclusion from premises that are no stronger, is a stronger argument. Call this an argument's *yield*. These twin notions of a stronger argument are additional to the more basic virtues of an argument's logical validity and the truth of its premises. Holding those things equal, an argument's strength depends on its efficiency.

The efficiency of an argument is essentially polemical in the sense that it is relative to an intended target interlocutor. That is, an argument's reliance on weaker premises is not any advantage at all from the standpoint of an interlocutor who fully accepts the less efficient argument's premises. He has no reason whatsoever to prefer a theory with weaker premises. This polemical relativity might be the best explanation of Occam's razor as well. A theory's ontological simplicity might only be an advantage from the standpoint of those who doubt some of the ontological commitments of the theory. On that reading of the principle, someone without any such doubts has no reason to prefer the theory that posits fewer entities.

This principle of normative efficiency is not the same as the general acceptability condition I am using as a requirement on political justification. That is a moral principle and serves a wholly different purpose, though it does employ the idea of moral efficiency. When we say that political justifications must be acceptable to all who are subject to them at least so long as their views are reasonable or qualified, we are saying that a certain kind of efficiency is morally required in political justification. If it is not there, then some or all of those to whom the justification is addressed remain unbound by the proposed obligations, and immune to political coercion the justification purports to permit.

It is also important not to confuse normative efficiency with points about a theory's demanding too much of people in the sense that it places unreasonable burdens on individuals. Here the sense in which a theory is more demanding is entirely different, meaning simply that the conditions it requires in order for laws to be legitimate are met in fewer possible worlds. That might happen because people find the conditions difficult to meet, but it could just as well happen for other reasons. As we have seen, something that is easy might still be unlikely.

Why go into this discussion of normative efficiency? I want to suggest that even theories that are (like mine) nonutopian, are nevertheless at a disadvantage if they impose requirements that are more difficult to meet—that is, met in fewer possible worlds—than mine. Fairness theories have undemanding conditions, but yield very little by way of authority or legitimacy. Correctness theories require more than can be expected, but that would not be a theoretical flaw. They also require more than necessary to account for authority, however, if my own less demanding theory is sound. This point uses the idea of normative efficiency. Theories (if any) in which legitimacy or authority are present only if the deliberation has met strict standards of civility, rationality, virtue, and public-spiritedness are, again, unlikely to be met, though that is no objection, since they are apparently not impossible to meet. But they demand too much if they demand more than necessary, which would be shown by developing a less demanding theory that accounts at least as well for authority or legitimacy.

Finally, recall our idea of a model deliberation: a hypothetical deliberative situation with apparent epistemic value. We can now refine the sense in which mirroring the model deliberation is not an appropriate practical goal. A standard should not be removed from normative political theory just because it will not be met. That is not a moral consideration, after all. The question is whether it could be met, never mind whether or not it will or is at all likely to be. We can safely say that the model deliberation is practically certain not to be instantiated in public political deliberation. That does not mean that it is impossible, however. If it is not impossible, we should accept it as a goal. I will not try to settle whether it is possible. But even it if is, and so counts as a goal by our non-utopophobic standards, we should still reject the mirroring view as it is normally formulated. Since the model deliberation's genuine instantiation will always be very unlikely, we should not seek to approximate it as closely as possible. The problem of second best takes over in all realistic cases for reasons discussed here and in chapter 10. This is all compatible with saying (if we should decide that it is true) that full instantiation of the model deliberation is something we can and should do. We are realistic about what is likely, and we adjust our aims accordingly. But to drop the standard because it will not be met would indicate a morally specious utopophobia.[18]

N o t e s

Chapter One Democratic Authority

1. *The Social Contract*, book II, chap. 5.
2. See Rawls 1993.
3. Nelson (1980, 18–19) notices that a coin flip could be said to be fair in the procedural sense, though he does not ask on what grounds fairness theories are entitled to prefer other fair procedures to this one.
4. See Sears and Funk 1990.

Chapter Two Truth and Despotism

1. Arendt 1967, 114. At several points in this chapter I draw on Estlund 1993.
2. Ibid., 115.
3. Ibid., 122.
4. Ibid., 133.
5. Ibid., 120.
6. Rawls 1993, 139–140.
7. Ibid., 129.
8. See Schumpeter 1976.
9. Arrow 1963, 22–23. Buchanan and Tullock 1962, 11–12: "We shall reject at the outset any organic interpretation of collective activity. . . . Only some organic conception of society can postulate the emergence of a mystical general will that is derived independently of the decision-making process in which the political choices made by the separate individuals are controlling." Tullock 1979, 31, 33 (cited in Mansbridge 1990): "The traditional view of government has always been that it sought something called the 'public interest,' [but] with public choice, all of this has changed. . . . the public interest point of view still informs many statements by public figures and the more old-fashioned students of politics."
10. Habermas 1996, 106.
11. Ibid., 285.
12. Rawls 1950, 317–35. On page 1 he calls the theories "authoritarian."
13. See Rawls 1971.
14. See Rawls 1993.
15. See Habermas 1999.
16. A note about this word I have invented for convenience. From the Greek *episteme*, meaning knowledge, the word is meant to stand for rule of the knowers. What I will mean by epistocracy is not quite this simple, as will emerge in the text, just as the idea of democracy is often more than the simple etymological

indication of rule of the people. An epistocrat might be a wise ruler or an advocate of epistocracy, depending on the context (the word is like "egoist" in this way). A democrat, by contrast, is an advocate of democracy, not a democratic citizen. A bureaucrat, however, is not an advocate of bureaucracy, but a person in administrative power. "Epistemocracy" would be truer to the Greek, but that gives us "epistemocrats," which seems too high a price.

17. *Gorgias* 446b–468e.

18. Supporting texts include *Crito* 47c9–d2, *Laches* 184e8–9, *Gorgias* 463d1–465e1, *Republic* I 341c4–342e11. This is also Richard Kraut's interpretation in *Socrates and the State* (see Kraut 1984, 231–44). Kraut calls this Socratic view authoritarian, but that seems inappropriate when the view is conjoined with another Socratic view (as Kraut agrees) that it is a permanent human fact that there are no experts of the relevant kind. At most, we could say that it is one of authoritarianism's central claims, although it is not by itself authoritarian.

19. Gregory Vlastos argues that precisely what Socrates meant when he denied that he or anyone had wisdom is a matter of some subtlety (and irony) (see Vlastos 1985). Vlastos argues that Socrates was a supporter of Athenian democracy (see Vlastos 1983).

20. The minimal sense of truth is defined above at page 25.

21. I slide freely between the ideas of actual wisdom, capacity for wisdom, and so on, so long as I believe my points hold equally well across these variants.

22. Here I agree in general terms with David Copp (see Copp 1993, 103–6). Noncognitivism might still be a way of avoiding the inference from expertise to authority, however. The reason is that noncognitivism is notoriously troubled by the phenomenon of rational inference. It is natural to suppose that if some elite had expert knowledge, at least in the minimal sense, and (the authority tenet) such experts had a special moral claim to rule, that it "follows" that there is an elite with a special moral claim to rule. But if the Authority Tenet is neither true nor false in the full, nonminimal sense, then we are lacking the normal "truth-functional" interpretation of what it means for the conclusion to follow from the premises. Noncognitivism, then, could resist the three-step case for epistocracy by exploiting these difficulties about inference. Of course, noncognitivism might itself be undone unless this lack can be made good. For recent discussions of these issues about noncognitivism and rational inference, see Van Roojen 2004.

23. Benn 1967, 39.

24. Rousseau 1968, 60 (book I, chap. 6).

25. See especially chapter 5, "The Flight from Substance," and chapter 13, "Rejecting the Democracy/Contractualism Analogy." I criticize Joshua Cohen's characterization of a qualified acceptability requirement as a "principle of deliberative inclusion" at page 91.

CHAPTER THREE AN ACCEPTABILITY REQUIREMENT

1. See Simmons 1999.

2. See page 134, where I point out that on my view there can be authority without legitimacy when normative consent is present.

3. Rawls 1993, 116. See also pages xx and 94 for similar statements.

4. It should not be thought that since the principle limits its application to questions of constitutional essentials, therefore since it does not address any constitutional essentials, it does not apply to itself. This principle is part of an account of the justification of the tenets of justice as fairness, Rawls's theory of constitutional essentials and matters of basic justice. Many things plainly fall under this principle of legitimacy even if they do not themselves address specific constitutional matters or principles of justice, such as metaphysical conceptions of the self, theological doctrines, or philosophical theories of the nature of morality. Rawls explicitly acknowledges the principle of legitimacy's application to these three matters at pp. 29 ff., 9–10, and Lecture III (passim), respectively.

5. Rawls 1993, 137.

6. Ibid., 10.

7. While I shall use the simple language of necessary conditions, sufficient conditions, if, only if, and so on, these are not meant (unless specified) in the sense of "material implication." For most purposes it suffices to think of the conditions discussed as rules or qualifications for membership. This will trigger the appropriate logical relations. I will sometimes substitute "required" for "necessary" and "decisive" for "sufficient" to mark this point. I give some more details about the logical issues in "The Insularity of the Reasonable: Why Political Liberalism Must Admit the Truth" (1998), note 12.

8. If C is a broad and diverse group, as I am assuming it is, it might seem unlikely that it will all accept any instance of AN. I take up this concern later.

9. Lyons 1986, 89.

10. The Branch Davidians are a religious cult many of whose members perished in a well-publicized battle with federal authorities in Waco, Texas, on April 19, 1993.

11. Remember, I am leaving open the possibility that actual acceptability is also required for admissibility, in addition to acceptability to all possible qualified views. If only one of the insular specifications were actually acceptable, there would be no troubling plurality of admissible insular groups. But, of course, more than one might be actually acceptable, and so this is no general solution to the theoretical difficulty.

12. I am grateful to Barry Miller for an instructive seminar paper that raises related questions, Brown University, Spring 1998.

13. I am grateful to Derek Bowman for pointing this out to me.

14. See Raz 1990.

15. Ibid., 15.

CHAPTER FOUR THE LIMITS OF FAIR PROCEDURE

1. Thomas Christiano reaches for the most minimal definitional common ground with "a society in which all or most of the population has the opportunity jointly to play an essential if not always very formative role in the determination of legislation and policy" (Christiano 1990, 151). This leaves out explicit mention of voting, so my account of the core idea may be slightly less minimal, but Christiano's would do for my purposes. Richard Arneson offers, as uncontroversial, a gloss essentially equivalent to mine, including voting. See Arneson 2003.

2. I will discuss Joshua Cohen's apparent dissent from this proposition in chapter 5, "The Flight from Substance."

3. George Sher and John Broome offer substantial accounts of procedural fairness, and my account differs significantly from both. They both link the equal chances involved in a random procedure to substantively equal claims on the goods in question. This is a highly implausible constraint on the use of random procedures. On my account procedural fairness comes into its own precisely when such substantive standards are not available. For Broome's main discussion of fairness, see Broome 1991. See also Sher 1980.

4. Broome holds fairness to be a defeasible value in this way. See Broome 1991.

5. On my account of fairness, it is procedural in a way that is more specific than the idea of impartiality. But this is not to be assumed here, so let the term *fairness* apply to impartialist moralities for the sake of argument.

6. Here I depart from Broome's view, according to which fairness is always *pro tanto* good or right.

7. My point is different from Williams's famous use of the example, which in his hands is meant to count against an impartialist structure to ethics at any level. My point is compatible with granting that ethics or morality is ultimately a form of impartiality.

8. Broome's view is closer to a theory of substantive fairness or justice than it is to procedural fairness. See note 3 above.

9. I do not call it "instrumentally" fair, partly to avoid, for now, questions of the value of fairness. That term might seem to build in the claim that such procedures are instrumentally valuable. Also my qualms about the idea of substantive fairness apply here too. Prospective procedural fairness may be better called *prospective justice*.

10. It seems to be the idea of procedural fairness that Barry discusses in *Political Argument*, chap. 6 (see Barry 1965). The principle of "fair play" as used by Rawls and others refers to something else entirely. "Playing fair" in ordinary language seems to refer to what I call *noncheating retrospective fairness*. The

Hart/Rawls idea I will call *fair cooperation*. It is not about the fairness of collective decision procedures at all. See Hart 1955; Rawls 1964, 3–18.

11. I do not mean that in that case there would be, in effect, an informal procedure and a unanimous decision, which would be a fair procedure in any case. That is not obvious. Even if all agreed about the correct decision, in a fair decision procedure there might be opposing groups because some might press their own interests rather than what they thought ought to be done.

12. Riker 1982, 116.

13. I say more about this distinction at page 76, where I distinguish my view from Pettit's "tracking" criterion.

14. In Estlund (1990) I exploit this fact to suggest that the concept of democracy strongly suggests that votes should not be conceived as expressions of preferences.

15. Philip Pettit argues that putting people's preferences in control of policy keeps them free from an important kind of domination by the state as it makes policy. For this moral purpose it is apparently sufficient if policy is forced to track preferences. I am grateful to him for illuminating discussion of the question whether there is something more to people being in charge than their preferences being in charge. See Pettit 1997 and 1999b.

16. The structure of my argument echoes the familiar antidrug dialectic (and I thank Nomy Arpaly for noticing the clever bridge term *substance abuse*). In reaction to substance abuse, some antidrug rhetoric retreats all the way to zero tolerance. Critics respond by observing that virtually everyone uses *some* drugs (caffeine, alcohol, antihistamine, tranquilizers, etc.). The zero-tolerance stance is criticized as hypocritical, and the debate is shifted to the question of which substance use is to be criticized and which is not. Fair proceduralism is the zero-tolerance stance in democratic theory's debates about the appropriate use of substance.

Chapter Five The Flight from Substance

1. For two overviews of the deliberative democracy movement, see the introduction to Bohman and Rehg 1997, and Freeman 2000. The deliberative democracy literature and the normative social choice theory literature are brought into vigorous engagement in John Dryzek, *Deliberative Democracy and Beyond* (2000, chap. 2).

2. A good example is Sunstein, "Preferences and Politics," *Philosophy and Public Affairs* (1991). Sunstein's discussion shows the influence of Jon Elster, *Sour Grapes: Studies in the Subversion of Rationality* (1983); and "The Market and the Forum," in Elster and Hylland 1986. The latter piece is explicitly under the influence of Habermas. Habermas states this approach clearly in *Between Facts and Norms* (1996, 181).

3. See Habermas 1996, 285. See also Cronin and De Greiff 1999, 255–56.

4. Habermas 1996, 453.

5. See Cronin and De Greiff 1999, 260.

6. See discussion and citations in Kenneth Baynes, *The Normative Grounds of Social Criticism* (1992, 112–15).

7. See Habermas 1979, 186; Cronin and De Greiff 1999, 31, 34, 259; and Habermas 1999, 103–4.

8. Rawls 1995, 176.

9. Cohen 1989, 22.

10. Ibid.

11. Cohen 1996, 103.

12. Ibid. Gutmann and Thompson, in "Deliberative Democracy beyond Process" (2002), suggest that while substantive principles are not to be avoided, they are also not to be treated as somehow outside of democratic theory properly conceived. Cohen's claim seems to me more ambitious: that the substantive principles that may be appealed to are themselves distinctively democratic values.

13. Rawls 1993, 137.

14. Hobbes, *Leviathan*, any edition; and Kavka 1986, chap. 10.

15. In a recent piece, Cohen attributes this same view to Rawls and defends it in new detail: laws or policies violating the liberal principle of legitimacy (acceptability to all reasonable citizens) can be criticized on the basis of distinctively democratic values, since there is no "collective authorization" by the people if this principle is violated (see Cohen 2002). But Cohen is happy to acknowledge that such a principle incorporates "substantive" or procedure-independent standards. And he rightly denies that this alone would compromise political autonomy. And since he shows that Rawls's view is deeply democratic in two other ways—by requiring democratic political institutions, and by resting on a conception of society as composed of free equals—I fail to see what is gained by construing this principle of legitimacy, which says nothing about any actual acts of willing, or voting, or authorizing, as a conception of democratic collective authorization. Stretching the idea of democracy in order to reach this view risks giving the impression that if the principle could not be accounted for democratically it would be incompatible with democracy, or in some other way inappropriate or unavailable. But Cohen's own discussion is ammunition against that conclusion.

16. Waldron 2000, 529.

17. Several points in the following paragraphs draw from previous work of mine: see Estlund 1997, 2000a, and 2000b.

CHAPTER SIX EPISTEMIC PROCEDURALISM

1. This chapter draws on Estlund (1997).

2. This is one natural reading of the views of Jürgen Habermas and Joshua Cohen. James Fishkin also seems to hold to a view of this type. See my 1994 review of his book *The Dialogue of Justice: Toward a Self-Reflective Society* (1992).

3. I owe this example to Derek Bowman.

4. If you think the value here is simply one of education for the future, let it be a prom at a senior center where few if any will be around for the next prom.

5. I agree with William Nelson (1980) that the question whether a political system will yield substantively fair legislation seems at least as important as the question whether it is fair in the procedural sense. This point, however, leads Nelson in a more instrumentalist direction than is taken here.

6. Rousseau 1968, 77 (book II, chap. 4).

7. Locke 1980, 52–53 (chap. VIII, pars. 96–98).

8. Rousseau 1968, 153 (book IV, chap. 2).

9. Rawls 1950, 319. Rawls goes on to identify the proper source of moral authority as the *collective* sense of right. This raises interesting questions that cannot be pursued here.

10. Rawls 1971, 356–57.

11. Notice that Cohen's definition of democratic legitimacy (". . . if and only if [the outcomes] would be the object of an [ideal] agreement . . .") commits him to a correctness theory rather than a proceduralist criterion of legitimacy; when actual procedures fail to match the answer of the hypothetical ideal procedure, they are not democratically legitimate, even though (as he seems to think) they are reliable evidence, to some degree, about that ideal standard. This is a crucial difference from epistemic proceduralism as developed here.

12. See chapter 12, "The Irrelevance of the Jury Theorem."

13. See the end of chapter 14, "Utopophobia," for more on this point.

14. This is the epistemic conception of democracy defended in Carlos Nino's *The Ethics of Human Rights* (see Nino 1991, 245–55). For example, "The democratic origin of a legal rule provides us with a reason to *believe* that there is good reason to accept its content and to *act* accordingly" (255). This is deference to the expertise of the procedure with a vengeance.

15. I do not mean to be assuming that moral noncognitivism is false (see the earlier discussion in chapter 2). I wish there were a better word than "cognitive" to mark that the participants address questions whose correct answers are independent of the answers arrived at by individuals or the collective decision process. Even noncognitivists can recognize such a thing. They can say that some things are just whether or not anyone holds that they are just.

16. Rousseau 1968, 153 (book IV, chap. 2)

17. See Wolff 1998.

18. This point leaves open whether the exceptions can still be accounted for without going beyond distinctively democratic values. This is a popular claim, as we saw from our treatment of Habermas and Cohen in chapter 5, "The Flight from Substance." For a recent account that explains the exceptions by reference to other democratic values alone, see Corey Brettschneider (2007).

19. The idea and possibility of a public conception of justice is elaborated in great depth by John Rawls, in Rawls 1993.

20. I'm grateful to Philip Pettit for pressing this point.

21. There remains, as I point out in chapter 4, an element of fairness in epistemic proceduralism's use of majority rule.

CHAPTER SEVEN AUTHORITY AND NORMATIVE CONSENT

1. See Raz 1986, chap. 2. This definition of authority is not committed to Raz's important view about when and why this moral power is present.

2. I thank John Deigh for the example.

3. John Simmons comes pretty close to what I call consent theory, with the following qualification. He argues only that there is no (state) authority without consent *unless*, as, for example, Kantian views of authority claim, accepting authority is necessary to discharge some moral duty or obligation. If, as I think, there can be a duty to accept authority as such, he has allowed that there might be authority without consent. But he doubts that there is ever such a duty. See part 4 of his essay "Justification and Legitimacy," in the volume of his papers, *Justification and Legitimacy* (2001).

4. *Of the Original Contract* (1968, original 1748), par. 4.

5. See discussion in chapter 3 of this feature of the qualified acceptability requirement.

6. That is, unless Joe has already consented by getting on the plane. I assume that he has not, since you cannot consent without realizing it.

7. In Estlund 2005a I argue that normative consent theory does not rely on hypothetical scenarios any more than actual consent theories. I skip that here for reasons of space.

8. I give more support for this interpretation of Rawls and Scanlon in chapter 13, "Rejecting the Democracy/Contractualism Analogy."

9. This comes up again below in chapter 8, at page 151.

10. For the leading criticisms of such attempts in the context of state authority, see Simmons 1979.

11. With all their differences, Kant (1979), Anscombe (1978), and Wellman (1996) all arguably provide examples of this general approach.

12. This is Scanlon's example, for slightly different purposes, in "Preference and Urgency" (see Scanlon 1975).

13. Nozick 1974, 90–96.

14. For example, see Klosko 1992, and replies by John Simmons in Simmons 2001, chaps. 1–2.

CHAPTER EIGHT ORIGINAL AUTHORITY AND THE DEMOCRACY/JURY ANALOGY

1. See chapter 3, "An Acceptability Requirement."

2. Locke writes: "no one ought to harm another in his life, health, liberty or possessions" (see Locke 1980, 9 [chap. II, §6]).

3. Elsewhere, I explore the implications of the anti-reverse-vigilante idea for jailers and executioners, and then in a broader context than just punishment, also for soldiers who are commanded to pursue unjust wars. See Estlund (2007).

4. This is related to the case of the tyrant's child at page xxx.

5. Here are a few sources: Simmons 1979; Edmundson, 1999; and Wellman and Simmons 2005.

6. Simmons presses this point in *Moral Principles and Political Obligation* (1979) in the chapter on fair play theories.

7. This is too simple in the end, since there might be some fair arrangement in which responsibility is apportioned in a way that takes some of us off the hook.

8. This is similar to examples that Nozick (1974) gives on pp. 90–95.

9. Klosko (1992) has pursued the fair play approach in a way that concentrates on especially weighty matters. His approach differs from mine by staying with the idea of benefits to the agent, however.

10. Simmons 1979.

11. Wellman and Simmons 2005, 183.

12. While charity is sometimes defined as morally optional, here it obviously is not.

13. At page 186 (Wellman and Simmons 2005), he admits at least the "intelligibility" of the claim that we are all "naturally bound to humanity," and that this generates a fair distribution of what he calls the duties of charity.

14. See Waldron 1993b. It is also separate from the agent-neutrally urgent task to which the districted system of obligation is meant to be a solution.

15. By global I do not mean a problem that afflicts people the world over, but rather a problem that, as it were, calls out to all agents, not just to those in some locale or those in certain associations.

16. See page 131.

17. Simmons is persuasive on this. See Simmons 1979, chap. 5.

18. The situation is complicated by the fact that, according to the normative consent approach, if consent would, hypothetically, have been required if it were solicited, then in the nonhypothetical world there is authority, and the question of actual consent is moot. That is, in the real condition there is no important general commitment task in those cases. But this should not confuse us. The question is whether there is such a task in the hypothetical condition where there is not authority but consent to new authority is solicited, not whether there is such a commitment task in the condition in which there is authority because consent would, hypothetically, have been required. In the hypothetical pre-authority condition the general commitment task, I claim, would be important enough that we would all have duties to commit ourselves by promising to obey the appropriate local justice system. That would be a morally required contribution to the general commitment task, a task that would be pressing in that imaginary condition. Now, stepping back from the hypothetical, since there would be such a

duty to consent to the proposed authority, there is (as argued in chapter 7) in the real condition, an obligation to obey just as if one had consented. For Prejurians, there is political authority based on normative consent. They were not asked for consent to new authority, but if they had been, they would have been morally required to give that consent as a contribution to what would have been an important commitment task. As a result, they are obligated now as if they had actually consented to authority.

19. See Wellman 1996; and Wellman and Simmons 2005.

20. "The death-penalty inflicted upon criminals may be looked on in much the same light: it is in order that we may not fall victims to an assassin that we consent to die if we ourselves turn assassins. In this treaty, so far from disposing of our own lives, we think only of securing them, and it is not to be assumed that any of the parties then expects to get hanged" (Rousseau 1968, 79 [book II, chap. 5]).

CHAPTER NINE HOW WOULD DEMOCRACY KNOW?

1. More precisely, the claim to investigate is that democracy tends to make the best decisions of any alternative political arrangement so far as can be ascertained within public reason, and does better than random.

2. For discussion and literature on this point, see Sinnott-Armstrong 2003.

3. Recall, we do not rely on a full account of reasonableness or qualification and then deduce that non-Christians are qualified. At several points, and this is one, we see where we would need to draw that line in order for the theory to have plausible implications.

4. Waldron 1999b, 253–54.

5. In science and in politics, we might use inductive inference from a procedure's ability to get the right answer in areas other than the one in question. This leaves entirely aside how those other truths came to be known. Still, such inductive arguments are within the category of formal rather than substantive epistemic approaches, since they do not judge the method's reliability on the question at hand by evaluating its performance on the question at hand.

6. I draw loosely on Habermas's ideal speech situation and Cohen's ideal democratic deliberation, although, as I say, the theoretical role I give to this imaginary situation is explicitly epistemic, answering to some further and prior moral standards. The ideal deliberative situations in Habermas and Cohen are evidently more constitutive and morally fundamental.

7. See Sunstein 2006.

8. Hayek discussed this point often. See, for example, his 1936 lecture, "Economics and Knowledge" (Hayek 1981).

9. Lavoie 1986.

10. See Schumpeter 1976, chap. 21. See also Brennan and Lomasky 1993.

11. See Sunstein 2006. Sunstein's book surveys some of the growing empirical literature on democratic deliberation. Engagement with the often skeptical orientation of those studies is beyond my scope in this book. My remarks in chapter 14, "Utopophobia," are relevant here, but empirical critiques will ultimately have to be considered one by one.

12. See List and Pettit 2005.

13. I borrow this from Christian List (2006). List's article contains a good introduction to the issues and a useful bibliography of related pieces.

14. There is an interesting practical problem (the main topic of List's paper [List 2006]) about whether the committee should have the authority to decide the tenure question, or whether it would be better for it only to decide the teaching and research questions, with the tenure question being settled automatically by those decisions. Epistemic proceduralism says to choose the one that is, so far as can be determined in a generally acceptable way, epistemically best.

Chapter Ten The Real Speech Situation

1. For a good discussion and guide to the texts, see Thomas McCarthy's classic discussion, *The Critical Theory of Jürgen Habermas* (1979).

2. A clear and influential example is Joshua Cohen, who writes, "The ideal deliberative procedure provides a model for institutions, a model that they should mirror, so far as possible" (1989, 26).

3. Meiklejohn 1960.

4. The idea was initially formulated in an economic context. See Lipsey and Lancaster 1957.

5. Marcuse 1969.

6. Mill 1991.

7. Marcuse 1969, 89.

8. Marcuse speaks of "freedom of thought and expression as preconditions of finding the way to freedom" (1969, 88). While he never clearly says that tolerance would promote truth under proper conditions, the structure of his argument seems to assume this, at least for the sake of argument. He argues that the conditions under which pure tolerance might be thought to support truth do not, anyway, obtain.

9. Ibid., 90.

10. The crucial idea here, as we will see, is countervailing distortions, so its application is not limited to views of the ideal deliberation in which the only thing counted as a distortion is power. I will nevertheless describe the point in those simple terms for the sake of concision. Of course, reason could itself be called a kind of power. A deeper objection would be to claim that this kind of power is not normatively less objectionable than any other. That sort of critique cannot be considered here. See my "Deliberation and Wide Civility: Response

to the Discussants," a reply to comments on my "Deliberation Down and Dirty" (Estlund 2001a).

11. See Habermas 1979, 186; Cronin and De Greiff 1999, 31, 34, 259; and Habermas 1996, 103–104.

12. Habermas 1990, 67.

13. A longer discussion of the ideas in this section can be found in Estlund 2000b.

14. The name "progressive" might connote three relevant things: (a) promotes quantity of input in a politically Pareto superior way, (b) promotes quality of decisions by independent standards of, e.g., justice, (c) involves progressive rates for marginal vouchers.

15. Only about 8 percent of eligible voters contribute any money to political campaigns. Miller and the National Election Studies 1994.

16. My interpretation puts a lot of weight on Habermas's discussion in *Between Facts and Norms* (1996, chaps. 7–8). For one important passage about the advantages of "unrestricted communication," see pp. 307–8. See also his reference at page 323 to "the projection of ideals, in the light of which we can identify deviations," and the legitimacy of using "such a projection for a thought experiment." I do not suggest that my view in this chapter is Habermas's, only that there are some instructive similarities.

17. The metaphor of a template is meant to evoke a draftsman's template, a flat, clear sheet with certain shapes cut through. The shapes can be used to draw those shapes, but also to see exactly how and where existing shapes deviate from the model. It is this identification of deviations that I propose as the template-like value of the model deliberation.

18. This is how I interpret Habermas's discussion in *Between Facts and Norms* (1996, chap. 7). For example, "The normative self-understanding of deliberative politics certainly requires a discursive mode of sociation *for the legal community,* but this mode does not extend to the whole of society in which the constitutionally organized political system is *embedded*" (301–2).

19. Bessette 1980.

20. I reflect on one concrete example of actual political protest in "Deliberation Down and Dirty: Must Political Expression Be Civil?" (2001b, 49–67).

CHAPTER ELEVEN WHY NOT AN EPISTOCRACY OF THE EDUCATED?

1. Plato 2000, book IV.

2. Ibid.

3. The groups Mill proposes to privilege electorally are (1) employers, managers, and professionals rather than workers, because they are likely to be more intelligent; (2) graduates of universities, or those achieving other suitable academic degrees. I will concentrate on the second only, for simplicity, though I believe the direction of my argument would apply more generally.

4. Sara Monoson argues for a less rigidly authoritarian reading of Plato than is common, but even her reading would not undermine the contrast (see Monoson 2000).

5. Plato 2000, 138 (book IV, 442e).

6. Thanks to Jed Silverstein for discussion of the subtleties here.

7. For a recent argument in favor of the Millian idea, see Caplan 2007. For my critique of Caplan, see Estlund 2006, and the vigorous exchange with Caplan at that Web site.

8. Mill 1991, 331.

9. Ibid., 334.

10. Plato 2000, book IV.

11. For a useful discussion of these texts, see "Aristotle's Multitude" in Waldron 1999a.

12. Aristotle, *Politics* (1984) 1284b32.

13. 1284a4–14.

14. It would seem to follow that if there are several equally preeminent people it would be better for them to rule as a group than any one of them alone. He says something along these lines at 1286b1–8, but the element of special preeminence is again missing, as he speaks of "a number of men equal in excellence." Also, at 1283b17–30: "In an aristocracy, . . . if one citizen is better than the other members of the government, however good they may be, he too, upon the same principle of justice, should rule over them." But he then regards this and similar arguments as *reductio*: "To those who claim to be masters of the government on the ground of their excellence or their wealth, the many might fairly answer that they themselves are often better and richer than the few— I do not say individually, but collectively."

15. It is therefore crucially different from Condorcet's jury theorem (to which it is often compared) that makes no use of communication. That discussion is central to Aristotle's account as is well shown by Waldron (see Waldron 1999a). I discuss these points further in chapter 12, "The Irrelevance of the Jury Theorem."

16. Mill 1991, 334.

17. A good critical survey of empirical work on various such dimensions of political knowledge in the United States is Delli Carpini and Keeler 1996. In chapter 14, "Utopophobia," I question whether the sorts of knowledge I list in the text are necessary for good ruling. There is no inconsistency between that and what I am suggesting here: that, other things equal, those sorts of knowledge (or some such list that the reader may construct) improve the ability to rule wisely.

18. See Rawls 1971, 357; and Green 2003.

19. Mill 1991, 337.

20. I try to make this puzzle vivid in the deck of cards example at page 105.

21. Mill 1991, 331.

22. At page 36.

23. I benefited from Joshua Tropp pressing this objection in a seminar paper.

24. Karen Jones discusses the idea of an epistemic privilege for victims of injustice in "Second-Hand Moral Knowledge" (1999). Claudia Card (1996) discusses the idea that such privilege might be limited by damage that accompanies the victimization.

25. The same methodological point goes for my assumption that some kind of education promotes wise rule, and that this is beyond qualified denial.

26. There may be the appearance of inconsistency in my argument. If we cannot assume that the discounted groups have any special insight, then what warranted the objection that privileging certain demographic groups might do enough epistemic damage to offset the gains from their being educated? But this is all consistent. Special insight can be denied or believed without disqualification. Since it can be believed, the demographic objection is not unreasonable or disqualified. But since it can be denied, no special insight can be appealed to as a justification for topping up the voting power of discounted groups, as I have been arguing. Fortunately, as I say in the text, I am not arguing for equal voting power, but only against a certain kind of argument for unequal voting power.

CHAPTER TWELVE THE IRRELEVANCE OF THE JURY THEOREM

1. Aristotle 2002, book 3, chap. 11.

2. For a good accessible survey of the varieties of collective wisdom, see Surowiecki 2004.

3. Originally published by Marquis de Condorcet (1785).

4. This paragraph borrows wording from Goodin and Estlund 2004.

5. See, for example, Goodin (2003, 125–26); Waldron (in Estlund, Waldron, Grofman, and Feld 1989, 1327).

6. The claims in this paragraph are defended in Estlund 1994b. See other similar literature in Goodin 2003, 96 (note 18).

7. Here I borrow from my review of Goodin's *Reflective Democracy* (Estlund, 2005b).

8. Goodin and List 2001.

9. Goodin and List say this themselves at page 284.

10. I am very grateful to Christian List and Kai Spiekermann for running some unpublished calculations at my request, which tend to support this conjecture.

11. For further worries along these lines, see Waldron's contribution to Estlund et al., 1989, 1317–22.

12. A useful discussion of this approach in democratic theory is in Goodin 2003, chap. 6.

13. *Politics* 3.11.

14. For a good survey of these challenges with an eye to democratic theory, see Sunstein 2006.

CHAPTER THIRTEEN REJECTING THE DEMOCRACY/CONTRACTUALISM ANALOGY

1. Since I will reject the analogy, no evaluation of contractualism is necessary. Epistemic proceduralism neither relies on it nor rejects it.

2. Scanlon 1998, 153.

3. See Rawls 1993, 137. Rawls gives a broadly contractualist reason for this, but many others accept it on more general liberal grounds. Waldron is an example. See "Theoretical Foundations of Liberalism," in Waldron 1993a, 56–57.

4. I will use *outcome* and *decision* interchangeably, but outcome is less ambiguous as between process and product.

5. In Estlund 2003 I argue that William Nelson, Brian Barry, and Joshua Cohen are among those who have influentially taken this view.

6. Rawls 1993, 330, emphasis added. Here Rawls echoes a point from *A Theory of Justice* (1971, 221–22).

7. See above at pages 240–41.

8. See Rawls 1993, 219.

9. For Jürgen Habermas's view, see Habermas 1996.

10. Nelson 1980.

11. Sen 1994.

12. See Samuel Freeman's instructive discussion of this point as it figures in the views of Cohen and Habermas, in "Deliberative Democracy: A Sympathetic Comment" (Freeman 2000).

13. Nelson 1980, 111–18.

14. Ibid., 119.

15. Philip Pettit observes that when we, actual moral agents, justify our actions to others, "we suppose in the very act of trying to justify ourselves . . . that there is an independent sense of right." This supposition is not available to the hypothetical contractors, which marks a decisive disanalogy. See Pettit 1999a.

16. Rawls writes, "The point of the original position is to understand our conception of justice . . . by seeing how this conception is limited by and can be constructed from other notions that it is natural to think of as more basic and abstract. . . . This is the reason for bracketing conceptions of the right in the construction of the original position" (Rawls 1999a, 269).

17. Michael Ridge instructively defends Scanlon against these charges in "Debate: Saving Scanlon: Contractualism and Agent-Relativity." See Ridge 2001, 472–81. My interpretation of Scanlon is indebted to Ridge's article.

18. "If we were to appeal to a prior notion of rightness to tell us which considerations are morally relevant and which are entitled to prevail in cases of conflict, then the contractualist framework would be unnecessary, since all the work would already have been done by this prior notion" (Scanlon 1998, 213). See also page 214, where he says it would be circular to appeal to a "noncontractualist theory of right."

19. Scanlon resists the complaint that the theory has little value unless all this content is made explicit so results can be cranked out mechanically (Scanlon 1998, 217–18). This is not my complaint. The objection I raise in the text is about the structure of the account regardless of what particular content is given to the key ideas such as reasonableness.

20. Ibid., 218.

21. Ibid., 218–23.

22. Ibid., 5.

23. Barry explicitly rejects veto power for individuals or minorities despite noting that this is suggested by his democracy/contractualism analogy. See Barry 1995, 107.

24. See Nelson 1980, chap. 6. Cohen says that, "when properly conducted, then democratic politics involves public deliberation focused on the common good" (Cohen 1989, 19).

25. I believe Barry's idea of an "empirical approximation" of a Scanlonian original position conflates outcome similarity and procedural similarity. See Barry 1995, 100, where "circumstances of impartiality" are glossed as referring to "empirical conditions that approximate those of a Scanlonian original position," but are also *defined* as "the conditions under which the substantive rules of justice of a society will tend actually to be just."

CHAPTER FOURTEEN UTOPOPHOBIA: CONCESSION AND ASPIRATION
IN DEMOCRATIC THEORY

1. See Schumpeter 1976, esp. chaps. 21 and 22; and Arrow 1951, 1963.

2. For reference to much of this work, see Caplan 2007.

3. "Survey Reveals Child Development Knowledge Gap among Adults," http://www.zerotothree.org/parent_poll.html.

4. Ko, Ramsell, and Wilson 1992.

5. "What Do Parents Know about Contraception?" (2004).

6. Mehta and Binns 1998.

7. See Tetlock 2005; and Louis Menand's informative review, "Everybody's an Expert" (2005).

8. See Arneson 1995.

9. This strategy is popular among many authors broadly following Schumpeter. See Przeworski 1999; Posner 2003.

10. Rousseau 1979 (originally 1762), 34. For other editions, this is in the preface, paragraph 5.

11. Rawls 1999b, 4.

12. Whether an action is possible is not just a matter of whether the agent could do it if he wanted to, of course. It might be impossible that he will come to want to. Depending on what is making the wanting impossible, it might or might not preempt moral responsibility for the failure to perform the action. In

any case, my main point stands: moral responsibility is not preempted by small probability, but only by impossibility (or maybe extreme difficulty) of certain kinds. I am grateful to Joshua Tropp for pressing this issue.

13. I will discuss another important example in chapter 10, "The Real Speech Situation."

14. Lipsey and Lancaster 1956–57.

15. See discussions in Singer 1972; Williams 1985; Kagan 1989; and Scheffler 1982.

16. Posner 2003 is a recent example.

17. See Caplan 2007; and Hardin forthcoming.

18. I benefited from a discussion of this point with Reed Caster.

Bibliography

Anscombe, E. 1978. "On the Source of the Authority of the State." *Ratio: An International Journal of Analytic Philosophy* 20:1–28.

Arendt, Hannah. 1967. "Truth and Politics." In *Philosophy, Politics and Society*. 3rd ser. Ed. Peter Laslett and W. G. Runciman. Oxford: Blackwell.

Aristotle. 1984. *Politics*. Translated by Benjamin Jowett. In *The Complete Works of Aristotle*. Vol. 2. Ed. Jonathan Barnes. Princeton, NJ: Princeton University Press.

———. 2002. *Nicomachean Ethics*. Trans. Christopher Rowe. Oxford: Oxford University Press.

Arneson, Richard. 1995. "Democratic Rights at National and Workplace Levels." In *The Idea of Democracy*, ed. David Copp, Jean Hampton, and John E. Roemer. Cambridge: Cambridge University Press.

———. 2003. "Defending the Purely Instrumental Account of Democratic Legitimacy." *Journal of Political Philosophy* 11:122–32.

Arrow, Kenneth. 1963. *Social Choice and Individual Values*. 2nd ed. New Haven, CT: Yale University Press.

Barry, Brian. 1965. *Political Argument*. London: Routledge and Kegan Paul.

———. 1995. *Justice as Impartiality*. Oxford: Oxford University Press.

Baynes, Kenneth. 1992. *The Normative Grounds of Social Criticism: Kant, Rawls, and Habermas*. Albany: SUNY Press.

Beitz, Charles. 1990. *Political Equality: An Essay in Democratic Theory*. Princeton, NJ: Princeton University Press.

Benhabib, Seyla, ed. 1996. *Democracy and Difference: Contesting the Boundaries of the Political*. Princeton, NJ: Princeton University Press.

———. 1996. "Toward a Deliberative Model of Democratic Legitimacy." In *Democracy and Difference: Contesting the Boundaries of the Political*, ed. Seyla Benhabib. Princeton, NJ: Princeton University Press.

Benn, S. 1967. "Equality." In the *Encyclopedia of Philosophy*. Vol. 3. Ed. Paul Edwards. New York: Macmillan.

Bessette, J. M. 1980. "Deliberative Democracy: The Majority Principle in Republican Government." In *How Democratic Is the Constitution?* ed. Robert Goldwin and William Schambra. Washington, DC: American Enterprise Institute for Public Policy Research.

Bohman, James, and William Rehg, eds. 1997. *Deliberative Democracy: Essays on Reason and Politics*. Cambridge, MA: MIT Press.

———. 1998. "The Coming of Age of Deliberative Democracy." *Journal of Political Philosophy* 6:400–425.

Brennan, Geoffrey, and Loren Lomasky. 1993. *Democracy and Decision: The Pure Theory of Electoral Preference.* Cambridge: Cambridge University Press.

Brettschneider, Corey. 2007. *Democratic Rights: The Substance of Self-Government.* Princeton, NJ: Princeton University Press.

Broome, John. 1991. "Fairness." *Proceedings of the Aristotelian Society* 91:87–101.

Buchanan, James M., and Gordon Tullock. 1962. *The Calculus of Consent.* Ann Arbor, MI: University of Michigan Press.

Caplan, Bryan. 2007. *The Myth of the Rational Voter.* Princeton, NJ: Princeton University Press.

Card, Claudia. 1996. *The Unnatural Lottery: Character and Moral Luck.* Philadelphia: Temple University Press.

Christiano, Thomas. 1990. "Freedom, Consensus, and Equality in Collective Decision Making." *Ethics* 101:151–81.

Cohen, Joshua. 1989. "Deliberation and Democratic Legitimacy." In *The Good Polity: Normative Analysis of the State,* ed. Alan Hamlin and Philip Petit. Oxford: Basil Blackwell.

———. 1996. "Procedure and Substance in Democratic Theory." In *Democracy and Difference,* ed. Seyla Benhabib. Princeton, NJ: Princeton University Press.

———. 2002. "For a Democratic Society." In *The Cambridge Companion to Rawls,* ed. Samuel Freeman. Cambridge: Cambridge University Press.

Condorcet, Marquis de. 1785, *Essai sur l'application de l'analyse a la probabilité des decisions rendues a la pluralité des voix.* Paris.

Copp, David. 1993. "Could Political Truth Be a Hazard for Democracy?" In *The Idea of Democracy,* ed. David Copp, Jean Hampton, and John E. Roemer. Cambridge: Cambridge University Press.

Copp, David, Jean Hampton, and John E. Roemer, eds. 1993. *The Idea of Democracy.* Cambridge: Cambridge University Press.

Cronin, Ciaran, and Pablo De Greiff, eds. 1999. *The Inclusion of the Other.* Cambridge, MA: MIT Press.

Dascal, Marcelo, and Ora Gruengard, eds. *Knowledge and Politics: Case Studies in the Relationship between Epistemology and Political Philosophy.* Boulder, CO: Westview Press.

Delli Carpini, Michael X., and Scott Keeler. 1996. *What Americans Know about Politics and Why It Matters.* New Haven, CT: Yale University Press.

Dryzek, John. 2000. *Deliberative Democracy and Beyond.* Oxford: Oxford University Press.

Dworkin, Ronald. 1989. "The Original Position." In *Reading Rawls,* ed. Norman Daniels. Palo Alto, CA: Stanford University Press.

Edmundson, William A., ed. 1999. *The Duty to Obey the Law.* Lanham, MD: Rowman and Littlefield.

Elster, Jon. 1983. *Sour Grapes: Studies in the Subversion of Rationality.* Cambridge: Cambridge University Press.

———. 1986. "The Market and the Forum: Three Varieties of Political Theory."

In *Foundations of Social Choice Theory*. ed. J. Elster and A. Hylland. Cambridge: Cambridge University Press.

Elster, J., and A. Hylland, eds. 1986. *Foundations of Social Choice Theory*. Cambridge: Cambridge University Press.

Estlund, David M. 1990. "Democracy without Preference." *Philosophical Review* 99:397–424.

———. 1993. "Making Truth Safe for Democracy." In *The Idea of Democracy*, ed. David Copp, Jean Hampton, and John F. Roemer. Cambridge: Cambridge University Press.

———. 1994a. "The Dialogue of Justice: Toward a Self-Reflective Society" [review]. *Ethics* 105:186–88.

———. 1994b. "Opinion Leaders, Independence, and Condorcet's Jury Theorem." *Theory and Decision* 36:131–62.

———. 1997. "Beyond Fairness and Deliberation: The Epistemic Dimension of Democratic Authority." In Bohman and Rehg 1997.

———. 1998. "The Insularity of the Reasonable: Why Political Liberalism Must Admit the Truth." *Ethics* 108:252–75.

———. 2000a. "Jeremy Waldron on Law and Disagreement." *Philosophical Studies: An International Journal for Philosophy in the Analytic Tradition* 99:111–28.

———. 2000b. "Political Quality." *Social Philosophy and Policy* 17:127–60.

———. 2001a. "Deliberation and Wide Civility: Response to the Discussants." In *The Boundaries of Freedom of Expression and Order in American Democracy*, ed. Thomas R. Hensley. Kent, OH: Kent State University Press.

———. 2001b. "Deliberation Down and Dirty: Must Political Expression Be Civil?" In *The Boundaries of Freedom of Expression and Order in American Democracy*, ed. Thomas R. Hensley. Kent, OH: Kent State University Press, 2001.

———. 2003. "The Democracy/Contractualism Analogy." *Philosophy and Public Affairs* 31:387–412.

———. 2005a. "Political Authority and the Tyranny of Non-consent." *Philosophical Issues* 15:351–67.

———. 2005b. "Reflective Democracy" [review]. *Ethics* 115:609–14.

———. 2006. "Outsmarting Democracy?" http://www.cato-unbound.org/2006/11/08/david-estlund/out-smarting-democracy/.

———. 2007. "On Following Orders." *Journal of Political Philosophy* 15.

Estlund, David M., Jeremy Waldron, Bernard Grofman, and Scott L. Feld. 1989. "Democratic Theory and the Public Interest: Condorcet and Rousseau Revisited." *American Political Science Review* 83:1317–40.

Fishkin, James S. 1992. *The Dialogue of Justice: Toward a Self-Reflective Society*. New Haven, CT: Yale University Press.

Foot, Phillipa. 1988. "Utilitarianism and the Virtues." In *Consequentialism and Its Critics*, ed. Samuel Scheffler. Oxford: Oxford University Press.

Freeman, Samuel. 2000. "Deliberative Democracy: A Sympathetic Comment." *Philosophy and Public Affairs* 29:371–418.

297

Goodin, Robert E. 2003. *Reflective Democracy.* Oxford: Oxford University Press.

Goodin, Robert E., and David Estlund. 2004. "The Persuasiveness of Democratic Majorities." *Politics, Philosophy and Economics* 3:131–42.

Goodin, Robert E., and Christian List. 2001. "Epistemic Democracy: Generalizing the Condorcet Jury Theorem." *Journal of Political Philosophy* 3:277–306.

Green, Leslie. 2003. "Legal Obligation and Authority." *Stanford Encyclopedia of Philosophy*, April 5, 2006. http://plato.stanford.edu/entries/legal-obligation/.

Gutmann, Amy, and Dennis Thompson. 2002. "Deliberative Democracy beyond Process." *Journal of Political Philosophy* 10:153–74.

Habermas, Jürgen. 1979. *Communication and the Evolution of Society.* Boston: Beacon Press.

———. 1990. "Discourse Ethics." In *Moral Consciousness and Communicative Action.* Cambridge, MA: MIT Press.

———. 1996. *Between Facts and Norms: Contributions to a Discourse Theory of Law and Democracy.* Translated by William Rehg. Cambridge, MA: MIT Press.

———. 1999. "A Short Reply." *Ratio Juris* 12:445–53.

Hardin, Russell. Forthcoming. *Why Know?* Princeton: Princeton University Press.

Hart, H.L.A. 1955. "Are There Any Natural Rights?" *Philosophical Review* 64:175–91.

Hayek, F. A. 1981. "Economics and Knowledge." In *L.S.E. Essays on Cost*, ed. James M. Buchanan and G. F. Thirlby. New York: New York University Press.

Hensley, Thomas R., ed. 2001. *The Boundaries of Freedom of Expression and Order in American Democracy.* Kent, OH: Kent State University Press.

Hume, David. 1748. *Of the Original Contract.*

Issacharoff, Samuel, Pamela S. Karlan, and Richard H. Pildes. 1998. *The Law of Democracy: Legal Structure of the Political Process.* Westbury, NY: Foundation Press.

Jones, Karen. 1999. "Second-Hand Moral Knowledge." *Journal of Philosophy* 96:55–78.

Kagan, Shelly. 1989. *The Limits of Morality.* Oxford: Clarendon Press.

Kant, I. 1979. *Metaphysics of Morals.* In *Kant's Political Writings*, ed. H. P. Reiss. Cambridge: Cambridge University Press.

Kavka, Gregory. 1986. *Hobbesian Moral and Political Theory.* Princeton, NJ: Princeton University Press.

Kinder, D. R., and D. R. Kiewiet. 1981. "Sociotropic Politics: The American Case." *British Journal of Political Science* 11:129–61.

Klosko, George. 1992. *The Principle of Fairness and Political Obligation.* Lanham, MD: Rowman and Littlefield.

Ko, M. L., N. Ramsell, and J. A. Wilson. 1992. "What Do Parents Know about Vitamins?" *Archives of Disease in Childhood* 9:1080–81.

Kraut, Richard. 1984. *Socrates and the State.* Princeton, NJ: Princeton University Press.

Larmore, Charles. 1987. *Patterns of Moral Complexity*. Cambridge: Cambridge University Press.

———. 1996. *The Morals of Modernity*. Cambridge: Cambridge University Press.

Lavoie, Don. 1986. "The Market as a Procedure for Discovery and Conveyance of Inarticulate Knowledge." *Comparative Economic Studies* 28:1–19.

Lipsey, R. G., and K. J. Lancaster. 1956–57. "The General Theory of Second Best." *Review of Economic Studies* 24:11–32.

List, Christian. 2006. "The Discursive Dilemma and Public Reason." *Ethics* 116:362–402.

List, Christian, and Philip Pettit. 2005. "On the Many as One." *Philosophy and Public Affairs* 33:377–90.

Locke, John. 1980. *Second Treatise of Government*. Ed. C. B. Macpherson. Indianapolis: Hackett.

Lyons, David. 1986. "Constitutional Interpretation and Original Meaning." *Social Philosophy and Policy* 4:75–101.

Mansbridge, Jane. 1990. *Beyond Self-Interest*. Chicago: University of Chicago Press.

Marcuse, Herbert. 1969. "Repressive Tolerance." In *A Critique of Pure Tolerance*, Boston: Beacon Press.

McCarthy, Thomas. 1979. *The Critical Theory of Jürgen Habermas*. Cambridge, MA: MIT Press.

Mehta, S., and H. J. Binns. 1998. "What Do Parents know about Lead Poisoning? The Chicago Lead Knowledge Test." *Archives of Pediatric and Adolescent Medicine* 152:1213–18.

Meiklejohn, Alexander. 1960. *Political Freedom*. New York: Harper and Row.

Menand, Louis. 2005. "Everybody's an Expert." *New Yorker*, December 5.

Mill, John Stuart. 1991. *On Liberty and Other Essays*. Ed. John Gray. Oxford: Oxford University Press.

Miller, Warren E., and the National Election Studies. 1994. *American National Election Studies Cumulative Data File, 1952–1992*. Ann Arbor, MI: University of Michigan, Center for Political Studies.

Monoson, S. Sara. 2000. *Plato's Democratic Entanglements: Athenian Politics and the Practice of Philosophy*. Princeton, NJ: Princeton University Press.

Nagel, Thomas. 1987. "Moral Conflict and Political Legitimacy." *Philosophy and Public Affairs* 16:215–40.

Nelson, William N. 1980. *On Justifying Democracy*. London: Routledge and Kegan Paul.

Nino, Carlos Santiago. 1991. *The Ethics of Human Rights*. Cambridge: Cambridge University Press.

Nozick, Robert. 1974. *Anarchy, State and Utopia*. New York: Basic Books.

Pettit, Philip. 1997. *Republicanism: A Theory of Freedom and Government*. Oxford: Clarendon Press.

———. 1999a. "Doing unto Others." *Times Literary Supplement*, June 25.

———. 1999b. "Republican Freedom and Contestatory Democratization." In

Democracy's Value, ed. Ian Shapiro and Casiano Hacker-Cordon. Cambridge: Cambridge University Press.

Plato, 1987. *Gorgias*. Translated by Donald J. Zeyl. Indianapolis: Hackett.

———. 2000. *The Republic*. Ed. G.R.F. Ferrari. Trans. by Tom Griffith. Cambridge: Cambridge University Press.

Posner, Richard A. 2003. *Law, Pragmatism, and Democracy*. Cambridge, MA: Harvard University Press.

Przeworski, Adam. 1999. "Minimalist Conception of Democracy: A Defense." In *Democracy's Values*, ed. Ian Shapiro and Casiano Hacker-Cordon. Cambridge: Cambridge University Press.

Rawls, John. 1950. "A Study in the Grounds of Ethical Knowledge: Considered with Reference to Judgments on the Moral Worth of Character." Ph. D. diss., Princeton University.

———. 1964. "Legal Obligation and the Duty of Fair Play." In *Law and Philosophy: A Symposium*, ed. Sidney Hook. New York: New York University Press.

———. 1971. *A Theory of Justice*. Cambridge, MA: Harvard University Press.

———. 1993. *Political Liberalism*. New York: Columbia University Press.

———. 1995. "Reply to Habermas's *Reconciliation through the Public Use of Reason*." *Journal of Philosophy* 92:132–80.

———. 1999a. "Fairness to Goodness." In *John Rawls: Collected Papers*, ed. Samuel Freeman. Cambridge, MA: Harvard University Press.

———. 1999b. *The Law of Peoples*. Cambridge, MA: Harvard University Press.

Raz, Joseph. 1986. *The Morality of Freedom*. Oxford: Clarendon Press.

———. 1990. "Facing Diversity: The Case of Epistemic Abstinence." *Philosophy and Public Affairs* 19:3–46.

Ridge, Michael. 2001. "Debate: Saving Scanlon: Contractualism and Agent-Relativity." *Journal of Political Philosophy* 9:72–81.

Riker, William. 1982. *Liberalism against Populism*. San Francisco: Freeman.

Rousseau, Jean-Jacques. 1968. *The Social Contract*. Translated by Maurice Cranston. London: Penguin Books.

———. 1979. *Emile: or On Education*. Trans. Allan Bloom. Basic Books.

Russell, Clifford S., ed. 1979. *Collective Decision Making: Applications from Public Choice Theory*. Baltimore: Johns Hopkins University Press.

Scanlon, T. M. 1975. "Preference and Urgency." *Journal of Philosophy* 72:655–69.

———. 1998. *What We Owe to Each Other*. Cambridge, MA: Belknap Press of Harvard University Press.

Scheffler, Samuel. 1982. *The Rejection of Consequentialism*. Oxford: Clarendon Press.

———, ed. 1988. *Consequentialism and Its Critics*. Oxford: Oxford University Press.

Schumpeter, Joseph A. 1976. *Capitalism, Socialism, and Democracy*. New York: Harper and Row.

Sears, David O., and Carolyn L. Funk. 1990. "Self-Interest in Americans' Political Opinions." In *Beyond Self-Interest*, ed. Jane Mansbridge, 147–70. Chicago: University of Chicago Press.

Sen, Amartya. 1994. "Freedom and Needs." *New Republic*, January 10 and 17.

Sher, George. 1980. "What Makes a Lottery Fair?" *Nous* 14:203–16.

Simmons, A. John. 1979. *Moral Principles and Political Obligation*. Princeton, NJ: Princeton University Press.

———. 1999. "Justification and Legitimacy" *Ethics* 109:739–71.

———. 2001. *Justification and Legitimacy: Essays on Rights and Obligations*. Cambridge: Cambridge University Press.

Singer, Peter. 1972. "Famine, Affluence, and Morality." *Philosophy and Public Affairs* 1:229–43.

Sinnott-Armstrong, Walter. 2003. "Consequentialism." *Stanford Encyclopedia of Philosophy*. http://plato.stanford.edu/entries/consequentialism.

Smith, Adam. 1982. *A Theory of the Moral Sentiments*. Indianapolis: Liberty Classics.

Sunstein, Cass R. 1991. "Preferences and Politics." *Philosophy and Public Affairs* 21:3–34.

———. 2006. *Infotopia: How Many Minds Produce Knowledge*. New York: Oxford University Press.

Surowiecki, James. 2004. *The Wisdom of Crowds: Why the Many Are Smarter Than the Few and How Collective Wisdom Shapes Business*. New York: Doubleday.

Tetlock, Philip. 2005. *Expert Political Judgment: How Good Is It? How Can We Know?* Princeton, NJ: Princeton University Press.

Tullock, Gordon. 1979. "Public Choice in Practice." In *Collective Decision Making: Applications from Public Choice Theory*, ed. Clifford S. Russell. Baltimore: Johns Hopkins University Press.

Van Roojen, Mark. 2004. "Moral Cognitivism vs. Non-Cognitivism." *Stanford Encyclopedia of Philosophy*, April 5, 2006, http://plato.stanford.edu/entries/moral-cognitivism/.

Vlastos, Gregory. 1983. "The Historical Socrates and Athenian Democracy." *Political Theory*, Vol. 11 no. 4, 495–516.

———. 1985. "Socrates' Disavowal of Knowledge." *Philosophical Quarterly* 35:1–31.

Waldron, Jeremy. 1993a. *Liberal Rights: Collected Papers, 1981–1991*. Cambridge: Cambridge University Press.

———. 1993b. "Special Ties and Natural Duties." *Philosophy and Public Affairs* 22:3–30.

———. 1999a. *The Dignity of Legislation*. Cambridge: Cambridge University Press.

———. 1999b. *Law and Disagreement*. Oxford: Clarendon Press.

———. 2000. "Speech: Legislation by Assembly." *Loyola Law Review* 46:507–34.

Wellman, Christopher H. 1996. "Liberalism, Political Legitimacy, and Samaritanism." *Philosophy and Public Affairs* 25:211–37.

Wellman, Christopher H., and A. John Simmons. 2005. *Is There a Duty to Obey the Law?* Cambridge: Cambridge University Press.

"What Do Parents Know about Contraception?" 2004. *Perspectives on Sexual and Reproductive Health* 36:50–57.

Williams, Bernard. 1985. *Ethics and the Limits of Philosophy.* Cambridge, MA: Harvard University Press.

Wolff, Robert Paul. 1998. *In Defense of Anarchism.* Berkeley: University of California Press.

Index

acceptability, 279n11; "acceptable standards" and "truth," 34; actual acceptance, 46–47, 49, 279n11; application of the acceptability requirement to itself, 53; general acceptability requirement, 23, 33–36, 38, 39, 43, 60, 112, 120, 165, 238; qualified acceptability requirement, 37–38, 47, 48, 49, 52, 167, 278n25; self-determination of, 90; unqualified acceptability requirement, 45. *See also* qualified acceptability requirement, objections to

accuracy. *See* political process/procedures, accuracy of

aggregativity, 73, 79; challenge to judgment aggregation (tenure example), 180, 287n14; definition of, 73–74; rules of aggregation, 74–75

anarchy, 146; juridical anarchy, 146

anonymity, 72–73; full, 78, 79–81; non-anonymity, 79; preference, 78–79

Arendt, Hannah, 21

argument, efficiency of, 273–74

aristocracy, 289n14

Aristotle, 208–9, 210, 232, 289n15

Arneson, Richard, 280n1

Arrow, Kenneth, 65, 258

aspirational theory, 259, 263–70; and institutional reticence, 270–71

authority (democratic/political), 2, 3, 7, 30, 32, 96–97, 117, 148, 273, 284n2; absence of, 120–21; and consent, 9–10; cost of accepting authority, 155; definition of, 30–31, 42, 118, 284n1; democratic basis of, 23; dependence of on justification(s), 4, 33–34; epistocratic account of, 35–36; and the general acceptability idea, 33–36; global/local model of, 150–51, 152, 285n15; and individual duty, 154–55;

justified, 33–34; limits of, 111–12; as the "moral power to require action," 118–19, 134, 143; Platonic conception of, 22; quasi-voluntarist constraint of, 131, 151, 152–53; and self-rule, 109–10; and the state's claim to, 41; and unjust law, 110–11. *See also* consent theory, of authority; jury system, authority of; proceduralism, epistemic, and democratic authority

Authority Tenet, 30, 31, 34–35, 278n22; revised, 35–36

authorization, 58–60; and alibi, 59; and stipulation, 59

Barry, Brian, 240, 256, 292n23; on "empirical approximation," 292n25

Bayes' theorem, 230–31

Between Acts and Norms (Habermas), 288n16

Branch Davidians, 55–56, 279n10

Broome, John, on procedural fairness, 280nn3, 8

charity, 148, 149, 285nn12–13

Christianity, 49–52

Christiano, Thomas, 280n1

citizens, 91, 98, 116, 264; norms of citizen participation, 184, 185; "reasonable," 54. *See also* democracy, as the authorization of laws by the people (citizens)

civil disobedience, 111

civility, 187, 189; and breakdown theory, 191–92; and collective action duties of, 191; narrow civility, 194, 200, 204; narrow civility and formal politics, 201–4; truth as the telos of, 193; wide civility, 185, 193–95